EIGHT HEROES WHO TOOK ON AN ARMY

ANDY—A tough South London orphan, he joined up at sixteen. Now he was in his thirties, a Special Forces commander, and the Gulf War was *his* war.

DINGER—A veteran of the Falklands, he had a football hooligan's face with a sharp brain behind it. He was also a rock—unmovable and hard as granite.

BOB—Of Swiss-Italian heritage, at 5'2" he was nicknamed the Mumbling Midget. But he was immensely strong both physically and in character.

CHRIS—Soft-spoken, a fanatical bodybuilder, cyclist, and skier, he was the most determined, purposeful, and deadly man in the Regiment.

VINCE—At thirty-seven, he was powerful—and an expert mountaineer, diver, and skier. The old man among them, he had two more years to serve.

LEGS—The new man, quiet, confident, dedicated to his family, he was an expert signaler, top motor mechanic, and exceptionally fast on his feet.

MARK THE KIWI—An Australian, a rugby player, he had legs like tree trunks and one word in his vocabulary. It began with the letter *f*.

STAN—Born in South Africa, witness to the terrorist war in Rhodesia, he trained to be a doctor. He quit medicine to join the Special Forces.

Also by Andy McNab

IMMEDIATE ACTION

ANDY McNAB

DCM MM

BRAVO TWO ZERO

Island
BOOKS

ISLAND BOOKS
Published by
Dell Publishing
a division of
Bantam Doubleday Dell Publishing Group, Inc.
1540 Broadway
New York, New York 10036

ISBN: 0-440-21880-2

Reprinted by arrangement with Bantam Press

Printed in the United States of America

September 1994

10 9 8 7 6 5 4

OPM

To the three who didn't come back

Contents

Maps

BRAVO TWO ZERO

1

Within hours of Iraqi troops and armor rolling across the border with Kuwait at 0200 local time on August 2, 1990, the Regiment was preparing itself for desert operations.

As members of the Counter Terrorist team based in Hereford, my gang and I unfortunately were not involved. We watched jealously as the first batch of blokes drew their desert kit and departed. Our nine-month tour of duty was coming to an end and we were looking forward to a handover, but as the weeks went by rumors began to circulate of either a postponement or cancellation altogether. I ate my Christmas turkey in a dark mood. I didn't want to miss out.

Then, on January 10, 1991, half of the squadron was given three days' notice of movement to Saudi. To huge sighs of relief, my lot were included. We ran around organizing kit, test firing weapons, and screaming into town to buy ourselves new pairs of desert wellies and plenty of Factor 20 for the nose.

We were leaving in the early hours of Sunday morning. I had a night on the town with my girlfriend Jilly, but she was too upset to enjoy herself. It was an evening of false niceness, both of us on edge.

"Shall we go for a walk?" I suggested when we got home, hoping to raise the tone.

We did a few laps of the block and when we got back I turned on the telly. It was *Apocalypse Now*. We weren't in the mood for talking so we just sat there and watched. Two hours of carnage and maiming wasn't the cleverest thing for me to have let Jilly look at. She burst into tears. She was always all right if she wasn't aware of the dramas. She knew very little of what I did, and had never asked questions—because, she told me, she didn't want the answers.

"Oh, you're off. When are you coming back?" was the most she would ever ask. But this time it was different. For once, she knew where I was going.

As she drove me through the darkness towards camp, I said, "Why don't you get yourself that dog you were on about? It would be company for you."

I'd meant well, but it set off the tears again. I got her to drop me off a little way from the main gates.

"I'll walk from here, mate," I said with a strained smile. "I need the exercise."

"See you when I see you," she said as she pecked me on the cheek.

Neither of us went a bundle on long good-byes.

The first thing that hits you when you enter squadron lines *(the camp accommodation area)* is the noise: vehicles revving, men hollering for the return of bits of kit, and from every bedroom in the unmarried quarters a different kind of music—on maximum watts. This time it was all so much louder because so many of us were being sent out together.

I met up with Dinger, Mark the Kiwi, and Stan, the other three members of my gang. A few of the unfortunates who weren't going to the Gulf still came in anyway and joined in the slagging and blaggarding.

We loaded our kit into cars and drove up to the top end of the camp where transports were waiting to take us to Brize Norton. As usual, I took my sleeping bag onto the aircraft with me, together with my Walkman, washing and shaving kit, and brew kit. Dinger took 200 Benson & Hedges. If we found ourselves dumped in the middle of nowhere or hanging around a deserted airfield for days on end, it wouldn't be the first time.

We flew out by RAF VC10. I passively smoked the twenty or so cigarettes that Dinger got through in the course of the seven-hour flight, honking at him all the while. As usual my complaints had no effect whatsoever. He was excellent company, however, despite his filthy habit. Originally with Para Reg, Dinger was a veteran of the Falklands. He looked the part as well— rough and tough, with a voice that was scary and eyes that were scarier still. But behind the football hooligan face lay a sharp, analytical brain. Dinger could polish off the *Daily Telegraph* crossword in no time, much to my annoyance. Out of uniform, he was also an excellent cricket and rugby player, and an absolutely lousy dancer. Dinger danced the way Virgil Tracy walked. When it came to the crunch, though, he was solid and unflappable.

We landed at Riyadh to find the weather typically pleasant for the time of year in the Middle East, but there was no time to soak up the rays. Covered transports were waiting on the tarmac, and we were whisked away to a camp in isolation from other Coalition troops.

The advance party had got things squared away sufficiently to answer the first three questions you always ask when you arrive at a new location: Where do I sleep, where do I eat, and where's the bog?

Home for our half squadron, we discovered, was a hangar about 300 feet long and 150 feet wide. Into it were crammed forty blokes and all manner of stores and equipment, including vehicles, weapons, and ammunition. There were piles of gear everywhere—everything from insect repellent and rations to laser target markers and boxes of high explosive. It was a matter of just getting in amongst it and trying to make your own little world as best you could. Mine was made out of several large crates containing outboard engines, arranged to give me a sectioned-off space that I covered with a tarpaulin to shelter me from the powerful arc lights overhead.

There were many separate hives of activity, each with its own noise—radios tuned in to the BBC World Service, Walkmans with plug-in speakers that thundered out folk, rap, and heavy metal. There was a strong smell of diesel, petrol, and exhaust fumes. Vehicles were driving in and out all the time as blokes went off to explore other parts of the camp and see what they could pinch. And of course while they were away, their kit in turn was being explored by other blokes. "You snooze, you lose," is the way it goes. Possession is ten tenths of the law. Leave your space unguarded for too long and you'd come back to find a chair missing—and sometimes even your bed.

Brews were on the go all over the hangar. Stan had brought a packet of orange tea with him, and Dinger and I wandered over and sat on his bed with empty mugs.

"Tea, boy," Dinger demanded, holding his out.

"Yes, bwana," Stan replied.

Born in South Africa to a Swedish mother and Scottish father, Stan had moved to Rhodesia shortly before the UDI (Unilateral Declaration of Independence). He was involved at first hand in the terrorist war that followed, and when his family subsequently moved to Australia he joined the TA (Territorial Army). He passed his medical exams but hankered too much for the active, outdoor life and quit in his first year as a junior doctor. He wanted to come to the UK and join the Regiment, and spent a year in Wales training hard for Selection. By all accounts he cruised it.

Anything physical was a breeze for Stan, including pulling women. Six foot three, big-framed and good-looking, he got them all sweating. Jilly told me that his nickname around Hereford was Doctor Sex, and the name cropped up quite frequently on the walls of local ladies' toilets. On his own admission, Stan's ideal woman was somebody who didn't eat much and was therefore cheap to entertain, and who had her own car and house and was therefore independent and unlikely to cling. No matter where he was in the world women looked at Stan and drooled. In female company he was as charming and suave as Roger Moore playing James Bond.

Apart from his success with women, the most noticeable and surprising thing about Stan was his dress sense: he didn't have any. Until the squadron got hold of him, he used to go everywhere in Crimplene safari jackets and trousers that stopped just short of his ankles. He once turned up to a smart party in a badly fitting check suit with drainpipe trousers. He had traveled a lot and had obviously made a lot of female friends. They wrote marriage proposals to him from all over the world, but the letters went unanswered. Stan never emptied his mailbox. All in all a very approachable, friendly character in his thirties, there was nothing that Stan couldn't take smoothly in his stride. If he hadn't been in the Regiment, he would have been a yuppie or a spy—albeit in a Crimplene suit.

Most people take tubes of mustard or curry paste with them to jazz up the rations, and spicy smells emanated from areas where people were doing supplementary fry-ups. I wandered around and sampled a few. Everybody carries a "racing spoon" about their person at all times. The unwritten rule is that whoever has the can or is cooking up has first go, and the rest has to be shared. You dip your racing spoon in so that it's vertical, then take a scoop. If it's a big spoon you'll get more out of a mess tin, but if it's too big—say, a wooden spoon with the handle broken off—it won't go into a can at all. The search for the perfect-sized racing spoon goes on.

There was a lot of blaggarding going on. If you didn't like the music somebody was playing, you'd slip in when they weren't there and replace their batteries with duds. Mark opened his bergen to find that he'd lugged a twenty-pound rock with him all the way from Hereford. Wrongly suspecting me of putting it there, he replaced my toothpaste with Uvistat sunblock. When I went to use it I bulked up.

I'd first met Mark in Brisbane in 1989 when some of us were being hosted by the Australian SAS (Special Air Service). He played against us in a rugby match and was very much the man of the moment, his tree-trunk legs powering him to score all his side's tries. It was the first time our squadron team had been beaten, and I hated him—all 5'6" of the bastard. We met again the following year. He was doing Selection, and the day I saw him he had just returned to camp after an eight-mile battle run with full kit.

"Put in a good word for us," he grinned when he recognized me. "You lot could do with a fucking decent scrum-half."

Mark passed Selection and joined the squadron just before we left for the Gulf.

"Fucking good to be here, mate," he said as he came into my room and shook my hand.

I'd forgotten that there was only one adjective in the Kiwi's vocabulary and that it began with the letter *f*.

The atmosphere in our hangar was jovial and lively. The Regiment hadn't been massed like this since the Second World War. It was wonderful that so many of us were there together. So often we work in small groups of a covert nature, but here was the chance to be out in the open in large numbers. We hadn't been briefed yet, but we knew in our bones that the war was going to provide an excellent chance for everybody to get down to some "green work"—classic, behind-the-lines SAS soldiering. It was what David Stirling had set the Regiment up for in the first place, and now, nearly fifty years later, here we were back where we'd started. As far as I could see, the biggest restrictions in Iraq were likely to be the enemy and the logistics: running out of bullets or water. I felt like a bricklayer who had spent my entire life knocking up bungalows and now somebody had given me the chance to build a skyscraper. I just hoped that the war didn't finish before I had a chance to lay the first brick.

We didn't have a clue yet what we'd have to do, so we spent the next few days preparing for anything and everything, from target attacks to setting up observation posts. It's all very well doing all the exciting things—abseiling, fast roping, jumping through buildings—but what being Special Forces is mostly about is thoroughness and precision. The real motto of the SAS is not "Who Dares Wins" but "Check and Test, Check and Test."

Some of us needed to refresh our skills a bit swiftly with explosives, movement with vehicles, and map reading in desert conditions. We also dragged out the heavy weapons. Some, like the 50mm heavy machine gun, I hadn't fired for two years. We had revision periods with whoever knew best about a particular subject—it could be the sergeant major or the newest member of the squadron. There were Scud alerts, so everybody was rather keen to relearn the NBC (*nuclear, biological, chemical*) drills they had not practiced since being in their old units. The only trouble was that Pete, the instructor from our Mountain Troop, had a Geordie accent as thick as Tyne fog and he spoke with his verbal safety catch on full automatic. He sounded like Gazza on speed.

We tried hard to understand what he was on about but after a quarter of an hour the strain was too much for us. Somebody asked him an utterly bone question, and he got so wound up that he started speaking even faster. More questions were asked, and a vicious circle was set in motion. In the end we decided among ourselves that if the kit had to go on, it would stay on. We wouldn't bother carrying out the eating and drinking drills Pete was demonstrating, because then we wouldn't have to carry out the shitting and pissing drills—and they were far too complicated for the likes of us. All in all, Pete said, as the session disintegrated into chaos, it was not his most constructive day—or words to that effect.

We were equipped with aviator sunglasses, and we enjoyed a few Foster Grant moments, waiting outside the hangar for anybody to pass, then slipping on the glasses as in the TV commercial.

We had to take pills as protection against nerve agents, but that soon stopped when the rumor went around that they made you impotent.

"It's not true," the sergeant major reassured us a couple of days later. "I've just had a wank."

We watched CNN news and talked about different scenarios.

We guessed the parameters of our operations would be loose, but that wouldn't mean we could just go around blowing up power lines or whatever else we saw. We're strategic troops, so what we do behind enemy lines can have serious implications. If we saw a petroleum line, for example, and blew it up just for the fucking badness of it, we might be bringing Jordan into the war: it could be a pipeline from Baghdad to Jordan which the Allies had agreed not to destroy so that Jordan still got its oil. So if we saw an opportunity target like that, we'd have to get permission to deal with it. That way we could cause the maximum amount of damage to the Iraqi war machine, but not damage any political or strategic considerations.

If we were caught, we wondered, would the Iraqis kill us? Too bad if they did. As long as they did it swiftly—if not, we'd just have to try and speed things up.

Would they fuck us? Arab men are very affectionate with each other, holding hands and so on. It's just their culture, of course; it doesn't necessarily mean they're shit stabbers, but the question had to be asked. I wasn't that worried about the prospect, because if it happened to me I wouldn't tell. The only scenario that did bring me out in a sweat was the possibility of having my bollocks cut off. That would not be a good day out. If the rag heads had me tied down naked and were sharpening their knives, I'd do whatever I could to provoke them into slotting me.

I'd never worried about dying. My attitude to the work I am expected to do in the Regiment has always been that you take the money off them every month and so you're a tool to be used—and you are. The Regiment does lose people, so you cater for that eventuality. You fill in your insurance policies, although at the time only Equity & Law had the bottle to insure the SAS without loading the premium. You write your letters to be handed to next of kin if you get slotted. I wrote four and entrusted them to a mate called Eno. There was one for my parents that said: "Thanks for looking after me; it can't have been easy for you, but I had a rather nice childhood. Don't worry about me being dead, it's one of those things." One was for Jilly, saying: "Don't mope around—get the money and have a good time. PS £500 is to go behind the bar at the next squadron piss-up. PPS I love you." And there was one for little Kate, to be given to her by Eno when she was older, and it said: "I always loved you, and always will love you." The letter to Eno himself, who was to be the executor of my will, said: "Fuck this one up, wanker, and I'll come back and haunt you."

At about 1900 one evening, I and another team commander, Vince, were called over to the squadron OC's table. He was having a brew with the squadron sergeant major.

"We've got a task for you," he said, handing us a mug each of tea. "You'll be working together. Andy will command. Vince will be 2 i/c. The briefing will be tomorrow morning at 0800—meet me here. Make sure your people are informed. There will be no move before two days."

My lot were rather pleased at the news. Quite apart from anything else, it meant an end to the hassle of having to queue for the only two available sinks and bogs. In the field, the smell of clean clothes or bodies can disturb the wildlife and in turn compromise your position, so for the last few days before you go you stop washing and make sure all your clothing is used.

The blokes dispersed, and I went to watch the latest news on CNN. Scud missiles had fallen on Tel Aviv, injuring at least twenty-four civilians. Residential areas had taken direct hits, and as I looked at the footage of tower blocks and children in their pajamas, I was suddenly reminded of Peckham and my own childhood. That night, as I tried to get my head down, I found myself remembering all my old haunts and thinking about my parents and a whole lot of other things that I hadn't thought about in a long while.

2

I had never known my real mother, though I always imagined that whoever she was she must have wanted the best for me: the carrier bag I was found in when she left me on the steps of Guy's Hospital came from Harrods.

I was fostered until I was 2 by a South London couple who in time applied to become my adoptive parents. As they watched me grow up, they probably wished they hadn't bothered. I binned school when I was 15½ to go and work for a haulage company in Brixton. I'd already been bunking off two or three days a week for the last year or so. Instead of studying for CSEs (Certificate of Secondary Education) I delivered coal in the winter and drink mixes to off-licenses in the summer. By going full-time I pulled in £8 a day, which in 1975 was serious money. With forty quid on the hip of a Friday night you were one of the lads.

My father had done his National Service in the Catering Corps and was now a minicab driver. My older brother had joined the Royal Fusiliers when I was a toddler and had served for about five years until he got married. I had exciting memories of him coming home from faraway places with his holdall full of presents. My own early life, however, was nothing remarkable. There wasn't anything I was particularly good at, and I certainly wasn't interested in a career in the army. My biggest ambition was to get a flat with my mates and be able to do whatever I wanted.

I spent my early teens running away from home. Sometimes I'd go with a friend to France for the weekend, expeditions that were financed by him doing over his aunty's gas meter. I was soon getting into trouble with the police myself, mainly for vandalism to trains and vending machines. There were juvenile court cases and fines that caused my poor parents a lot of grief.

I changed jobs when I was 16, going behind the counter at McDonald's in Catford. Everything went well until round about Christmas time, when I was arrested with two other blokes coming out of a flat that didn't belong to us in Dulwich village. I got put into a remand hostel for three days while I waited to go in front of the magistrates. I hated being locked up and swore that if I got away with it I'd never let it happen again. I knew deep down that I'd have to do something pretty decisive or I'd end up spending my entire life in Peckham, fucking about and getting fucked up. The army seemed a good way out. My brother had enjoyed it, so why not me?

When the case came up the other two got sent to Borstal. I was let off with a caution, and the following day I took myself down to the army recruiting office. They gave me a simple academic test, which I failed. They told me to come back a calendar month later, and this time, because it was exactly the same test, I managed to scrape through by two points.

I said I wanted to be a helicopter pilot, as you do when you have no qualifications and not a clue what being one involves.

"There's no way you are going to become a helicopter pilot," the recruiting sergeant told me. "However, you can join the Army Air Corps if you want. They might teach you to be a helicopter refueler."

"Great," I said, "that's me."

You are sent away for three days to a selection center where you take more tests, do a bit of running, and go through medicals. If you pass, and they've got a vacancy, they'll let you join the regiment or trade of your choice.

I went for my final interview, and the officer said, "McNab, you stand more chance of being struck by lightning than you do of becoming a junior leader in the Army Air Corps. I think you'd be best suited to the infantry. I'll put you down for the Royal Green Jackets. That's my regiment."

I didn't have a clue about who or what the Royal Green Jackets were or did. They could have been an American football team for all I knew.

If I'd waited three months until I was 17, I could have joined the Green Jackets as an adult recruit, but like an idiot I wanted to get stuck straight in. I arrived at the Infantry Junior Leaders battalion in Shorncliffe, Kent, in September 1976 and hated it. The place was run by Guardsmen, and the course was nothing but bullshit and regimentation. You couldn't wear jeans, and had to go around with a bonehead haircut. You weren't even allowed the whole weekend off, which made visiting my old Peckham haunts a real pain in the arse. I landed in trouble once just for missing the bus in Folkestone and being ten minutes late reporting back. Shorncliffe was a nightmare, but I learned to play the game. I had to—there was nothing else for me. The passing-out parade was in May. I had detested every single minute of my time there but had learned to use the system and for some reason had been promoted to junior sergeant and won the Light Division sword for most promising soldier.

I now had a period at the Rifle Depot in Winchester, where us junior soldiers joined the last six weeks of a training platoon, learning Light Division drill. This was much more grown-up and relaxed, compared with Shorncliffe.

In July 1977 I was posted to 2nd Battalion, Royal Green Jackets, based for the time being in Gibraltar. To me, this was what the army was all about—warm climates, good mates, exotic women, and even more exotic VD. Sadly, the battalion returned to the UK just four months later.

In December 1977 I did my first tour in Northern Ireland. So many young soldiers had been killed in the early years of the Ulster emergency that you had to be 18 before you could serve there. So although the battalion left on December 6, I couldn't join them until my birthday at the end of the month.

There must have been something about the IRA and young squaddies because I was soon in my first contact. A Saracen armored car had got bogged down in the cuds *(countryside)* near Crossmaglen, and my mate and I were put on stag *(sentry duty)* to guard it. In the early hours of the morning, as I scanned the countryside through the night sight on my rifle, I saw two characters coming towards us, hugging the hedgerow. They got closer and I could clearly see that one of them was carrying a rifle. We didn't have a radio so I couldn't call for assistance. There wasn't much I could do except issue a challenge. The characters ran for it, and we fired off half a dozen rounds. Unfortunately, there was a shortage of night sights at the time so the same weapon used to get handed on at the end of each stag. The night sight on the rifle I was using was zeroed in for somebody else's eye, and only one of my rounds found its target. There was a follow-up with dogs, but nothing was found. Two days later, however, a well-known player *(member of the Provisional IRA)* turned up at a hospital just over the border with a 7.62 round in his leg. It had been the first contact for our company, and everybody was sparked up. My mate and I felt right little heroes, and both of us claimed the hit.

The rest of our time in Ireland was less busy but more sad. The battalion took some injuries during a mortar attack on a position at Forkhill, and one of the members of my platoon was killed by a booby-trap bomb in Crossmaglen. Later, our colonel was killed when the Gazelle helicopter he was traveling in was shot down. Then it was back to normal battalion shit at Tidworth, and the only event worth mentioning during the next year was that, aged all of 18, I got married.

The following year we were back in South Armagh. I was now a lance corporal and in charge of a brick *(four-man patrol)*. One Saturday night in July our company was patrolling in the border town of Keady. As usual for a Saturday night the streets were packed with locals. They used to bus it to Castleblaney over the border for cabaret and bingo, then come back and boogy the night away. My brick was operating at the southern edge of the town near a housing estate. We had been moving over some wasteland and came into a patch of dead ground that hid us from view. As we reappeared over the brow, we saw twenty or so people milling around a cattle truck that was parked in the middle of the road. They didn't see us until we were almost on top of them.

The crowd went apeshit, shouting and running in all directions, pulling their kids out of the way. Six lads with Armalites had been about to climb onto the truck. We caught them posing in front of the crowd, masked up and ready to go, their rifles and gloved fists in the air. We later discovered they had driven up from the south; their plan was to drive past the patrol and give us a quick burst.

Two were climbing over the tailgate as I issued my warning. Four were still in the road. A lad in the back of the truck brought his rifle up to the aim, and I dropped him with my first shot. The others returned our fire, and there was a severe contact. One of them took seven shots in his body and ended up in a wheelchair. One player who was wounded was in the early stages of an infamous career. His name was Dessie O'Hare.

I was flavor of the month again, and not just with the British army. One of the shop owners had taken a couple of shots through his window during the firefight, and the windscreen of his car had been shattered. About a month later I went past on patrol and there he was, standing behind his new cash register in his refurbished shop, with a shiny new motor parked outside. He was beaming from ear to ear.

By the time we returned to Tidworth in the summer of 1979 I was completely army barmy. It would have taken a pick and shovel to get me out. In September I was placed on an internal NCOs' cadre. I passed with an A grade and was promoted to corporal the same night. That made me the youngest infantry corporal in the army at the time, aged just 19. A section commanders' battle course followed in 1980. I passed that with a distinction, and my prize was a one-way ticket back to Tidworth.

The Wiltshire garrison town was, and still is, a depressing place to live. It had eight infantry battalions, an armored regiment, a recce regiment, three pubs, a chip shop, and a launderette. No wonder it got on my young wife's nerves. It was a pain in the arse for the soldiers too. We were nothing more than glorified barrier technicians. I even got called in one Sunday to be in charge of the grouse beaters, who were also squaddies, for a brigadier's shoot. The incentive was two cans of beer—and they wondered why there was such a turnover of young squaddies. By September my wife had had enough. She issued me with an ultimatum: take her back to London or give her a divorce. I stayed, she went.

In late 1980 I got posted back to the Rifle Depot for two years as a training corporal. It was a truly excellent time. I enjoyed teaching raw recruits, even though with many of them it meant going right back to basics, starting with elementary hygiene and the use of a toothbrush. It was also round about this time that I started to hear stories about the SAS.

I met Debby, a former RAF girl, and we got married in August 1982. I married her because we were getting posted back to the battalion, which was now based at Paderborn in Germany, and we didn't want to be parted. All my worst fears about life in Germany were confirmed. It was Tidworth without the chip shop. We spent more time looking after vehicles than using them, with men working their fingers to the bone for nothing. We took part in large exercises where no one really knew what was going on, and after a while no one even cared.

I felt deprived that the Green Jackets had not been sent to the Falklands. Every time there was some action, it seemed to me, the SAS were involved. I wanted some of that—what was the point of being in the infantry if I didn't? Hereford sounded such a nice place to live as well, not being a garrison town. At that time, you were made to feel a second-class citizen if you lived in a place like Aldershot or Catterick; as an ordinary soldier you couldn't even buy a TV set on hire purchase unless an officer had signed the application form for you.

Four of us from the Green Jackets put our names down for Selection in the summer of 1983, and all for the same reason—to get out of the battalion. A couple of our people had passed Selection in the previous couple of years. One of them was a captain, who wangled us onto a lot of exercises in Wales so we could travel back to the UK and train. He personally took us up to the Brecon Beacons and put us through a lot of hill work. More than that, he gave us advice and en-

couragement. I owe a lot to that man. We were lucky
to know him: some regiments, especially the corps,
aren't keen for their men to go because they have skills
that are hard to replace. They won't give them time
off, or they'll put the application in "File 13"—the
wastepaper basket. Or they'll allow the man to go but
make him work right up till the Friday before he goes.

None of us passed. Just before the endurance phase,
I failed the sketch-map march of 18 miles. I was pissed
off with myself, but at least it was suggested to me
that I try again.

I went back to Germany and suffered all the slag-
gings about failing. These are normally dished out by
the knobbers who wouldn't dare attempt it themselves. I didn't care. I was a young thruster, and the
easy option would have been to stay in the battalion
system and be the big fish in a small pond, but I'd lost
all enthusiasm for it. I applied for the Winter 1984 Selection and trained in Wales all through Christmas.
Debby didn't care too much for that.

Winter Selection is fearsome. The majority of people
drop out within the first week of the four-week endurance phase. These are the Walter Mitty types, or those
who haven't trained enough or have picked up an injury. Some of the people who turn up are complete
nuggets. They think that the SAS is all James Bond and
storming embassies. They don't understand that you
are still a soldier, and it comes as quite a shock to them
to find out what Selection is all about.

The one good thing about Winter Selection is the
weather. The racing snakes who can move like men
possessed across country in the summer are slowed by
the snow and mist. It's a great leveler for every man to
be up to his waist in snow.

I passed.

After this first phase you are put through a four-
month period of training which includes an arduous
spell in the jungle in Asia. The last main test is the

Combat Survival course. You are taught survival skills for two weeks, and then sent in to see the doctor. He puts a finger up your arse to check for Mars bars, and you're turned loose on the Black Mountains dressed in Second World War battledress trousers and shirt, a greatcoat with no buttons, and boots with no laces. The hunter force was a company of Guardsmen in helicopters. Each man was given the incentive of two weeks' leave if he made a capture.

I had been on the run for two days accompanied by three old grannies—two Navy pilots and an RAF loadmaster. You had to stay together as a group, and I couldn't have been cursed with a worse trio of millstones. It didn't matter for them: the course was just a three-week embuggerance, and then they'd go home for tea and medals. But if SAS candidates didn't pass Combat Survival, they didn't get badged.

We were waiting for one particular RV (rendezvous) when the two on stag fell asleep. In swooped a helicopter full of Guardsmen, and we were bumped. After a brief chase we were captured and taken to a holding area.

Some hours later, as I was down on my knees, my blindfold was removed and I found myself looking up at the training sergeant major.

"Am I binned?" I said pitifully.

"No, you nugget. Get back on the helicopter and don't fuck up."

I'd caught him in a good mood. An ex-Household Division man himself, he was delighted to see his old lot doing so well.

For the next phase I was on my own, which suited me fine. Our movement between RVs was arranged in such a way that everybody was captured at the end of the E&E (escape and evasion) phase and subjected to tactical questioning. You are taught to be—and you always try to be—the gray man. The last thing you want is to be singled out as worthy of further questioning. I didn't find this stage particularly hard because despite the verbal threats nobody was actually filling you in, and you knew that nobody was going to. You're cold and wet and hungry, uncomfortable as hell, but it's just a matter of holding on, physically rather than mentally. I couldn't believe that some people threw in their hand during these last few hours.

In the end a bloke came in during one of the interrogations, gave me a cup of soup, and announced that it was over. There was a thorough debriefing, because the interrogators can learn from you as well as you from them. The mind does get affected; I was surprised to find that I was six hours out in my estimation of the time.

Next came two weeks of weapon training at Hereford. The instructors looked at who you were, and they expected from you accordingly. If you were fresh from the Catering Corps they'd patiently start from scratch; if you were an infantry sergeant they'd demand excellence. Parachute training at Brize Norton was next, and after the rigors of Selection it was more like a month at Butlins.

Back at Hereford after six long, grueling months, we were taken into the CO's office one by one. As I was handed the famous sand-colored beret with its winged dagger, he said: "Just remember: it's harder to keep than to get."

I didn't really take it in. I was too busy trying not to dance a jig.

The main bulk of the new intake, as usual, was made up of people from the infantry, plus a couple of engineers and signalers. Out of 160 candidates who had started, only eight passed—one officer and seven men.

Officers only serve for a three-year term in the SAS, though they may come back for a second tour. As an other rank, I had the full duration of my 22-year army contract to run—in theory, another fifteen years.

We went to join our squadrons. You can say whether you'd like to be in Mountain, Mobility, Boat, or Air Troop, and they'll accommodate you if they can. Otherwise it all depends on manpower shortages and your existing skills. I went to Air.

The four squadrons have very different characters. It was once said that if you went to a nightclub, A Squadron would be the ones along the wall at the back, not saying a word, even to each other, just giving everybody the evil eye. G Squadron would be talking, but only to each other. D Squadron would be on the edge of the dance floor, looking at the women. And B Squadron—my squadron—would be the ones out there on the floor, giving it their all—and making total dickheads of themselves.

Debby came back from Germany to join me in Hereford. She had not seen much of me since I started Selection way back in January, and she wasn't too impressed that the day after she arrived I was sent back to the jungle for two months of follow-up training. When I returned it was to an empty house. She had packed her bags and gone home to Liverpool.

In December the following year I started going out with Fiona, my next-door neighbor. Our daughter Kate was born in 1987, and in October that year we got married. My wedding present from the Regiment was a two-year job overseas. I came back from that trip in 1990, but in August, just a couple of months after my return, the marriage was dissolved.

In October 1990 I met Jilly. It was love at first sight—or so she told me.

3

We assembled at 0750 at the OC's table and headed off together for the briefing area. Everybody was in a jovial mood. We had a stainless steel flask each and the world's supply of chocolate. It was going to be a long day, and saving time on refreshment breaks would allow us to get on with more important matters.

I was still feeling chuffed to have been made patrol commander and to be working with Vince. Approaching his last two years of service with the Regiment, Vince was 37 and a big old boy, immensely strong. He was an expert mountaineer, diver, and skier, and he walked everywhere—even up hills—as if he had a barrel of beer under each arm. To Vince, everything was "fucking shit," and he'd say it in the strongest of Swindon accents, but he loved the Regiment and would defend it even when another squadron member was having a gripe. The only complaint in his life was that he was approaching the end of his 22 years' engagement. He had come from the Ordnance Corps and looked rough in a way that most army people would expect a member of the Regiment to look rough, with coarse, curly hair and sideboards and a big mustache. Because he'd been in the Regiment a bit longer than I had, he was going to be a very useful man to have around when it came to planning.

The briefing area, we discovered, was in another hangar. We were escorted through a door marked *NO UNAUTHORIZED PERSONNEL*. As a regiment we were in isolation, but the briefing area was isolation within isolation. OPSEC *(operational security)* is crucial. Nobody in the Regiment would ever ask anybody else what he was doing. As unwritten rules go, that one is in red ink, capital letters, and underlined. Doors either side of us were labeled *AIR PLANNING, D SQUAD-RON, INT CORPS, MAP STORE*. There was nothing fancy about the signs; they were A4 sheets of paper pinned to the door.

The atmosphere in this building was markedly different. It was clinical and efficient, with the ambient hiss and mush of radio transmissions in the background. Intelligence Corps personnel, known to us as "spooks" or "green slime," moved from room to room with bundles of maps in their arms, being meticulous about closing doors behind them. Everybody spoke in low voices. It was an impressive hive of professional activity.

We knew many of the spooks by name, having worked with them in the UK.

"Morning, slime," I called out to a familiar face. "How's it going?"

I got a mouthed word and a jerk of the wrist in return.

The place had no windows and felt as though it had been derelict for a long time. There was an underlying smell of mustiness and decay. On top of that were the sort of ordinary office smells you'd get anywhere— paper, coffee, cigarettes. But this being what we called a remf *(rear echelon motherfucker)* establishment and early in the morning, there was also a strong smell of soap, shaving foam, toothpaste, and aftershave.

"Morning, remfs!" Vince greeted them with his

Swindon accent and a broad grin. "You're fucking shit, you are."

"Fucking shit yourself," a spook replied. "Could you do our job?"

"Not really," Vince said. "But you're still a remf."

The B Squadron room was about 15 feet square. The ceiling was very high, with a slit device at the top that gave the only ventilation. Four tables had been put together in the center. Silk escape maps and compasses were laid out on top.

"Freebies, let's have them," Dinger said.

"Never mind the quality, feel the width," said Bob, one of Vince's gang.

Bob, all 5'2" of him, was of Swiss–Italian extraction and known as the Mumbling Midget. He'd been in the Royal Marines but wanted to better himself, and had quit and taken a gamble on passing Selection. Despite his size he was immensely strong, both physically and in character. He always insisted on carrying the same load as everybody else, which at times could be very funny—all you could see was a big bergen (*backpack*) and two little legs going at it like pistons underneath. At home, he was a big fan of old black-and-white comedies, of which he owned a vast collection. When he was out on the town, his great hobbies were dancing and chatting up women a foot taller than himself. On the day we left for the Gulf, he'd had to be rounded up from the camp club in the early hours of the morning.

We looked at the maps, which dated back to the 1950s. On one side was Baghdad and surroundings, on the other Basra.

"What do you reckon, boys?" said Chris, another from Vince's team, in his broad Geordie accent. "Baghdad or Basra?"

A spook came in. I knew Bert as part of our own intelligence organization in Hereford.

"Got any more of these?" Mark asked. "They're fucking nice."

Typical Regiment mentality: if it's shiny, I want it. You don't even know what a piece of equipment does sometimes, but if it looks good you take it. You never know when you might need it.

There were no chairs in the room, so we just sat with our backs against the wall. Chris produced his flask and offered it around. Good-looking and softspoken, Chris had been involved with the Territorial SAS as a civilian when he decided he wanted to join the Regiment proper. For Chris, if a job was worth doing it was worth doing excellently, so in typical fashion he signed up first with the Paras because he wanted a solid infantry background. He moved to Hereford from Aldershot as soon as he'd reached his intended rank of lance corporal and had passed Selection.

If Chris had a plan, he'd see it through. He was one of the most determined, purposeful men I'd ever met. As strong physically as he was mentally, he was a fanatical bodybuilder, cyclist, and skier. In the field he liked to wear an old Afrika Korps peaked cap. Off duty he was a real victim for the latest bit of biking or skiing technology, and wore all the Gucci kit. He was very quiet when he joined the Regiment, but after about three months his strength of character started to emerge. Chris was the man with the voice of reason. He'd always be the one to intervene and sort out a fight, and what he said always sounded good even when he was bullshitting.

"Let's get down to business," the OC said. "Bert's going to tell you the situation."

Bert perched on the edge of a table. He was a good spook because he was brief, and the briefer they are the easier it is to understand and remember what they're telling you.

"As you know, Saddam Hussein has finally carried out an attack on Israel by firing modified Scud missiles at Tel Aviv and Haifa. The actual damage done is very small, but thousands of residents are fleeing the cities for safer parts of the country. The country has come to a standstill. Their prime minister is not impressed.

"The rag heads, however, are well pleased. As far as they're concerned, Saddam has hit Tel Aviv, the recognized capital of Israel, and shown that the heart of the Jewish state is no longer impregnable.

"Saddam obviously wants Israel to retaliate, at whatever cost, because that will almost certainly cause a split in the anti-Iraqi Coalition, and probably even draw Iran into the war on the Iraqi side to join the fight against Israel.

"We knew this was a danger, and have been trying from day one to locate and destroy the Scud launchers. Stealth bombers have attacked the six bridges in central Baghdad that cross the river Tigris. These bridges connect the two halves of the city, and they also carry the landlines along which Baghdad is communicating with the rest of the country and its army in Kuwait— and with the Scud units operating against Israel. Since Iraq's microwave transmitters are already bombed to buggery and its radio signals are being intercepted by Allied intelligence, the landlines are Saddam's last link. For the air planners, they have become a priority target.

"Unfortunately, London and Washington want the attacks to stop. They think the news footage of kids playing next to bombed-out bridges is bad PR. But gents, Saddam has got to be denied access to those cables. And if Israel and Iran are to be kept out of the war, the Scuds have to be immobilized."

Bert got up from the table and went over to a large-scale map of Iraq, Iran, Saudi, Turkey, Syria, Jordan, and Kuwait that was tacked to the wall. He jabbed his finger at northwest Iraq.

"Here," he said, "be Scuds."

We all knew what was coming next.

"From Baghdad there are three MSRs (*main supply*

routes) running east to west," he went on, "mostly into Jordan. These MSRs are used for the transportation of fuel or whatever—and for moving Scuds. Now, it appears the Iraqis are firing the Scuds in two ways. From fixed-launcher sites, which are presurveyed, and from unfixed sites where they have to stop and survey before they fire. These are more tactical. We have hosed down most of the presurveyed sites. But the mobiles . . ."

We had even more of an idea now.

"Landlines are giving information to these mobile launchers, because all other comms are down. And I doubt there are that many people left in the country who can repair these things. And that, basically, is the situation."

"Your task is in two parts," said the boss. "One, to locate and destroy the landlines in the area of the northern MSR. Two, to find and destroy Scud."

He repeated the tasking statement, as is standard tasking procedure. His task now became our mission.

"We're not really bothered how you do it, as long as it gets done," he went on. "Your area of operation is along about 150 miles of this MSR. The duration of task will be fourteen days before resupply. Has anybody got any questions?"

We didn't at this stage.

"Right, Bert here will get you everything you want. I'll be coming back during the daytime anyway, but any problems, just come and get us. Andy, once you've got a plan sorted out, give me a shout and I'll have a look at it."

Rather than dive straight in, we took time out to have a breather and a brew. If you fancy a drink, you take one from the nearest available source. We emptied Mark's flask, then looked at the map.

"We'll need as much mapping as you've got," I said to Bert. "All the topographical information. And any photography, including satellite pictures."

"All I've got for you is one-in-a-half-million air navigation charts. Otherwise, there's jack shit."

"What can you tell us about weather conditions and the going?" Chris said.

"I'm getting that squared away. I'll go and see if it's ready."

"We also need to know a lot more about the fiber optics, how they actually operate," said Legs. "And Scuds."

I liked Legs. He was still establishing himself in the Regiment, having come from Para Reg just six months before. Like all newcomers he was still a bit on the quiet side, but had become firm friends with Dinger. He was very confident in himself and his ability as patrol signaler, and having started his army life in the engineers, he was also an excellent motor mechanic. He got his name from being a real racing snake over the ground.

Bert left the room, and discussions started up amongst the blokes. We were feeling relaxed. We appeared to have plenty of time, which is rare for the Regiment's operations, and we were in a nice, sterile environment; we weren't having to do our planning tactically, in the pouring rain in the back of beyond. There is a principle in the infantry that's referred to as "The Seven Ps": Proper Planning and Preparation Prevents Piss Poor Performance. We had perfect planning conditions. We'd have no excuses for Piss Poor Performance.

While we waited for Bert to come back, blokes wandered off to fill their flasks or make use of the remfs' plumbing facilities.

"I've got the mapping for you," Bert said as he came through the door a quarter of an hour later. "And I've got the information on the ground—but not a lot of it. I'll try to get more. There are some better escape maps coming through. I'll get you those before you leave."

We had already pocketed the others as souvenirs in any event.

We'd now had time to think things through a bit more, and Bert was bombarded with requests for information on enemy positions; areas of local population; the nature of the border with Syria because we were immediately thinking of an E&E plan and that frontier was the closest; what type of troops were near our area and in what concentrations, because if there were massive concentrations of troops, there was going to be a lot of movement up and down the MSR, which would make the task harder; what type of traffic moved up and down the MSR and in what volume; plus everything he could find out about how landlines worked, what they looked like, how easy they were to detect, and whether, having been found, they could be destroyed with ten pounds of plastic explosive or just a bang with a hammer.

Bert left with our new shopping list.

Looking at the map on the wall, I saw an underground oil pipe that had been abandoned. "I wonder if it's laid parallel to the MSR," I said, "and if the cable runs through it?"

"There's a boy in the squadron who used to lay landlines for Mercury," Stan said. "I'll see if he knows the score."

Bert came back with piles of maps. While some of us taped the separate sheets together to make one big section, two lads went out and nicked chairs.

The atmosphere was rather more serious now. We mulled things over in general for another half an hour before we launched into planning proper. Chris studied the maps and made pertinent comments. Legs scribbled memos to himself about radio equipment. Dinger opened another packet of Benson & Hedges.

The first point we had to consider was the location we were going to. We needed to know about the ground, and areas of civilian and military population. The information available was very sketchy.

"The actual MSR isn't a metaled road but a system of tracks amalgamated together," Bert said. "At its widest point it's about one and a half miles across, at its narrowest about two thousand feet. Over 10 miles either side of the MSR there's only a 150 foot drop in the ground. It's very flat and undulating, rocky, no sand. As you start moving north towards the Euphrates, the ground obviously starts to get lower. Going south, it's flat area most of the way down to Saudi, but then you start coming into major wadi-type features, which are good for navigation and good for cover, and then it flattens out again."

The tactical air maps didn't have contours but elevation tints, rather like a school atlas. Ominously, the whole area of the MSR was one color.

"This country's fucking shit," Vince said.

We laughed, but a bit uneasily. We could see it was not going to be easy terrain to hide in.

In remote regions, everything tends to be near a road or a river. The MSR went through built-up areas of population, three or four airfields, and several pumping stations for water, which we could take for granted would be defended by troops. It was also a fair assumption that there would be pockets of local population all along the MSR, either in fixed abodes or as bedu on the move, and plantations scattered all along the area to take advantage of the availability of transportation and water.

The MSR hit the Euphrates in the northwest at the major town of Banidahir; then it ran southwest all the way to Jordan. Traffic would be in the form of transports to and from Jordan, military transport going to airfields, and local militia in the built-up areas. They weren't likely to be on the alert, because they would not be expecting Allied troops in such a remote spot.

As far as they would be concerned, there was nothing of great strategic importance up there.

So, where along the MSR should we operate? Not at its widest point, that was for sure, because if we had to call up an air strike we wanted to keep the potential target area tight. What we really needed was a point where the MSR was at its narrowest, and common sense dictated that this would be at a sharp bend: no matter where you are in the world, drivers always try to cut a corner. We looked for a choke point that was as far away from habitation and military installations as possible. This was hard to do because an air chart only shows towns and major features. However, Legs pinpointed a suitable bend at a position midway between an airfield and the town of Banidahir, and about 18 miles from both. As a bonus, the underground pipeline crossed at the same point, which might provide a useful navigation marker.

The weather, Bert informed us, would be a bit nippy but not uncomfortably cold. Like a spring day in the UK, we could expect it to be chilly at night and early morning, warming up in the afternoons. Rainfall was very rare. This was good news, because there's nothing worse than being wet and cold, particularly if you are hungry as well. Keep those three things under control and life becomes very easy indeed.

We knew where we were going to go. Next, we had to decide how we were going to get there.

"The options are to patrol in on foot, take vehicles, or have a heli drop-off," Vince said.

"Tabbing in is a nonstarter," Chris said. "We wouldn't be able to carry sufficient kit such a distance —and we'd have to be resupplied after a while by a heli that might just as well have dropped us off there in the first place."

We agreed that vehicles could get us away from trouble quickly and let us relocate on the MSR or get to another area altogether for retasking. Pinkies or one-tens *(long-wheelbase Land-Rovers)* would also give us the increased firepower of vehicle-mounted GPMGs *(general purpose machine guns)* and M19 40mm grenade launchers, or anything else we wanted. We could take more ammunition and explosives and equipment as well, and generally make ourselves more self-sufficient for a longer period. But vehicles had two major disadvantages.

"We would be limited as to the amount of fuel we could take with us," Dinger said, puffing on his cigarette, "and besides, the possibilities for concealment in the area around the MSR look bugger all."

Since our mission required us to stay in the same area for a long time, our best form of defense was going to be concealment, and vehicles wouldn't help us with that at all. In this territory they'd stick out like a dog's bollocks. Every time we went on patrol we'd have to leave people with the wagons to keep them secure. Otherwise we wouldn't know if they'd been booby-trapped or we were walking into an ambush, or if they had been discovered by the local population and knowledge of their existence passed on. What was more, for eight men we would need two vehicles, and two vehicles equaled two chances of compromise. With one patrol on foot, there was only one chance of getting discovered. On the other hand, it might just be that two weeks' supply of ordnance and other equipment would be too much for us to carry, and despite their shortcomings we would have to go in vehicles after all. We'd have to work out the equipment requirements first and take it from there.

We worked out that we would need explosives and ammunition, two weeks' worth of food and water per man, NBC clothing, and, only if there was room, personal kit. Vince did the calculations and reckoned that we could just about lug the lot ourselves.

"So we're going to patrol on foot," he said. "But do

we get people to take us in vehicles, or are we going to get a heli and patrol in?"

"More chance of compromise in vehicles," Mark said. "We might not even get there without a resupply of fuel."

"If we need a resupply by heli, why not just fly in anyway?" Legs said.

In the end the team consensus was for a heli drop-off.

"Can we get an aircraft?" I asked Bert.

He went to the operations room to check it out.

I looked at the map. It must have been going through all of our minds how isolated we'd be. If we got into trouble, there'd be nobody up there to bail us out.

Bob said, "At least if we're in the shit we don't have too many hills to hump over to get away."

"Mmm, good one," Dinger grunted.

Bert reappeared. "We can get you an aircraft, no problems."

I opened the next debate. "Where should they drop us off then?"

The good news about helicopters is that they get you there quickly. The bad news is that they do it noisily and can draw antiaircraft fire. The landing, too, is quite compromising. We didn't want it to be associated with the task, so we would want to choose a site that was at least 12 miles from the MSR itself. We wouldn't want to be landed east or west of the bend in the MSR because it would be harder to navigate to. Navigation is not a science but a skill. Why make the skill harder by putting in problems? The object was to reach the LUP (*lying-up point*) as quickly as we could.

"Should we fly north over the MSR and then tab back south, or should we approach it from the south?" I said.

Nobody saw any advantage in crossing the MSR with the aircraft, so we chose to be dropped due south of our chosen point. Then all we had to do was navigate due north and we'd hit the MSR.

We would march on a bearing and measure distance by dead reckoning. Everybody knows his own pacing, and it's common practice to keep tally with a knotted length of paracord in your pocket. I knew, for example, that 112 of my paces on even ground equaled 325 feet. I would put ten knots in a length of paracord and feed it through a hole in my pocket. For every 112 paces I marched, I would pull one knot through. When I'd pulled ten knots through, I would know that I'd covered six-tenths of a mile, at which point I would check with the "check pacer." If his distance was different from mine, we'd take the average. This would be done in conjunction with Magellan, a handheld satellite navigation system. SatNav is an aid but it cannot be relied upon. It can go wrong and batteries can run out.

We couldn't yet work out when we would want to be dropped off; we would do the time and distance evaluation later, depending on what the pilots said. It was up to them to gauge the problem of antiaircraft emplacements and troop concentrations, together with the problem of fitting us into a slot that didn't conflict with the hundreds of other sorties being flown every day—a factor known as deconfliction.

By this stage of the planning we knew where we were going, how we were getting there, and more or less where we would like to get dropped off.

There was a knock at the door.

"We've got the pilot here if you want to talk with him," said a spook.

The squadron leader was shorter than Mike, with ginger hair and freckles.

"Could you get us to this point?" I asked, showing him the map.

"When?" he asked in a flat Midlands monotone.

"I don't know yet. Some time after two days."

"At the moment, yes. However, I'd have to do my planning on deconfliction, et cetera. How many of you?"

"Eight."

"Vehicles?"

"Just equipment."

"No problem."

I sensed that in his mind he was already calculating fuel loads, visualizing ground contours, thinking about antiaircraft capabilities.

"Have you got any other information—as in maps?"

"I was going to ask you the same question," I said.

"No, we've got jack shit. If we can't get you there, where else do you want to go?"

"All depends where you can get us to."

The pilot would run the whole show from pickup to drop-off, even though he'd have no idea what the task was. We would trust his judgment totally; we would just be passengers.

He left and we organized another brew before we tackled the tricky bit: how to attack the landlines and Scud.

We wanted to work out how to inflict the maximum amount of damage with the minimum of effort. With luck, the cables would run alongside the MSR, and every 5 miles or so there would be inspection manholes. We didn't know if we would find a signal-booster system inside the manholes, or what. But Stan suggested that because of the economics of laying lines, there might even be a land communication line inside as a bonus.

More questions for Bert. Would the manhole covers be padlocked? Would they have intruder devices, and if so would we be able to defeat them? If not, would we have to start digging for the landline itself? Might they be encased in concrete or steel or other protective devices? If so, we might have to make a shaped charge to pierce the steel. Would the manholes be flooded to prevent attack? Strangely enough, this would actually be an advantage, because water acts as a tamping for explosives and would therefore increase the force of the explosion.

We worked out that, depending on the ground, we'd do an array of four, five, or six cuts along the cable, and each one of them would be timed to detonate at different times over a period of days. We'd lay all the charges in one night, and have one going off, say, in the early evening next day. That would give one whole night when, at best, it was incapable of being repaired, or at least they would be slowed down, and they'd come probably at first light to fix it. They'd eventually find out where the cuts had been made and send a team down to repair them. It made sense for us to try and include these people in the damage if we could, thereby reducing the Iraqis' capability to carry out other repairs. Mark came up with the idea of putting down Elsie mines, which are small antipersonnel mines that work on pressure. When you step on them, they explode.

If everything went to plan, the first charge would make the cut and when they came down, possibly at first light, to repair it, the technician or a guard would lose his foot to an Elsie mine. The next evening, number two would go off, but we'd have laid the charge without Elsie mines. However, the boys that came down would be very wary, take their time, or maybe even refuse to do the job. The following day, another would go off, and this time we would have laid Elsie mines. Maybe they'd be more confident, and they'd get hit again. The only problem would be that we couldn't place the Elsie mines too near the site we were blowing, or the explosion might dislodge or expose them.

In the worst scenario, we'd have rendered the cable inoperable over six days. At best, we might have wrecked it for ever after the first day. It was a brilliant

thought of Mark's, and we added two boxes of Elsies
—twenty-four in all—to the equipment list.

In essence, we would do as many cuts as we could
with the ordnance and time available. It might be that
we'd have to do cuts that were 12 miles apart, and take
two nights doing it. I hoped we wouldn't have to blow
the manholes to get at the cables, because if they
checked other covers they'd be sure to find the other
devices. To cater for that, we would put an antihandling device on all the timers. It would either be a
pull switch or a pressure release, which would detonate the charge if they lifted it.

I was starting to feel tired. It was time for a break, or
we'd begin to make mistakes. You only rush your
planning if you have to.

We had a brew and stretched our legs before getting
down to the business of how to destroy Scud.

Thirty-seven feet long and about 3 feet wide, the Rus-
sian-built SS-1C Scud-B had a range of 100–175 miles.
It was transported on, and fired from, an eight-
wheeled TEL *(transporter erector launcher)*. Crews were
trained to operate from points of maximum concealment. Not very accurate, Scud was designed to strike
at major storage sites, marshaling areas, and airfields,
and was almost more of a propaganda weapon. As
well as conventional high explosive, it could carry
chemical, biological, or nuclear warheads.

When our armored divisions were sent to Saudi, a
rumor had circulated that if Saddam Hussein used
chemicals against British forces, Mrs. Thatcher had in-
structed the generals to go tactical nuclear. I never
thought that in my lifetime I'd find myself up against
chemical agents. No one in their right mind would use
them, but here was a man who had done so against
Iran and his own people and would no doubt do so
again in this war if the need arose.

"There are maybe fifteen to twenty TELs but many

more missiles," Bert said. "You can expect the TEL to be accompanied by a command vehicle, like a Land Cruiser, with the commander and/or the surveyor aboard. In the TEL itself will be the crew, two in the front, and other operators in the back. The command post within the TEL itself is in the center of the vehicle, entry being via a door on the left-hand side. There might be infantry in support, but we don't know how many—nor whether there might be several TELs together in convoy, or operating individually."

It became clear that the surveyor was the main personality at a Scud launch. After the transporter rumbled up to an unprepared site, there was a wait of about an hour before the Scud could be launched. The time was spent in accurate site surveying, radar tracking of upper atmosphere balloons, calculating such factors as angle of deflection, and pumping in of propellants.

There were a couple of lesser players, too—the commander, and the operators in the control center who tapped in the coordinates. That made a minimum of three people to be killed in order to render the launcher totally inoperable. However, they could be replaced. We'd still have to deal with the Scud.

How would we destroy it? Air strikes are all very well, but we knew that the Iraqis had excellent DF *(direction finding)* capability, and we had to assume the worst scenario—that their DF equipment was intact and operational. It worked via a series of listening posts dotted around the country that shot a bearing out to the source of a radio signal. It only took two such bearings to pinpoint a position; it would then be very easy for them to get hold of us, especially if we were on foot. Calling in an air strike would effectively mean that we had gone overt.

We'd only use air strikes if the Iraqis made us an offer we couldn't refuse—say, the world's supply of Scuds in convoy. Then we'd just have to get on the net *(radio network)* and take a chance of getting DF'd. We had to assume that they'd know we were there anyway just because the strike had been directed in.

If we were going to attack the missile itself, there were dangers with the warhead. We wouldn't know if it was chemical, biological, nuclear, or conventional, and we didn't want to have to take the precaution of attacking with NBC protective clothing on because it takes time to put on and slows you down badly. The fuel was also a problem, being highly noxious.

The TEL itself would be a better target, because without it the rockets couldn't be launched.

"Can we destroy it?" Bob said.

"Probably, but we don't know how easy it would be to repair," Dinger said. "And anyway, it's too near the missile."

"What about the flight information that has to be installed into the rockets?" Chris said.

The more we thought about it, the more sense it made to do a hands-on attack to destroy the control center in the middle of the vehicle.

"We could just put a charge in there which would fuck things up nice without any problems to us," Vince suggested. "The TEL must be protected against the rocket blast—enough to stop our charge affecting the missile."

We knew what to attack, but how would we do it? We finally decided that when we saw a Scud being launched, which shouldn't be too difficult given the billiard-table terrain, we would take a bearing and find it. Hopefully if the landlines were destroyed there would not be any launches anyway.

We knew the vulnerable points. We knew there would be no problems finding the Scuds. We would go to the area, pinpoint the launch site, and put in a CTR *(close target recce)* to find out how many troops there were, how many launchers were left, and where the stags were. In a typical CTR, we'd probably find the

Scud, then move back and stop at an FRV *(final RV)* about a mile away, depending on the ground. From there, four blokes would go and carry out a 360-degree recce of the position itself, looking for vulnerable points. Two of us would then go in as far as we had to in order to complete the information. Then we'd withdraw to the FRV. I'd have to give a quick brief for that CTR—how we were going to do it, how we were going to get there, what direction we were going to come back in, what the recognition signal was as we came back into the FRV. You always come back in exactly the same direction you left from, to cut down confusion. My normal recognition signal was to walk in with both arms outstretched in a crucifix position, my weapon in my right hand. Different patrols use different signs. The aim is to cut out the noise of a challenge and be easily ID'd. FRVs have to be somewhere easily identifiable and defendable, because navigating back to them in pitch darkness is not as easy as it sounds. Back at the FRV, I'd mentally prepare a quick set of orders for the attack and then tell everybody what was "on target."

Until we actually got on the ground, we would work on the assumption that we'd have at least three "points of contact": i.e., we'd kill the surveyor, control-center commander, and operators. This would normally be done with silenced weapons. A man will always drop if you put a round into his body T—the imaginary line from one temple running across the eyebrows to the other temple and from that line down the center of the face from the bridge of the nose to the base of the sternum. Pop in a round anywhere along the T, and your man will always go down. It must be done from close up, almost right on top of him. You go from a "rolling start line" and just keep going until he turns round; then you must be quick. You cannot hesitate. It's all down to pure speed, aggression, and surprise.

So much for the theory. Vince had brought a silenced weapon with him from the UK, but another squadron had come and begged it off him for a specific task and there were none left. D Squadron had got to Saudi before us, and down at the stores there had been a nasty outbreak of Shiny Kit Syndrome. They had snaffled everything in sight, and there was no point in us going and asking them nicely if we could please have our ball back. They'd only say they needed it—and probably they did. In the absence of silenced weapons we'd probably have to use our fighting knives—weapons resembling the famous Second World War commando dagger—if we wanted the attack to remain covert for as long as possible.

A fire-support base consisting of four men would be positioned, and then the other four would move out and infiltrate the Scud area. We'd take out the surveyor, then the characters sleeping or sitting in the TEL. Then we'd lay a charge made from PE4 plastic explosive. My guess was that about 2 pounds of explosive on a 2-hour timer inside the TEL would do the trick. We'd close the door and up it would go, well after we'd exfiltrated. We'd put an antihandling device on the PE as well, so that even if they found it and went to lift it, it would detonate.

Also on the charge we would have a compromise device. This would be a grip switch that would initiate a length of safety fuse, which in turn would initiate the detonator after about 60 seconds. So if the shit hit the fan, we could just place the charge and run. There would be three different initiations on the charges, hopefully covering any eventuality: the timing device, an antihandling device—pull, pressure, or pressure-release, whichever was appropriate—and a compromise device.

It was 1600. One or two of the faces around me were beginning to look tired, and I guessed that I looked the same. We'd really motored. We knew how we were going to do the task, even down to such detail as "actions on." Actions on contact for the 4-man fire-support group were to give covering fire to allow the attack group, if possible, to complete their task and extract themselves. Actions on for the 4-man attack group were to give support to each other and attempt to complete the target attack using the compromise device. One way or another, they should extract to the ERV *(emergency RV)* and quickly regroup. They should then move to the patrol RV and regroup with the fire-support team.

We wouldn't know, of course, if any of this was feasible until we saw the disposition on the ground. There might be four TELs together, which would pose problems of compromise as there would be many more targets. Or maybe there'd be just one TEL which we couldn't get in to attack, in which case we'd do a stand-off attack with lots of firepower—but not at the expense of the patrol to take out only one objective. In a stand-off attack we wouldn't get "hands on" but would use 66s to try and destroy the target. Such an attack must be short and sharp, but whether or not to carry one out would be a decision that could only be made on the ground. It's only when you have seen the problem that you can make your appreciations and work out what you will do. We would always try a covert target attack if at all possible.

The third option would be an air strike. Deciding between a stand-off attack and an air strike would be a fine balance, probably swayed by the numbers involved. Both, however, would advertise the fact that we were close by in the area. The compromise would be bearable if the numbers were high enough to warrant it, but if we were successful in cutting the cable, there would be no need for this at all.

By now the place was stinking of sweat, farts, and cigarettes. There were bits of paper everywhere with pictures of Scuds and matchstick men and fire-support group movement diagrams. Planning is always exhaustive, but only because we want to work everything out to the finest detail. When we got to the TEL and the door was closed, where was the handle? How did you operate it? Which way did the door go, out or in? Was it a concertina door? Did the door hinge from the top? Would the door be padlocked as it is on many armored vehicles? What would we do then? People didn't know, so we studied pictures and tried to work it out. Detail, detail, detail. It's so important. You might be pushing a door when you should be pulling. Minor detail missed equals fuckup guaranteed.

We moved on to thinking about the equipment required to execute our plans.

You can destroy a power station with a shaped charge of 2 pounds of explosive in just the right place; you don't have to blow the whole installation into the sky. It can be done by a small specific-to-task charge, because you know the vulnerable point you're going for. With Scud we knew the vulnerable points, but not for sure how we were going to get at them. I was keen to take just charges of PE, each weighing about 2 pounds, rather than specific-to-task explosives, because we might not be able to use specifics any other way. Again, we wouldn't have the information until we got there on the ground.

We'd need PE4 explosive, safety fuse, grip switches, nonelectric and electric dets, timers, and det cord. You don't put detonators straight into plastic explosive, which is how it's portrayed in films. You put det cord between the detonator and the explosives. We'd make up these charges in advance, and just before the attack place the dets and timers on to them.

Vince and Bob disappeared to go and organize these items, and came back a quarter of an hour later.

"That's all squared away," said Vince. "It's all under your bed."

All the main points had now been covered.

We would be on foot, carrying everything in, so we'd need a cache area, which would be our LUP (*lying-up point*). Ideally, the LUP would provide cover from fire and cover from view, because we'd be manning it all the time. It's very dangerous to leave equipment and go back to it—even though this sometimes has to be done—because it might be ambushed or booby-trapped if discovered. We'd work from a patrol base and move out from there to carry out our tasks. It might happen that we'd find a better site for our LUP during a patrol, in which case we'd move all the kit again under cover of darkness.

We now worked out the E&E plan. We would be 185 miles from Saudi, but only 75 from neighboring countries. Some were part of the Coalition, so in theory would be perfect places to head for.

"What are the borders like?" Vince asked Bert.

"I'm not entirely sure. Might be like the border with Saudi, a tank berm and that's all. But they could be heavily defended. Whatever, if you cross a border, for heaven's sake make sure they don't think you're Israeli—it's not that far away."

"Fair one, Bert," said Stan, nodding his head in Bob's direction and grinning. "But I'm not going across any border with that spick."

Bob certainly looked the part, with tight black curly hair and a large nose.

"Yeah, well, who'd want to go with Zorro there?" Bob pointed at Mark's big nose.

Everything was going well. It's when people stop the slagging and start being nice to each other that you have to worry.

"What's the ground like going up there?" Mark asked.

"Much the same. Basically flat, but when you get up

to the areas of Krabilah and the border there is some high ground. The further west, the higher the ground."

"What's the score on the Euphrates?" Dinger said. "Is it swimmable?"

"It's almost a half mile wide in places, with small islands. It'll be in fierce flood this time of the year. All around there is vegetation, and where there's vegetation, there's water, and where there's water there's people. So there'll always be people around the river. It's rather green and lush—Adam and Eve country, actually, if you remember your Bible."

We looked at the options. If we were compromised, did we tab it all the way south or did we move northwest? We'd probably have a lot of drama getting across any border, but we'd have that going south as well. They'd guess we were going south anyway, and it was a hell of a long distance to run.

Dinger piped up in his best W. C. Fields voice, "Go west, young man, go west."

"Nah, fuck that," Chris said, "it's full of rag heads. If we're on the run, let's go somewhere nice. Let's go to Turkey. I went there for my holidays once. It was rather nice. If we get to Istanbul, there's a place called the Pudding Club, where all the international travelers meet and leave messages. We could leave a message for the search and rescue team and then just go on the piss while we wait for them to pick us up. Sounds good to me."

"Bert, what sort of reception committee would we get elsewhere?" Legs asked. "Any info from downed pilots yet?"

"I'll find out."

"Unless we're told otherwise, Bert," I said, "we're not going south."

You always keep together as a team for as long as you can, because it's better for morale and firepower, and your chances of escape are higher than as individuals. But if the patrol were split, the beauty of choosing north was that you could be the world's worst navigator and still find your way there. Due north and hit the river, hang a left, heading west. But even if we managed to cross the border we couldn't count ourselves as being on safe ground. There was no information to suggest otherwise.

The one thing we dreaded was getting captured. As far as I knew, the Iraqis were not signatories to either the Geneva or Hague Conventions. During the Iran/Iraq War we'd all seen reports of atrocities they'd committed while carrying out interrogations. Their prisoners had been flogged, electrocuted, and partially dismembered. I was very concerned that if we were captured and just went into the "Big Four"—number, rank, name, date of birth—these people wouldn't be satisfied and would require more from us, as their gruesome track record had shown. I therefore decided that, contrary to military conventions and without telling my superiors, the patrol should prepare itself with a cover story. But what should it be?

We were clearly an attacking force. We would be stuck up in northwest Iraq, carrying the world's supply of ammunition, explosive ordnance, food, and water. You wouldn't need the brains of an archbishop to realize that we weren't there as members of the Red Cross.

The only thing we could think of was that we were a search and rescue team. These teams came as quite a big package, especially when the Americans were out to rescue one of their downed pilots. The pilots had a TACBE *(tactical beacon)* which transmitted on the international distress frequency, which AWACS *(Airborne Warning and Control System)* continuously listened to and got a fix on. Of course, everybody else was listening in as well, including the Iraqis. AWACS would locate the pilot from his beacon and relay the message. A search and rescue mission would then be stood to *(made ready)*. The package would be a heli with an extraction party of eight to ten men ready to give covering fire from the air, with machine guns mounted on the helicopter. The party might even be joined by a couple of Apache attack helicopters giving cover so that the bigger helicopter could come down and do the snatch. There would probably be top cover as well, a couple of jets like A10s to add to the hosing down if needed. There was a big emphasis on getting people back, and so there should be. Then you know that if you get in the shit, there'll be every effort made to come and save you, especially if you're a pilot. It's good for morale and flying efficiency, and quite apart from anything else there's the purely financial angle—millions of pounds' worth of training have gone into every single pilot.

The Iraqis would be aware of these big rescue packages, and of the fact that inside the pickup helicopter there would be a medical team, mainly for trauma management. We were about the right numbers, and we would be dressing more or less uniformly. Contrary to common belief, we don't all walk around in what we like. You need a form of recognition so your own troops can identify you. You don't want to be shot by your own side: that's rather unprofessional. So for this sort of op you resemble some form of soldier.

Because it was just normal PE4 that we would be carrying, we could say it was for our own protection—that sometimes we had to man an RV point while AWACS talked the downed pilot on to us. In such a case we'd put local protection out. "They've given us all this stuff," we would say, "but we don't really have a clue how to use it."

Everybody had medical experience. The whole Regiment is trained to a high standard. Chris, being a patrol medic, was partly NHS *(National Health Service)* trained. Stan, of course, had a medical degree and a year of clinical experience. Search and Rescue is concerned mainly with trauma management, so people of our standard would be involved.

The TACBEs would blend in with our story, but in my heart of hearts I knew it wouldn't hold up for long, especially if we were caught with the cache equipment. We knew we wouldn't get more than two or three days out of the story, but that would be long enough for the Head Shed to do their assessment of the damage we could do to OPSEC. What do they know? our Head Shed would ask—and how can it affect our future operations? They would have to assume that everything we knew, we would have told. That's why we are only told what we need to know—for our own good as well as everybody else's. At best, we'd just be giving them time.

It was about six o'clock in the evening now and time for another break. The room really stank, and you could see the signs of strain on people's faces. We went and had a scoff, and for a change we all sat together. Normally you'd be off with your own mates and doing your own thing.

"I was in the doghouse for watching *Apocalypse Now* on the box the night before we left," Vince said as he stirred his coffee.

"Me too," Mark said. "But there was nothing else to do: the pubs were shut."

Most people had experienced that same horrible lull when it was the early hours of the morning and they were just sitting there and waiting. Jilly and I had spent the day and night in strained silence. Only Bob had had a different time of it, boogying the night away at the club, rather badly as usual, apparently.

We talked about how good the task was and how much we were looking forward to getting on the ground, but the excitement was tempered a bit by the thought of how isolated we would be. We knew it was risky, but it wasn't the first time and it wouldn't be the last—after all, this was what we were paid for.

We filled our flasks ready for the next session.

The mood was more lighthearted now as I summarized twelve hours of planning.

"Right. We fly in by Chinook to a DOP (*drop-off point*) twenty kilometers south of the MSR, then tab one night, maybe two, depending on the terrain and population, to the LUP-cum-cache. From there we'll carry out recce patrols to locate the landline. This hunt might take two or three nights: we just don't know until we get on the ground. Initially we will be preoccupied with finding the landline, but at the same time we'll OP (*put an observation post on*) the MSR, watching for Scud movement. If we see the world's supply of Scud moving along the MSR, we will assess and call in an air strike. If we see a Scud launch, we'll take a bearing, locate it, recce, then carry out a target attack. We'll then move back to the LUP and carry on with our tasking. All of this is very flexible until we get on the ground. We might get a Scud launch on our very first night. But we'll do nothing about it until we are firmly in an LUP-cum-cache position. There's no point screaming 'banzai!' and getting our arse kicked just for the sake of a bit of bravado and a solitary Scud. Better to take our time and do more damage. So we sort ourselves out, then we go and give it max. After fourteen days we'll exfiltrate to a pickup point prearranged with the aircrew before we infil, or we will give them an RV with our Sit Rep. They will come and either resupply us and redeploy us, or bring us back for retasking. All very simple really."

And so it was. You must keep things that way if you can; then there's less to forget and less to go wrong. If a plan has many facets and depends on split second timing—and sometimes it does—it's more likely to fuck up. Plenty of plans have to be like this, of course, but you must always try to keep it simple. Keep it simple, keep it safe.

We had a patrol radio for comms between the FOB *(forward operating base)* in Saudi and the patrol. There was unlikely to be room for a spare because of the weight. Having just one was no problem because we were working as one patrol. We also had four TACBEs; it would have been ideal to have one each, but the kit just wasn't available. They are dual-purpose devices. Pull one tab out, and it transmits a beacon which is picked up by any aircraft.

"I remember a story about a unit in Belize," I said. "Not from the Regiment, but they were jungle training. They were issued with TACBEs while they were in the jungle. One officer put his TACBE in his locker, and as he put it in, the tab of the distress beacon was pulled out and set off. Commercial aircraft were radioing in, everybody was running around. It took two days for them to find the beacon in his locker."

"Dickhead."

Pull out another tab, and you can use it like a normal radio, speaking within a limited range to aircraft overhead. You can also use TACBE to communicate with each other on the ground—a system known as working one-to-one—but it has to be line of sight and has a limited range. Its main use, however, would be to talk to AWACS if we were in trouble. We were informed that AWACS would be giving us twenty-four-hour coverage and would answer our call within fifteen seconds. It was comforting to know that there'd be someone talking back to us in that nice, sedate, polite voice that AWACS always use to calm down pilots in distress. The problem was, TACBE was very easily DF'd *(detected by direction-finding equipment)*. We'd only use it in an emergency, or if everything was going to rat shit on the air strikes.

We also had another radio, operating on "Simplex" —the same principle as TACBE but on a different frequency, which worked over a range of about a kilometer. This was so we could talk to the helicopter if we had a major drama and call him back, or to direct him in. Because the transmission wattage was minuscule, it was almost impossible to DF, and we could use it quite safely.

The main elements in our belt kit would be ammunition, water, emergency food, survival kit, shell dressings, a knife, and a prismatic compass as a backup for the Silva compass and for taking a bearing off the ground. Water and bullets: those are always the main considerations. All other kit is secondary, so personal comfort items would be the last to go in—and only if we had room. Survival kit is always suitable to theater and task, so out came the fishing lines, but we kept the heliograph, thumb saw, and magnifying glass for fire making. We also carried basic first aid kit, consisting of suture kit, painkillers, rehydrate, antibiotics, scalpel blades, fluid, and fluid-giving sets. The SOP *(standard operating procedure)* is to carry your two Syrettes of morphine around your neck, so that everybody knows where it is. If you have to administer morphine, you always use the casualty's, not your own: you might be needing your own a few minutes later.

We wouldn't bother with sleeping bags because of the bulk and weight, and because the weather would not be too bad. I would take a set of lightweight GoreTex, however, and everybody else took their poncho liner or space blanket. I also took my old woolly hat, since you lose a massive amount of body heat through your head. When I sleep, I pull it right over my face, which has the added advantage of giving that rather pleasant sense of being under the covers.

In our bergens we carried explosives, spare batteries for the patrol radio, more intravenous fluids and fluid-giving sets, water, and food. Bob was elected to carry the piss can, a one-gallon plastic petrol container.

When it was full, one of us would carry it a mile or so into the bush while on patrol, move a rock and dig a hole underneath it, empty the can, and replace the earth and rock. This would prevent detection by smell, animal interest, or insect activity.

I delegated various other tasks.

"Chris, you sort out the medic kit."

He would automatically get trauma equipment, including a complete intravenous set and field dressings for everybody.

"Legs will sort out the scaley kit."

For some reason unknown to me, signalers are usually called scaleys. I knew that among other tasks Legs would make sure we had spare antennas for the patrol radio, so that if we were compromised when the antenna was out we could just leave it out and move. We would still be able to communicate using the spare antenna. He would also check that everything had a fresh battery, that we had spare batteries, and that everything was actually working.

"Vince and Bob, can you sort out the dems kit?"

They would take the PE out of all its packaging and wrap it in masking tape to keep its shape. This would save the noise of unpacking in the field and any risk of compromise as a result of dropped rubbish. "If the enemy see as much as a spent match on the ground in front of them, they'll know you were there," the instructor on my Combat Survival course had said. "And if they find it behind them they'll know it was Special Forces."

"Mark, you can sort out the food and jerricans."

The Kiwi would draw eight men's rations for fourteen days from Stores. You strip it all down, and keep just one set of brew kit in your belt kit. I throw away the toilet paper because in the field I shit by squatting and therefore don't need it. But everybody keeps the plastic bags for shitting into. You simply tie a knot in them after use and put the contents into your bergen.

Everything must go with you, as nothing can be left to compromise your position, old or present. If you just buried shit it would create animal interest, and if discovered the ingredients could be analyzed. Rice content, for example, would indicate Iraqis; currants or chili would point to Westerners.

There's always a lot of banter to swap menus. The unwritten rule is that whatever you don't want you throw into a bin liner for the other blokes to sort through. Stan didn't like Lancashire hot pot but loved steak and vegetables, so unbeknownst to him we swapped the contents. He would go over the border with fourteen days' worth of his least favorite meal. It was just a stitch; once we were out there we would swap around.

We still needed cam nets to conceal ourselves and our kit.

"I'll do it," Dinger volunteered.

He would cut rolls of hessian into six-by-six-foot squares. Brand-new hessian needs to be messed up with engine oil. You put the hessian into a puddle of it and rub it in well with a broom. Then you turn it over and put it in the mud and rub it all in. Give it a good shake, let it dry, and Bob's your uncle—your very own cam net.

"Everything to be done by 1000 tomorrow," I concluded.

We would check and test, check and test. This wouldn't prevent things going wrong or not working, but it would at least cut down the odds.

It was about 2230, and Dinger announced that he had just run out of fags.

I got the hint. We'd covered everything and to carry on would just be reinventing the wheel. As the blokes left, they put every scrap of paper into a burn bag to be destroyed.

Vince and I stayed behind. We still had to go into the Phases (*outline plan*) with the squadron OC and sergeant major. They would hit us with a lot of questions of the "what if?" variety, and their different track of thinking might put a new angle on things. With luck, they might even approve the plan.

4

I couldn't sleep because my mind was going at a hundred miles an hour. It was people's lives I was playing with here, my own included. The squadron OC had given the plan his approval, but that didn't stop me wondering if there was a better way of going about it. Were other people just nodding and agreeing with what I said? Probably not, since they all had a vested interest in our success and they were outspoken individuals. Was there anything I'd left out or forgotten? But you reach the point where you have to press on regardless. You could spend the rest of your life thinking about the different options.

I got up and made a brew. Legs had just finished sorting out the signals kit, and he came over and joined me. There was no sign of Stan or Dinger. Those two could sleep on a chicken's lip.

"The signals Head Shed have just given me our call sign," Legs said. "It's Bravo Two Zero. Sounds good to me."

We had a bit of a chat about possible shortages. As I watched him head back to his bed, I wondered if he was thinking about home. He was a strong family man, with a second child that was just five months old. My mind drifted to Jilly. I hoped she wasn't getting upset by anything she was reading in the media.

There was the constant noise of kit being lugged and blokes mooching around sorting themselves out. I put my Walkman on and listened to Madness. I wasn't really listening because my mind was screaming in so many directions, but I must have nodded off at about three, because at six, when I woke, the lead singer had dropped two octaves and they were just about grinding to a halt.

It was quite a frenzy that morning. We checked that we still knew how to activate the distress signals on the small TACBE radios and use them one-to-one so we could actually talk line of sight on them.

Vince had collected the 5.56 ammunition for the Armalites and as many 40mm bombs for the grenade launchers as he could get his hands on. We had a lot of shortages on these bombs because the grenade launcher is such a formidable, excellent weapon. The bombs are quite a commodity; when you've got them, you hoard them. I explained the problem to a mate in A Squadron, and he poached about and got us some more.

All the 5.56 had to be put into magazines, and the magazines checked to make sure they were working. The magazines are as important as the weapon itself, because if the springs don't push the round into position, the working parts can't push the round into the breech. So you check and recheck all your mags, and then recheck them a third time. The Armalite magazine normally takes 30 rounds, but many of us choose to put in just 29, which gives a little bit of extra push in the spring. It's easier and quicker to put on a new mag than to clear a stoppage.

We checked the 203 bombs and explosives. PE4 doesn't smell and feels very much like plasticine. It's surprisingly inert. You can even light a stick of it and watch it burn like a frenzied candle. The only trouble with PE4 is that when it's cold, it's quite brittle and hard to mold into shapes. You have to make it pliable by working it in your hands.

We checked and rechecked all the detonators. The nonelectric ones that we'd be using for the compromise device are initiated by the safety fuse burning into them, and cannot be tested. Electric dets can be put on a circuit tester. If the electric circuit is going through the det, we can be sure that the electric pulse will set off the explosive inside and, in turn, detonate the charge. Fortunately, misfires are very rare.

It takes quite a while to test the timers. You have to set the time delay and check that it's working. If it works for one hour, it will work for forty-eight hours. Then you time the device and see if it is working correctly. In theory, if it is more than five seconds early or late, you exchange it for another. In practice, I bin any timer that I have doubts about.

The last item for testing was the wiring for the claymore antipersonnel mines, which was also done on a circuit tester.

We then ran through the rigging and derigging of the little Elsie antipersonnel mines. For many of us it had been a while since we'd had our hands on this sort of kit. We made sure we could remember how to arm them and, more importantly, how to disarm them. There might be a situation where we'd lay the explosive and Elsie mines on target, but for some reason have to go in and extract them. This makes life more difficult when you're placing them, because not only do you have to keep a record of where they are on the ground, but also the person who sets the antihandling device should be the one to lift it.

There was a severe shortage of claymores, which was a problem because they are excellent for defense and antipursuit. The solution was to go round to the cookhouse, get a pile of ice-cream containers, and make our own. You make a hole in the center of the carton, run a det cord tail into it, and tie a knot inside the container. You make a shaped charge with PE4 and put it in the bottom of the tub, making sure that the knot is embedded. You then fill the carton with nuts and bolts, little lumps of metal, and anything else nasty you can find lying around, put on the lid, and wrap lots of masking tape around to seal it. Once the claymore is in position, all you have to do is put a det onto the det cord and Bob used to be your uncle.

Next, we sorted out the weapons, starting with a trip down to the range to "zero" the sights. You lie down in the prone position, aim at the same place on a target 300 feet away, and fire five rounds. This is then called a group. You look where the group has landed on the target and then adjust the sights so that the next group will land where you want it to—which is where you are aiming. If you do not zero and the group is, say, 4 inches to the right of where you are aiming at 300 feet, then at 600 feet it will be 8 inches to the right, and so on. At 1200 feet you could easily miss a target altogether.

One individual's zero will be different from another's because of many factors. Some are physical size and "eye relief"—the distance between the eye of the firer and the rear sight. If you used another person's weapon the zero could be off for you. This is not a problem at short ranges of up to 900 feet, but at greater distances it could be a problem. If this was the case and you could see where the rounds were going, you could "aim off" to adjust.

We spent a whole morning down at the range—first to zero the weapons, and second to test all the magazines. I was going to take ten magazines with me on the patrol, a total of 290 rounds, and every magazine had to be tested. I would also be carrying a box of 200 rounds for a Minimi, which takes the same round as the Armalite and can be either belt- or magazine-fed.

We also fired some practice 203 bombs, which throw out a chalk puff when they land to help you see if you've got to aim higher or lower—it's a crude form of zero.

We rehearsed for many different scenarios. The situation on the ground can change very rapidly, and you have to expect everything to be rather fluid. The more you practice, the more flexible you can be. We call this stage of planning and preparation "walk through, talk through," and operate a Chinese parliament while we're doing it. Everybody, regardless of rank, has the right to contribute his own ideas and rip to shreds those of others.

We practiced various kinds of LUP because we weren't sure of the lie of the ground. The terrain might be as flat as a pancake, in which case we'd LUP in two groups of four that gave each other mutual support. We discussed the way we would communicate between the two groups—whether it would be by comms cord, which is simply a stretch of string that can be pulled in the event of a major drama, or by field telephone, a small handset attached to a piece of two-flex D10 wire running along to the next position. In case we decided to go ahead with the landline, we practiced running the D10 out and how we were actually going to speak. Legs went off and came back with a pair of electronic field telephones that even he wasn't familiar with. They had been running from one office to another between Portakabins before he nicked them. We sat with them like children with a new Fisher-Price toy, pressing this, pushing that. "What's this do then? What if I push this?"

The priority when filling a bergen is "equipment to task"—in our case, ordnance and equipment that could help us to place or deliver that ordnance. Next came the essentials to enable you to survive—water and food, trauma-management equipment, and, for this op, NBC protection.

The equipment in our bergens was what we would need on the ground to operate. However, radio batteries run down and, along with many other things, would have to be replaced during our two weeks of being self-sufficient. Therefore more equipment had to be taken along and cached, simply to resupply the bergens. This was what was in the jerricans and two sandbags, one containing more NBC kit, the other more food plus any batteries and odds and sods.

It added up to an awesome weight of kit. Vince was in charge of distribution. Different types of equipment have to be evenly placed in the patrol. If all the explosives were placed in one bergen and that was lost, for whatever reason, we would then lose our attack capability using explosives. In the Falklands, the task force's entire supply of Mars bars was sent on one ship, and everybody was flapping in case it sank. They should have got Vince to organize it. Besides the tactical considerations behind equal distribution, people want and expect equal loads, whether they're 5'2" or 6'3". We have a scale that weighs up to 200 lb, and it showed that we were carrying 154 lb per man in our bergens and belt kit. On top of that we had a 5-gallon jerrican of water each—another 40 lb. We carried our NBC kit and cache rations, which weighed yet another 15 lb, in two sandbags that had been tied together to form saddlebags that could go around our necks or over our shoulders. The total weight per man was therefore 209 lb, the weight of a 15-stone man. Everybody packed their equipment the way they wanted. There's no set way of doing this, as long as you've got it and can use it. The only "must" was the patrol radio, which always goes on top of the signaler's bergen so that it can be retrieved by anybody in a contact.

Belt kit consists of ammunition and basic survival requisites—water, food, and trauma-care equipment, plus personal goodies. For this op we would also take TACBEs in our belt kit, plus cam netting to provide cover if we couldn't find any natural, and digging tools to unearth the cables if necessary. Your belt kit should never come off you, but if it does it must never be more than an arm's length away. At night you must always have physical contact with it. If it's off, you sleep on top of it. The same goes for your weapon.

The best method of moving the equipment proved to be a shuttle service in two groups of four, with four giving the protection, four doing the humping, and then changing around. It was hard work, and I didn't look forward to the 12 mile tab that first night—or maybe two—from the heli drop-off to the MSR. We certainly wouldn't practice carrying it now: that would be a bit like practicing being wet, cold, and hungry, which wouldn't achieve anything.

We did practice getting off the aircraft, and the actions we would carry out if there was a compromise as it was happening or the heli was leaving.

Everything now was task-oriented. If you weren't physically doing something to prepare for it, you were thinking about it. As we "walked through, talked through," I could see the concentration etched on everybody's face.

We were getting centrally fed, and the cooks were sweating their butts off for us. Most of the Regiment had already disappeared on tasks, but there were enough blokes left to pack the cookhouse and slag each other off. The boys in A Squadron had given themselves the most outrageous crewcuts, right down to the bone. They had suntanned faces in front and sparkly white domes behind. Some of them were the real Mr. Guccis, the lounge lizards downtown of a Friday, and there they were with the world's worst haircuts, no doubt desperately praying the war was going to last long enough for it to grow again.

Because a lot of Regiment administration was also being run centrally, I kept bumping into people that I hadn't seen for a long time. You'd give them a good slagging, see what reading material they had, then nick it. It was a really nice time. People were more sociable than usual, probably because we were out of the way, there were no distractions, just the job at hand. Everybody was euphoric. Not since the Second World War and the days of David Stirling had there been so much of the Regiment together at any one time in one theater.

We had some very nasty injections at one stage against one of the biological warfare agents it was thought Saddam Hussein might use. The theory was that you got one injection, then waited a couple of days and went back for another, but the majority of us were out of the game after the first jab. It was horrendous: our arms came up like balloons, so we didn't go back.

We were told on the 18th that we were going to move forward to another location, an airfield, from where we would mount our operations. We sorted out our personal kit so that if it had to be sent to our next of kin anything upsetting or pornographic had been removed. This would be done by the blokes in the squadron as well, to make sure your rubber fetish was never made public. To make less drama for your family you usually put military kit in one bag and personal effects in another. We labeled it and handed it in to the squadron quartermaster sergeant.

We flew out from the operating base on a C130 that was packed with pinkies and mountains of kit. It was tactical, low-level flying, even though we were still in Saudi airspace. There was too much noise for talking. I put on a pair of ear defenders and got my head down.

It was pitch-dark when we landed at the large Coalition airbase and started to unload the kit. Noise was constant and earsplitting. Aircraft of all types took off and landed on the brightly lit runway—everything from spotter aircraft to A10 Thunderbolts.

We were much closer to the Iraqi border here, and I noticed that it was much chillier than we had been used to. You definitely needed a jumper or smock to keep yourself warm, even with the work of unloading. We laid out our sleeping bags on the grass under the palm trees and got a brew going from our belt kit.

I was lying on my back looking up at the stars when I heard a noise that started as low, distant thunder and then grew until it filled the sky. Wave after wave of what looked like B52s were passing overhead en route to Iraq. Everywhere you looked there were bombers. It could have been a scene from a Second World War recruitment poster. Tankers brought out their lines and jets moved in to fill up. The sky roared for five or six minutes. Such mighty, heart-stirring airpower dominating the heavens—and down below on the grass, a bunch of dickheads brewing up. We had been self-contained and self-obsessed, seeing nothing of the war but our own preparations. Now it hit home: the Gulf War was not just a small number of men on a task; this was something fucking outrageously major. And bar one more refuel, we were within striking distance of adding to the mayhem.

Just before first light Klaxons started wailing, and people ran in all directions. None of us had a clue what was going on, and we stayed put in our sleeping bags. "Get in the shelter!" somebody yelled, but it was too warm where we were. Nobody budged, and quite rightly so. If somebody wanted us to know what was going on, they'd come and tell us. Eventually somebody shouted, "Scud!" and we jumped. We'd just about got to our feet when the order came to stand down.

Every hour on the hour during the day, somebody would tune in to the BBC World Service. At certain times you'd hear the signature tune of the Archers as well. When you're away there's always somebody who's listening to the everyday tale of country folk, even if they will not admit it.

We were told we were going in that night. It was quite a relief. We'd got to the airfield with only what we stood up in.

In the afternoon I gave a formal set of orders. Everybody who was involved in the task was present—all members of the patrol; the squadron OC; the OPS officer who oversees all the squadron's operations.

After I had delivered them verbally, the orders would be handed over to the operations center. They would stay there until the mission was completed, so that if anything went wrong, everybody would know what I wanted to happen. If we ought to have been at point A by day 4, for example, and we weren't, they'd know that I wanted a fast jet flying over so I could make contact by TACBE.

The top of each orders sheet is overprinted with the words *Remember Need to Know* to remind you of OPSEC. It's critically important that nobody should know anything that does not concern him directly. The pilots, for example, would not attend the orders.

I started by describing the ground we were going to cover. You have to explain your orders as if nobody's got a clue what's going on—so in this case I started by pointing out where Iraq was and which countries bordered it. Then you go into the area in detail, which for us was the bend in the MSR. I described the lie of the ground and the little topographical information I had. Everything that I knew, they had to know.

Next I gave times of first and last light, the moon states, and the weather forecast. I had been confidently informed by the met blokes that the weather should be cool and dry. Weather information is important because if, for example, you have been briefed in the orders that the prevailing wind is from the northeast, you can use that information to help you with your navigation. Since the weather was still forecast as fairly clement for the duration of our mission, we had again elected to leave our sleeping bags behind. Not that there would have been any room to take them anyway.

I now gave the Situation phase of the orders. I would normally tell at this point everything I knew about the enemy that concerned us—weapons, morale, composition, and strengths, and so on—but the intelligence was very scanty. I would also normally mention the location of any friendly forces and how they could help us, but for our op there was nothing to tell.

Next was the mission statement, which I repeated twice. It was just as the OC had given it to us in the briefing room: one, to locate and destroy the landline in the area of the northern MSR, and two, to find and destroy Scud.

Now came Execution, the real meat of the orders— how we were actually going to carry out the mission. I gave a general outline, broken down into phases, a bit like telling a story.

"Phase 1 will be the infiltration, which will be by the Chinook. Phase 2 will be moving up to the LUP-cum-cache area. Phase 3 will be LUP routine. Phase 4 will be the recce, then target attack on the landline. Phase 5 will be the actions on Scud location. Phase 6 will be the exfiltration, or resupply and retasking."

Then, for each phase, I would go into the detail of how we were going to do it. This has to be as detailed as possible to eliminate gray areas. After every phase I then gave the "actions on"—for instance, actions on compromise during the drop-off, if the patrol came under fire just as the heli took off again. Then people would know what I wanted to happen when there was no drama, and they'd also know what needed to happen if there was.

That was all very fine in theory, of course, but for

each of these actions on, you also need to describe every detail of how you want things to be done. All of this had to be talked about and worked out beforehand and then given in the formal orders. Forward planning saves time and energy on the ground because people then know what is required of them. For example, what happens if the heli is required to return to the patrol at some stage to replace a damaged radio? When the heli lands do we go around to the back of the aircraft? Do we take the new radio out of the loadmaster's side door? How do we actually call the heli in? What is the authentification code? The answer to this one was that we'd give a phonetic code, the letter Bravo, as recognition. The heli pilot would know that at a certain grid, or in a certain area within that grid, he was going to see us flashing Bravo on infrared. He'd be looking through his PNG *(passive night goggles)*, and because I'd told him so, he'd know he would land 15 feet to the left-hand side of the B when he saw it. Then, because he was landing on my right-hand side, all I'd have to do was walk past the cockpit to the loadmaster's door, which is behind the cockpit on the left-hand side on the Chinook, throw a radio in, and catch the radio that they threw out. If there were any messages they'd grab my arm and give them to me on a bit of paper. The exchange would be all over in a minute.

It took about an hour and a half to go through all the details of each phase. Next were coordinating instructions, the nitty-gritty details like timings, grid references, RVs, locations of interest. These had already been given but would be said again to confirm. This stage also included actions on capture, and details of the E&E plan.

I covered service support, which was an inventory of the stores and equipment we were taking with us. And finally I described the chain of command and signals—types of radio, frequencies, schedules, codes and codewords, and any field signals that were unique to the task.

"As I'm sure you all know by now," I said, "our call sign is Bravo Two Zero. The chain of command is myself as patrol commander and Vince as 2 i/c. The rest of you can fight for it."

It was now the patrol's chance to ask questions, after which we synchronized watches.

The air brief was given by the pilot, since he would be in command during the infil and exfil phases. He showed us a map of the route we were going to take, and talked at some length about the likely difficulty of antiaircraft sites and attack by Roland ground-to-air missiles. He told us what he wanted to happen in the back of the aircraft, and the actions on crashing. I had talked to him about this before and was secretly glad that he wanted us to split up, with the aircrew and the patrol taking their own chances. To be honest, we wouldn't have wanted a bunch of aircrew with us, and for some reason they were not particularly keen to come with us anyway. He spoke, too, about deconfliction, because there were going to be air raids going in on surrounding targets—a number of fixed-launch sites were going to be hosed down within 6 miles of our drop-off point. Our deconfliction was arranged to enable us to slip in under these air strikes and use them for cover.

The orders group ended at about 1100. Everybody now knew what they had to do, where they were doing it, and how they were going to do it.

At lunchtime, we were told that because of deconfliction we might not be able to get in. However, we were going to attempt it anyway—you don't know until you try. We would refuel just short of the Saudi/Iraq border, then go over with full tanks. We did a final round of checks, loaded the kit onto wagons, and ate as much fresh food as we could get down us.

We were eager to go. The mood was very much one of let's just get in there and do it. We'd leave it to the other blokes to run round stealing tents and kit and generally square everything away. The camp would be sorted out by the time we returned.

At 1800 we climbed into the vehicles and drove across to the Chinook. It was all rather casual, with blokes from the squadron coming up and saying, "What size are those new boots of yours—you won't be needing them again, will you?" At our first location four or five of us had nicked some foam mattresses, operating on the usual principle: if it's there and it's shiny, take it. Now some of the other patrols started coming over and saying, "You won't be needing it ever again, will you, so you can leave it for us." They accompanied it with the motion of digging our graves.

Even the RSM (Regimental Sergeant Major) appeared. "Get in there, do the business, and come back." That was the extent of his brief.

Bob suddenly remembered something. "I've fucked up," he said to a mate. "I haven't completed the will form. My mum's name is down and I've signed it—you'll have to dig in my kit for her address. Can you make sure it's all sorted and handed in?"

I had a quick chat with the pilots. They'd been given sets of body armor and were going through big decisions about what to do with it—whether to sit on it so they didn't get their bollocks shot off, or actually wear it so they didn't get shot in the chest. They came to the conclusion that it was better to wear it on the chest, because they could live without their balls.

"Not that he has any," said the copilot, "as you will soon find out."

It was still light and we could see the downwash of the rotors kicking up a fierce sandstorm as the helicopter took off. When the dust settled, all we could see was blokes looking skywards and waving.

We flew low-level across the desert. At first we watched the ground, but there wasn't much to see—just a vast area of sand and a few hills. Dotted across the desert there were peculiar circles that looked like corn circles in reverse—crops growing up rather than pushed down. They were horticultural sites that looked from the air like green sewage-treatment plants, with large watering arms turning constantly to irrigate the crops. They looked so out of place in the barren landscape.

It was last light and we were about 12 miles short of the border when the pilot spoke into the headsets.

"Get the blokes up to the window and have a look at this."

Countless aircraft were in the sky a thousand feet above us. Orchestrated by AWACS, they were flying with split second timing along a complex network of air corridors to avoid collision. Every one of them had its forward lights on. The sky was ablaze with light. It was like *Star Wars*, all these different colored lights from different sizes of aircraft. We were doing about 100 knots; they must have been flying at 500 or 600. I wondered if they knew about us. I wondered if they were saying to themselves: let's hope we can do a good job so these guys can get in and do their thing. I doubted it.

Two fighters screamed down to check us out, then flew back up.

"We're 5Ks short of the border," the pilot said. "Watch what happens now."

As he spoke, and as if a single fuse controlling the Blackpool illuminations had blown, the sky was suddenly pitch-black. Every aircraft had dowsed its lights at once.

* * *

We landed in inky blackness for a hot refuel, which meant staying on board with the rotors moving. We were going to receive the final "go" or "no go" here regarding the vital deconfliction, and as the ground crew loomed out of the darkness, I watched anxiously for somebody to give an encouraging signal. One of them looked at the pilot and revolved his hand: Turnaround.

Bastard!

Another bloke ran up to the pilot with a bit of paper and pushed it through the window.

The pilot's voice came over our headsets a moment later: "It's a no go, no go; we've got to go back."

Dinger was straight on the intercom. "Well, fuck it, let's get over the border anyway, just to say we've been over there—come on, it's just a couple of Ks away: it won't take long to get there and back. We need to get over, just to stop the slagging when we return."

But that wasn't the way the pilot saw it. We stayed on the ground for another twenty minutes while he did his checks and the refueling was completed; then we lifted off and headed south. Wagons were waiting for us. We unloaded all the kit and were taken to the half-squadron location, which by this time had been moved to the other side of the airfield. People had dug shell scrapes and covered them with ponchos and bits of board and cardboard to keep out the wind. It looked like a dossers' camp, bodies in little huddles everywhere, around hexy-block fires.

The patrol were in dark moods, not only because of the anticlimax of not getting across the border, but also because we weren't sure what was going to happen next. I was doubly unimpressed because I had given my mattress away.

All during the day of the 20th we just hung loose, waiting for something to happen, waiting for a slot.

We checked the kit a couple more times and tried to make ourselves a bit of a home in case we had a long wait. We got some camouflage netting up—not from the tactical point of view, because the airfield was in a secure area—but just to keep the wind off and give us some shade during the day. It gives you an illusion of protection to be sheltered under something. Once we had made ourselves comfy, we screamed around the place in LSVs *(light strike vehicles)* and pinkies seeing what we would nick. The place was a kleptomaniac's dream.

We did some good exchanges with the Yanks. Our rations are far superior to the American MREs *(meals ready to eat)*, but theirs do contain some pleasant items —like bags of M&M's and little bottles of Tabasco sauce to add a little *je ne sais quoi* to the beef and dumplings. Another fine bit of Yank kit is the strong plastic spoon that comes with the MRE pack. You can burn a little hole through the back of it, put some string through, and keep it in your pocket: an excellent, almost perfect racing spoon.

Because our foam mattresses had been whisked away to a better world during the abortive flight, we tried to get hold of some comfy US issue cots. The Americans had kit coming out of their ears, and bless their cotton socks, they'd happily swap you a cot for a couple of boxes of rations.

Little America was on the other side of the airfield. They had everything from microwaves and doughnut machines to Bart Simpson videos screening twenty-four hours a day. And why not—the Yanks sure know how to fight a stylish war. Schoolkids in the States were sending big boxes of goodies to the soldiers: pictures from 6-year-olds of a good guy with the US flag, and a bad guy with the Iraqi flag, and the world's supply of soap, toothpaste, writing material, combs, and antiperspirant. They were just left open on tables in the canteen for people to pick what they wanted.

The Yanks could not have made us more welcome, and we were straight in there, drinking frothy cappuccino and having a quick root through. Needless to say, we had most of it away.

Some of the characters were outrageous and great fun to talk to, especially some of the American pilots who I took to be members of the National Guard. They were all lawyers and sawmill managers in real life, big old boys in their forties and fifties, covered in badges and smoking huge cigars, flying their Thunderbolts and whooping "Yeah boy!" all over the sky. For some of them, this was their third war. They were excellent people, and they had amazing stories to tell. Listening to them was an education.

During the next two days we went over the plan again. Now that we had a bit more time, was there anything we could improve on? We talked and talked, but we kept it the same.

It was frustration time, just waiting, as if we were in racing blocks and the starter had gone into a trance. I was looking forward to the relief of actually being on the ground.

We had a chat with a Jaguar pilot whose aircraft had been stranded at the airfield for several days. On his very first sortie he had had to abort because of problems with a generator.

"I want to spend the rest of the war here," he said. "The slagging I'll get when I fly back will be way out of control."

We felt quite sorry for him. We knew how he felt.

Finally, on the 21st, we got the okay to go in the following night.

On the morning of the 22nd we woke at first light. Straightaway Dinger got a fag on.

Stan, Dinger, Mark, and I were all under one cam net, surrounded by rations and all sorts of boxes and plastic bags. In the middle was a little hexy-block fire for cooking.

Stan got a brew going from the comfort of his sleeping bag. Nobody wanted to rise and shine because it was so bloody cold. We lay there drinking tea, gobbing off, and eating chocolate from the rations. Our beauty sleep had been ruined by another two Scud alerts during the night. We were sleeping with most of our kit on anyway, but it was a major embuggerance to have to pull on your boots, flak jacket, and helmet and leg it down to the slit trenches. Both times we only had to wait ten minutes for the all clear.

Dinger opened foil sachets of bangers and beans and got them on the go. Three or four cups of tea and, in Dinger's case, three cigarettes later, we tuned in to the World Service. Wherever you are in the world, you'll learn what's going on from them before any other bugger tells you. We take small shortwave radios with us on all operations and exercises anyway, because if you're stuck in the middle of the jungle, the only link with the outside world you ever get is the World Service. Everywhere you go, people are always bent over their radios tuning in, because the frequencies change depending on the time of day. We were going to take them out on this job as well, because the chances were that it was the first we'd know that the war had ended. Nobody would be able to tell us until we made comms, and that could be the day after Saddam surrendered. We took the piss out of Dinger's radio because it's held together with bits of tape and string. Everybody else had a digital one, and Dinger still had his old steam-powered thing that took an age to tune in.

We had heard rumors that there was going to be some mail in that day, our first load since arriving in Saudi. It would be rather nice to hear from home before we went off. I was in the process of buying a house with Jilly, and I had to sign a form giving her power of attorney. I was hoping that was going to come through; otherwise, there would be major dramas for her to sort out if I got topped.

The pilot and copilot came over, and we had a final chat about stowing the equipment. I went through the lost comms routine and actions on contact at the DOP again, to make doubly sure we were both clear in our minds.

We spoke to the two loadies, lads in their twenties who were obviously great fans of *Apocalypse Now*, because the Chinook had guns hanging off it all over the place. The only things missing were the tiger-head emblems on their helmets and Wagner's ''Ride of the Valkyries'' coming out of their intercom speakers. For them, getting across the border was a once-in-a-lifetime opportunity. They were loving it.

The pilots knew of some more Roland positions and had worked out a route around them, but from the way the loadies were talking you'd have thought they actually wanted to be attacked. They were gagging to get in amongst it. I imagined it would be a huge anticlimax for them if they dropped us off and came back in one piece.

I checked my orders at a table on the other side of the airfield, undistracted. Because the first infil had been aborted, I would have to deliver an orders group all over again that afternoon—not in as much detail, but going over the main points.

We waited for the elusive mail. The buzz finally went round that it had arrived and was on the other side of the airfield about half a mile away. It was 1730, just half an hour to go before moving off to the aircraft. Vince and I got into one of the LSVs and screamed round and grabbed hold of the B Squadron bag.

One of the blokes received his poll tax demand. Another was the lucky recipient of an invitation to enter a

Reader's Digest draw. I was luckier. I got two letters. One was from my mother, the first letter from either of my parents since I was maybe 17. They didn't know I was in the Gulf, but it must have been obvious. I didn't have time to read it. If you're in a rush, what you can do is slit the letters open so that they appear to have been read, so as not to hurt anybody's feelings if you don't return. I recognized an A4 envelope from Jilly. Inside were some toffees, my favorite Pic 'n Mix from Woolies. Oddly enough there were eight of them, one for each of us in the patrol. There was also the power of attorney letter.

The Last Supper is quite a big thing before you go out on a job. Everybody turns up and takes the piss.

"Next time I see you I'll be looking down as I'm filling you in," somebody said, going through the motion of shoveling earth onto your grave.

"Nice knowing you, wanker," somebody else said. "What sort of bike you got at home then? Anyone here to witness he's going to give me his bike if he gets topped?"

It was a very lighthearted atmosphere, and people were willing to help out if they could in any preparation. At the same time, another lot of "fresh" turned up. The regimental quartermaster sergeant had got his hands on a consignment of chops, sausages, mushrooms, and all the other ingredients of a good fry-up. It was fantastic scoff, but one unfortunate outcome was that after being on rations for so long, it put us all in need of an urgent shit.

5

The ground crew had been up all night re-camouflaging the Chinook a splashy desert pattern that drew wolf whistles and applause from the blokes who'd come to see us off.

It was time for passing on last minute messages again. I saw my mate Mick and said: "Any dramas, Eno has got the letters. Make sure you look after the escape map because it's signed by the squadron. I don't want that to go missing: it would be nice for Jilly."

I overheard Vince saying: "Any drama, it's down to you to make sure Dee's sorted out."

Mick had a camera round his neck. "Do you want a picture?"

"Madness not to," I said.

We posed on the tailgate of the Chinook for the Bravo Two Zero team photo.

The blokes were busy taking the piss out of the air-crew, especially the loadies. One of them was a dead ringer for Gary Kemp from Spandau Ballet, even down to the 1980s sideboards. Two or three blokes from the squadron were standing by a wagon doing the old shu-wap, shu-wap routine, singing "You are gold. . . ." The poor lad was getting well embarrassed.

Some blokes got together and practiced doing the pallbearer bit, humming the death march. Others did a takeoff of the Madness video "It must be love," where the singer is standing over a grave and the undertaker's jumping up and down and across measuring him.

Interspersed with the banter was the odd muttering of "See you soon" and "Hope it all goes well."

The aircrew came round for a final quick chat in their body armor, and we climbed aboard.

Nobody flies Club Class in a Chinook. The interior was spartan, a bare hull with plastic coating over the frame. There were no seats, just nonslip flooring to sit on. The deck was littered with sand and grease. A large inboard tank had been fitted to allow us to carry extra fuel. The stink of aviation fuel and engines was overpowering, even at the back near the ramp. It was like sitting in an oven. The loadies kept the top half of the tailgate down to circulate air.

The engines sparked up, coughing fearsome clouds of fumes to the rear. From our position on the ramp we saw blokes dropping their kecks and mooning in the heat haze, and the Spandau Ballet gang were giving it some again. As the Chinook lifted, its downwash created a major sandstorm. By the time the dust had settled we had reached a hundred feet, and soon all we could see were the flashing headlights of the pinkies.

It was hot and I started to sweat and stink. I felt tired, mentally as well as physically. So many things were running through my mind. The infiltration worried me because we had no control over it: we'd just have to sit there and hope for the best. I've never liked it when my life was in somebody else's hands. There were Roland antiaircraft missiles along our route, and the bigger the machine, the bigger the chance of getting shot down. Chinooks are massive. There was also the added risk of getting hosed down by our own aircraft, since we were going in with the cover of three air raids.

I looked forward to getting on the ground, however. It felt good to be in command of such a classic SAS task. Everybody hopes for a major war once in his life, and this was mine, accompanied by a gang that the rest of the squadron was already calling the Foreign Legion.

The bergens were strapped down to stop them flying through the air and landing on top of us if the pilot had to take evasive action or crashed. Just before last light, the loadies cracked cyalume sticks and put them around the kit so we could see where it was, mainly to prevent injury. The sticks are like the ones kids buy at fun fairs—a plastic tube that you bend to crack the glass phials inside and bring two chemicals together to make a luminous mixture.

I put on a pair of headsets and talked to the pilot while the rest of the blokes rooted through all the RAF kit, sorting out the crew's sandwiches, chocolate, and bottles of mineral water.

We had a brief recap on the landing scenarios. If we came into a contact as we landed, we should stay on the aircraft. If we were getting off the aircraft, we should jump back on. But if the heli had already taken off and we had a contact, the Simplex radio gave us about a range of a mile to talk to him and summon him back.

"I'll just turn the aircraft and come screaming back in," he said, "and you just get on it however you can, fuck all the kit."

The RAF are sometimes thought of as glorified taxi drivers, taking you from point A to point B, but they're not: they're an integral part of any operation. For a pilot to bring in a Chinook like that would be totally outrageous. It's a big machine and an easy target, but he was willing to do it. Either he had no idea what would be happening on the ground, or he was blasé because that was his job. He obviously knew what he was talking about, so he was blasé. And if he was willing to do it, I wouldn't give a damn: I'd jump back in.

As we were flying across Saudi, we started to appreciate the lie of the ground. It looked like a brown billiard table. I'd been in the Middle East lots of times, but I'd never seen anything like this.

"We're on Zanussi," Chris said into his headset, using the Regiment term for somebody who's so spaced out and weird you can't get in touch with him; he's on another planet.

And Zanussi was what this looked like—another world. Our map studies told us the ground was like this all the way up. We were going to have problems, but it was too late to do anything about it. We were committed.

Now and again there'd be a bit of chat on the headphones as the pilots talked to AWACS. I loved watching the two loadie warlords getting ready for the Big One, checking their guns and hoping, no doubt, that they would get shot at soon.

All the time, there was the deafening zsh, zsh, zsh of the rotor blades. Not much was said between ourselves because of the noise. Everybody was just pleased that they weren't rushing around any more, that we were just lying around on the kit drinking water or pissing into one of the bottles we'd just emptied. I was wondering if my life might have been different if I'd stayed at school and got my CSEs. I might have been sitting up in the cockpit now, chatting away, looking forward to a pie and a pint later on.

The front loadie's door was half open, like a stable door. Wind rushed through it, cool and refreshing. The straps hanging off the insides of the Chinook flapped and slapped in the gale.

* * *

We got to the same refueling point as before. Again, the pilot kept the rotors turning. An engine failure at this stage would mean canceling the operation. We stayed on the aircraft, but the back loadie was straight off into the darkness. The Yanks, God bless 'em, have so much kit they just throw it at you. He returned with Hershey bars, doughnuts, and cans of Coke. For some unaccountable reason, the Yanks had also given him handfuls of Biros and combs.

We waited and waited. Bob and I jumped down and went for a dump on the side of the tarmac about 100 feet away. When we got back the loadie motioned for me to put on my headsets.

"We have the go," the pilot said, with just the faintest detectable hint of excitement in his voice.

We started to lose altitude.

"We're over the border," the pilot said matter-of-factly.

I passed the message on. The blokes started putting their webbing on.

Now the aircrew really started earning their money. The banter stopped. They were working with night-viewing goggles, screaming along at 80 knots just 70 feet off the ground. The rotor blades had a large diameter and we knew from the map that we were flying in amongst a lot of power lines and obstructions. One loadie looked out the front at the forward blades, and the other did the same at the rear. The copilot continuously monitored the instruments; the pilot flew by visual and instructions received from the rest of the crew.

The exchange between pilot, copilot, and loadies was nonstop as they flew low between features. The tone of the voices was reassuring. Everything was well rehearsed and well practiced. It was all so matter-of-fact they could have been in a simulator.

Copilot: "100 feet . . . 80 feet . . . 80 feet."

Pilot: "Roger that, 80 feet."

Copilot: "Power lines one mile."

Pilot: "Roger, power lines one mile. Pulling up."

Copilot: "120 . . . 150 . . . 180 . . . 200. That's half a mile. 500 feet now."

Pilot: "500 feet. I have the lines visual . . . over we go."

Loadie: "Clear."

Pilot: "Okay, going lower."

Copilot: "150 . . . 120 . . . 80 feet. 90 knots."

Pilot: "Roger, staying at 80 feet, 90 knots."

Copilot: "Reentrant left, one mile."

Pilot: "Roger that, I have a building to my right."

Loadie: "Roger that, building right."

Copilot: "80 feet. 90 knots. Power lines five miles."

Pilot: "Roger that, five miles. Breaking right."

The loadies were looking at the ground below as well. Apart from watching for obstructions, they checked for any "incoming."

Copilot: "80 feet. Metal road coming up, two miles."

Pilot: "Roger that. Metal road, two miles."

Copilot: "One mile to go. That's 100 knots, 80 feet."

At anything below 80 feet the blades would hit the ground as the aircraft turned. Meanwhile, the loadmasters were looking for obstructions and trying to ensure the blades had enough room to rotate as we hugged any feature that would give the heli some protection.

Pilot: "Break my right now. That's nice."

Copilot: "Right, that's 70 foot, 100 knots. 70 foot, 90 knots."

We had to cross a major obstruction that ran east–west across this part of the country.

Copilot: "Okay, that's the dual carriageway 5 miles."

Pilot: "Let's go up. 200 foot."

Copilot: "Okay, got it visual."

Us passengers were just sitting there eating Hershey bars when all of a sudden the front loadie manned his guns. We grabbed our rifles and jumped up as well. We didn't have a clue what was going on. There wouldn't be much we could do because if you put the barrel of your gun out into the slipstream, it's like putting your hand out of a car traveling at 100 mph. We could have done jack shit really, but we felt we had to help him.

There wasn't actually a drama. It was just that we were getting near the road and the loadie was hoping that somebody was going to fire at us so he could have a pop back.

It was the main carriageway between Baghdad and Jordan. We crossed it at 500 feet. There were a lot of lights from convoys, but we were unlit and they certainly couldn't hear us. It was our first sight of the enemy.

Sighting the road gave us a location fix because we knew exactly where it was on the map. I was just trying to work out how much longer we'd be in the air when I heard a Klaxon.

Dinger and I both had headsets on, and we looked at one another as we listened to the crew.

"Break left! Break right!"

All hell was let loose. The helicopter did severe swings to the left and right.

The loadies jumped around, torches on, pressing buttons all over the place as chaff was fired off.

The pilots knew where most of the Rolands were, but they obviously hadn't known about this one. The ground-to-air missile had "illuminated" us and set off the inboard warnings. To complicate matters, we were going fairly slowly when it locked on.

I saw the expression on Dinger's face in the glow of the cyalume sticks. We'd been lulled into a false sense of security listening to all the confident banter. Now I had the feeling you get when you're driving a car and

you glance down for a moment and look back up and
find that the situation ahead has suddenly changed
and you have to jump on the brakes. I didn't know if
the missile had actually fired, or locked on, or what.

"Fuck this!" he said. "If it's going to happen, I don't
fucking want to hear it!"

Simultaneously, we threw our headsets on the floor.
I got down and crunched up into a ball, ready to accept the landing.

The pilot threw the aircraft all over the sky. The engines groaned and strained as it did its gymnastics.

The Chinook leveled out and flew straight ahead.
The look on the loadies' faces told us that we'd got
away with it.

I put the headphones back on and said, "What the
fuck was that?"

"Probably a Roland, who knows? Not the best of
things. It's all right for you lot: we've got to come back
this way."

I wanted to get off this aircraft and be back in control of my own destiny. It's nice getting chauffeured to
a place, but not like this. And it wasn't over yet. If the
Iraqis on the ground reported a lock-on, their aircraft
might come looking for us. Nobody knew if the Iraqis
were getting aircraft into the sky, or if they had night-
flying capability, but you have to assume the worst
scenario. I was sweating like a rapist.

Half an hour later, the pilot gave us a two-minute
warning that we would be landing. I held up two fingers to the blokes, the same warning as for a parachute
drop. The rear loadie started to undo the straps that
held down the kit. The red glow from the penlight
torch that he held in his mouth made him look like the
devil at work.

Four of us had 203s, the American M16 Armalite rifle
with a grenade launcher attached that fires a 40mm
bomb that looks like a large, stubby bullet; the others

had Minimis, a light machine gun. For our purposes, the Armalite is a superior weapon to the Army's new SA80. It's lighter and is very easy to clean and maintain. It's a good, simple weapon that has been around in different variants since Vietnam days. The Regiment tried SA80s in jungle training when they came out, and found it not best suited to its requirements. With the M16 everything's nice and clean; there are no little bits and pieces sticking out. The safety catch is very simple and can be operated with the thumb—with the SA80 you have to use your trigger finger, which is madness. If you're in close country with the M16, you can flick the safety catch off easily with your thumb, and your finger is still on the trigger. What's more, if the safety catch will go to Automatic on your M16, you know it's made ready: this means it is cocked, with a round in the chamber. You see people patrolling with their thumbs checking the safety catch every few minutes; the last thing they want is a negligent discharge within earshot of the enemy.

The M16 has a quiet safety catch—another plus if you're patrolling—and there are no parts to go rusty. If rifles were cars, instead of going for a Ford Sierra 4×4 —good, reliable, tested, and enjoyed by the people who drive them—in the SA80 the Army went for a Rolls-Royce. But at the stage when it was first brought into service, it was still a prototype Rolls-Royce, and there were plenty of teething problems. In my opinion the one and only drawback with a 203 is that you can't put a bayonet on because of the grenade launcher underneath.

We didn't have slings on the M16s. A sling means a rifle is going over your shoulder: on operations, why would you want to have a weapon over the shoulder rather than in your hands and ready to fire? When you patrol with a weapon you always move with both hands on it and the butt in your shoulder. What's the point of having it if you can't bring it to bear quickly?

I'm not interested in how or where a weapon is made, as long as it does the job it needs to do and I know how to use it. As long as it fires ammunition and you've got lots of it, that's all you should be concerned about.

Weapons are only as good as their handlers, of course. There's a lot of inbred rivalry between the blokes when it comes to live firing drills. All our weapon training is live firing, and it has to be that way because only then do you get a sense of realism and perspective. In a firefight, the awesome noise will impair your ability to act if you're not well and truly used to it. An Armalite sounds surprisingly tinny when it fires, and there's not much kick. You tend to hear other people's weapons rather than your own. When the 40mm bomb fires, you just hear a pop; there's no explosion or recoil.

We had four Minimis, which are 5.56 light-support machineguns. They can take belted ammunition in disintegrating link in boxes of 200, or ordinary magazines. The weapon is so light that it can be used in the attack like a rifle as well as giving support fire, and it has a fearsome rate of fire. It has a bipod to guarantee good, accurate automatic fire if needed. The plastic prepacked boxes of ammo for the weapon are not its best design feature. As you're patrolling, the box is across your body; it can bang against you and fall off, but you just have to guard against it. Another problem can be that the rounds are not completely packed in the boxes and you get a rhythmic, banging noise, which is bad news at night as noise travels more easily.

Each man in the patrol also carried a disposable 66mm rocket. American-made, the 66 is designed for infantry antitank use. It's just over two foot long and consists of two tubes inside each other. You pull the two apart and the inner tube contains the rocket, all ready to go. As you pull it apart, the sights pop up.

You just fire the weapon and throw it away. It's good because it's simple. The simpler something is, the more chance there is that it'll work. The round has a shaped charge on the end, which is designed to punch through armor. The fuse arms itself after about 30 feet; even if you just graze the target, it blows up. The 66 doesn't explode in a big ball of fire as in the movies. HE never does that unless there is a secondary explosion.

We carried white phos grenades as well as the ordinary L2 explosive grenade. Phosphorus burns fiercely and lays down a rather good smokescreen if you need time to get away.

Grenades no longer have the old pineapple shape that people tend to think of. White phos is cylindrical, with the letters WP written across it. The L2 is more egg shaped and consists of tightly wound wire around an explosive charge. We splay the pins even more than they already are so that it takes more pressure to extract them. We also put masking tape around the grenade to hold the handle down as an extra precaution in case there's a drama with the pin. White phos is not much used in training because it's so dangerous. If you get it on you, you have to pour water very slowly from your water bottle to stop it getting oxygen, then pick it off. If you're not successful, it's not a nice way to die.

We had at least 10 magazines each, 12 40mm bombs, L2 and phos grenades, and a 66. The four Minimi gunners had more than 600 rounds each, plus 6 loaded mags. For an 8-man patrol it was a fearsome amount of firepower.

Those of us with 203s checked there was a bomb loaded. Bob was checking that the belts of ammunition for his Minimi weren't kinked—the secret of belt-fed ammunition is that it goes into the weapon smoothly. If it's twisted, you'll get a stoppage. I saw Vince checking the box of ammunition that clips on to the side of the weapon to make sure it was not going to fall off. His gang were going to provide all-round cover by moving straight out to points just beyond the wash of the aircraft. As they were running out, the rest of us would be throwing the kit off the tailgate as fast as we could.

Stan checked his white phos to make sure it was easy to get at. Everybody was mentally adjusting himself ready to go. Blokes jumped up and down to check that everything was comfy. You do simple things like undo your trousers, pull them up, tuck everything in, redo them, tighten your belt, make sure your belt kit is comfortable, make sure your pouches and buttons are done up. Then you check and recheck that you've got everything and haven't left anything on the floor.

I could tell by the grind of the blades that the heli was maneuvering close to the ground. The tailgate started to lower. I peered out. You're incredibly vulnerable during the landing. The enemy could be firing at the aircraft, but because of the engine noise you wouldn't know until you were on the ground. The ramp came down more. The landscape was a black-and-white negative under the quarter moon. We were in a small wadi with a 13-foot rise either side. Clouds of dust flew up, and Vince and his gang moved onto the tailgate, weapons at the ready. There was a strong smell of fuel. The noise was deafening.

The aircraft was still a few feet off the ground when they jumped. If there was a contact, we wouldn't know about it until we saw them jumping straight back on.

The pilot collapsed the Chinook the last couple of feet onto the ground. We hurled the kit, and Stan, Dinger, and Mark jumped after it. I stayed on board while the loadie went across the floor with a cyalume stick in his hand in a last-minute sweep. The noise of the rotors increased, and I felt the heli lift its weight off the undercarriage. I waited. It's always worth the extra ten seconds it takes to make sure, rather than discover when the heli has gone that you've only picked up half the equipment. The balance, as ever, is between speed and doing the job correctly.

The loadie gave the thumbs up and said something into his headset. The aircraft started to lift and I jumped. I hit the ground and looked up. The heli was climbing fast with the ramp still closing. Within seconds it was gone. It was 2100 and we were on our own.

We were on a dried-up riverbed. To the east was flatness and dark. To the west, the same.

The night sky was crystal clear, and all the stars were out. It was absolutely beautiful. I could see my breath. It was colder than we had been used to. There was a definite chill in the air. Sweat ran down the side of my face, and I started to shiver.

Eyes take a long time to adjust in darkness. The cones in your eyes enable you to see in the daytime, giving color and perception. But they're no good at night. What takes over then are the rods on the edge of your irises. They are angled at 45 degrees because of the convex shape of the eye, so if you look straight at something at night you don't really see it: it's a haze. You have to look above it or around it so you can line up these rods, which then will give you a picture. It takes forty minutes or so for them to become fully effective, but you start to see better after five. And what you see when you land and what you see those five minutes later are two very different things.

Vince with his hoods was still out giving cover. They had gone out about 30 meters to the edge of the rise of the wadi and were looking over. We moved off to the side to make a more secure area. It took each of us two trips to ferry the bergens, jerricans, and sandbags.

Mark got out Magellan and took a fix. He squinted at it with one eye. Even small amounts of light can wreck your night vision, and the process must start all over again. If you have to look at something, you close the eye that you aim with, the "master eye," and look with the other. Therefore you can still have 50 percent night vision, and it's in the eye that does the business.

We lay in all-round defense, covering the whole 360-degree arc. We did nothing, absolutely nothing, for the next ten minutes. You've come off a noisy, smelly aircraft, and there's been a frenzy of activity. You have to give your body a chance to tune in to your new environment. You have to adjust to the sounds and smells and sights, and changes in climate and terrain. When you're tracking people in the jungle you do the same: you stop every so often and look and listen. It happens in ordinary life, too. You feel more at ease in a strange house after you've been in it a little while. People indigenous to an area can sense instinctively if the mood is ugly and there's going to be trouble; a tourist will bumble straight into it.

We needed to confirm our position because there's often a difference between where you want to be and where the RAF put you. Once you know where you are, you make sure that everybody else in the patrol knows. Passage of information is vital; it's no good just the leader having it. We were in fact where we wanted to be, which was a shame, because now we couldn't slag the RAF when we got back.

The ground was featureless. It was hard bedrock with about two inches of rubbly shale over the top. It looked alien and desolate, like the set of *Dr. Who*. We could have been on the moon. I'd been in the Middle East many times on different tasks, and I thought I was familiar with the ground, but this was new to me. My ears strained as a dog barked in the distance.

We were very isolated, but we were a big gang, we had more weapons and ammunition than you could

shake a stick at, and we were doing what we were
paid to do.

Bombing raids were going on about 10–20 miles to
our east and our northeast. I saw tracer going up and
flashes on the horizon, and seconds later I heard the
muffled sound of explosions.

Silhouetted in one of the flashes I saw a plantation
about a mile to our east. It shouldn't have been there,
but it was—trees, a water tower, a building. Now I
knew where the barking had come from. More dogs
sparked up. They would have heard the Chinook, but
as far as any population were concerned a helicopter's
a helicopter. Problems would only come if there were
troops stationed there.

I worried about how good the rest of our information was. But at the end of the day we were there now:
there wasn't a lot we could do about it. We lay waiting
for signs of cars starting up but nothing happened. I
looked beyond the plantation. I seemed to be staring
into infinity.

I watched the tracer going up. I couldn't see any
aircraft, but it was a wonderful, comforting feeling all
the same. I had the feeling they were doing it just for
us.

"Fuck it, let's get on with it," Mark said quietly.

I got to my feet, and suddenly, to the west, the earth
erupted with noise and there was a blinding light in
the sky.

"Fucking hell, what's that?" Mark whispered.

"Helicopter!"

Where it had sprung from I didn't have a clue. All I
knew was that we'd just been on the ground ten minutes and were about to have a major drama. There was
no way the heli could be one of ours. For a start, it
wouldn't have had its searchlight on like that. Whoever it belonged to, it looked as if it was coming
straight towards us.

Jesus, how could the Iraqis be on to us so quickly?

Could they have been tracking the Chinook ever since
we entered their airspace?

The light seemed to keep coming and coming. Then
I realized it wasn't coming towards us but going upwards. The bright light wasn't a searchlight; it was a
fireball.

"Scud!" I whispered.

I could hear the sighs of relief.

It was the first one any of us had seen being
launched, and now that we knew what it was, it
looked just like an Apollo moon shot, a big ball of
exhaust flames about 6 miles away, burning straight
up into the air until it finally disappeared into the
darkness.

"Scud alley," "Scud triangle," both these terms had
been used by the media, and now here we were, right
in the middle of it.

Once everything had settled down, I went up and
whispered in Vince's ear for him to call the rest of the
guns in. There was no running or rushing. Shape,
shine, shadow, silhouette, movement, and noise are
some of the things that will always give you away.
Slow movement doesn't generate noise or catch the
eye so easily, which is why we patrol so slowly. Plus,
if you run and fall over and injure yourself, you'll
screw everybody up.

I told them exactly where we were, and confirmed
which way we would be going, and confirmed the RV
that was forward of us. So if there was any major
drama between where we were now and our proposed
cache area and we got split up, everybody knew that
for the next twenty-four hours there was a meeting
place already set up. They would go north, eventually
hit a half buried petroleum pipeline and follow that till
they hit a major ridgeline, and we'd meet there. It had
to be that vague because anything more precise would
mean nothing to a bloke in the middle of the desert
with just a map and compass: all the map shows is

rock. After that, and for the next twenty-four hours, the next RV would be back at the point of the landing site.

Now we had to patrol up to the proposed cache area. We did it in a shuttle, as we had practiced, four blokes ferrying the kit, the other four giving protection, then swapping over. Because we were patrolling, everything had to be done tactically: we'd stop, check the ground ahead, and every couple of miles, when we stopped for a rest, the 4-man protection would go out; then we'd check the kit to make sure that we hadn't dropped anything, that all pouches were still done up, and none of the sandbags had split.

The water was the worst because it was like carrying the world's heaviest suitcase in one hand. I tried mine on the top of my bergen until the strain on my back got too outrageous. But then, nobody said it would be easy.

Moving as quickly but as tactically as we could, we had to get to the MSR well before first light to give us time to find somewhere to cache the kit and hide up. In my orders I'd put a cutoff time of 0400 the next morning; even if we hadn't reached the proposed cache area by then, we'd have to start finding an LUP. That would give us an hour and a half of darkness to work in.

The ground worried me. If it carried on like this it was going to be too flat and too hard to hide up in. If we had to lie in open ground in broad daylight we'd stick out like the balls on a bulldog.

We navigated by bearings, time, and distance. We had Magellan, but it was only an aid. Patrolling as we were was not a good time to use it. Apart from the fact that it could not be depended upon, the machine emitted telltale light, and it would not be tactical anyway for the operator to be looking at a machine rather than the ground.

Every half hour or so we fixed a new ERV *(emer-*

gency rendezvous), a point on the ground where we could regroup if we had a contact and had to withdraw swiftly. If we came to a prominent feature like a pile of old burial ruins, the lead man would indicate it as the new ERV by a circular motion of the hand and this would be passed down the patrol.

All the time, you keep making appreciations. You've got to say to yourself: What if? What happens if we get an attack from the front? Or from the left? Where will I go for cover? Is this a good ambush point? Where was the last emergency RV? Who have I got in front of me? Who have I got behind me? You have to check all the time that you're not losing anyone. And you always have to cover your arcs and be conscious of the noise you're making.

As you patrol you start to get hot. When you stop you get cold again. You're sitting there with all the coldness down your back and under your armpits, and your face starts to feel it. The back of your hair starts to get that horrible, uncomfortable, sticky feeling, and the clothing around your belt is soaked. Then you move off again because you want to be warm. You don't want to stop for too long because you don't want to freeze. You've been like this plenty of times before, and you know that you'll dry out eventually, but that doesn't make it any less of a pain in the arse.

We finally got into the area of the bend of the MSR at about 0445. We couldn't see any lights or vehicles in the pitch-black. We cached the equipment, and Vince's gang stayed to protect it. The rest of us were going to go forward for a recce to find a place to hide.

"My cutoff time to be back here will be 0545," I whispered to Vince, my mouth right against his ear so that the sound didn't carry.

If we failed to return but they knew there hadn't been a contact because they hadn't heard any noise, we would meet at the patrol RV near the oil pipeline. If we weren't at the patrol RV by the twenty-four-hour

cutoff time, Vince was then to move back to the RV at
the heli-landing site, then wait a further twenty-four
hours before requesting an exfil. If we weren't there,
he'd just have to get on the helicopter and go. They
should also move back to the helicopter RV if they
heard a contact but it wasn't close enough for them to
give support.

I went through the actions on return. "I will come in
the same direction as I leave," I whispered to Vince,
"and as I come in I'll approach just on my own with
my weapon in my right arm and walk in as a crucifix."

I would then come forward and confirm with the
stag and go back and bring the other three in. I would
do all this on my own because as well as confirming
that it was me, I would want to confirm that it was
safe to come in—they might have been bumped, and
the enemy could be waiting in ambush. The other
three would be out supporting, so if there was any
drama, they would lay down fire and I could withdraw to them.

We set out on our recce patrol, and after about half an
hour we found a good site for the LUP—a watershed
where flash floods over thousands of years had carved
a small reentrant about 15 feet high into the rock so
that there was an overhang. We would be in dead
ground, covered from view and with limited cover
from fire. I couldn't believe our luck. We patrolled
straight back to fetch the others.

We moved all the equipment into the LUP. The cave
was divided by a large rock, so we centralized the
equipment and had the two gangs either side. At last I
felt secure, even though the problem with finding an
LUP at night is that in the morning everything can
look different. You can find that what you thought was
the perfect LUP is smack in the middle of a housing
estate.

Now was another period of stop, settle down, be

quiet, listen to what's going on, tune in to the new environment. The ground did not look so alien now, and we were feeling more confident.

It was time to get some sleep. There's an army saying, "Whenever there's a lull in the battle, get your head down," and it's true. You've got to sleep whenever you can, because you never know when you're going to get the opportunity again.

There were two men on stag, changing every two hours. They had to look and listen. If anything came towards us, it was their job to warn us and get us stood to. The rest of us slept covering our arcs, so we'd just have to roll over and start firing.

More jets went over that night. We saw flak going up and Baghdad erupting to our half right about 100 miles away. There were no incidents on the ground.

Just as it was coming up to first light, two of us moved out of the LUP position and checked that we hadn't left footprints on our way in to the LUP, dropped any kit, disturbed anything, or left any other "sign" to betray us. You must assume that everybody is better at everything than you—including tracking—and make your plans accordingly.

We arranged our claymores so that both men on stag could see them and their field of view, and be ready to detonate them with hand-held "clackers." If the stag saw or heard movement, he'd wake everybody else. There wouldn't be hectic running around, we'd just stand to. Everything is always done at a slow pace. You'd know if it had to be rushed because you'd hear the stag firing. If somebody was in a position to be hit with a claymore, we were in a position to be compromised, so it was down to the sentry whether or not he pushed the clackers. If they came as close as the kill zone of the claymores, which were positioned as a protection of last resort, we'd just have to initiate the contact. But still the best weapon we had was concealment.

I went up onto the dead ground to double-check. Looking north towards the MSR, I saw a flat area of 2000 feet, then a slight rise of about 15 feet, and then, another 1300 feet away, a plantation. Looking east and west, the ground was flat as far as the horizon. South, to my rear, I saw another plantation about 1500 meters away, with a water tower and buildings. According to the map and Bert's briefing these locations shouldn't have been there, but they were, and they were far too close for comfort.

I heard vehicles moving along the as yet uncon-firmed MSR, but that was of no concern. The only way anybody could see us was if they were on the opposite lip looking down. No one on our side of the wadi could see us because of the overhang. They could only see us if we could see them.

I went down and briefed everybody on what was above us. Only one man was needed on stag because from his vantage point he could look down the wadi as well as up on the lip. He had his back to us as I did the briefing, covering his arcs. I described what I'd seen on the high ground and went through our actions on if we had a contact during the day.

It was time to transmit the Sit Rep *(situation report)* to the FOB. Until we did, nobody knew where we were or what state we were in. On this task we would try to send a Sit Rep every day, telling them where we were, everything we had learned about the enemy in the area or done with them, our future intentions, and any other information. They would come back to us with instructions.

As I wrote it out, Legs prepared the radio. He en-coded the message and typed it in ready for transmis-sion. The patrol radio would transmit in a single, very short burst that was virtually undetectable by the en-emy. The burst would bounce off the ionosphere, and we would wait for some kind of an acknowledgment.

We got jack shit.

Legs tried again and again, but nothing happened. It was annoying but not desperate, because we had a lost comms procedure. The following night, we'd simply go back to the landing site and RV with a heli at 0400 to exchange the radios.

For the rest of that day we tried different antennas—everything from sloping wire to half-wave dipole. All of us were signals trained and we all had a go, but without success.

We each did two hours' stag, and half an hour before last light we stood to. The ideal conditions for an attack are just before last light and just before first light, so it is an SOP that everybody is awake at those times and everything is packed away ready to go. We got into the fire position with our weapons and prepared our 66s, removing the top cover and opening up the tube so it was ready to fire. Once last light had come, we closed everything up again and got ready for our recce patrol.

I left with my gang at 2100. Our cutoff time was to be 0500. If we weren't back by then, it would be because we'd had a drama—we'd got lost, got an injury, or had a contact, which Vince's lot should hear. If they didn't hear a contact, they were to wait at the LUP until 2100 the following night. If we weren't back by then, they were to move to the heli RV. If there was a contact, they were to move back to the heli RV that night, and we'd make our way back there as best we could, to get there for the following 0400 pickup.

Stan, Dinger, Mark, and I climbed over the lip of the wadi in total blackness. The task was to confirm the position of the Main Supply Route and to locate the landline. It's no good just sitting there on top of what you think is your objective unless you have checked. One mile further on for all we knew, there could be the proper MSR, so it had to be physically checked. We would patrol in an anticlockwise direction, generally heading north, using the lie of the ground, to see if we hit anything else which resembled the MSR.

First, we needed to locate a marker that would guide us back to the LUP if we got lost. We would take a bearing due north until we hit the other side of the road, where we'd try to find a rock or some other feature. Then if we did get lost, we'd know that all we'd have to do was go along the high ground, find the marker, and move due south back onto the watershed.

It was going to be difficult to map-read because there were no definite features. In most countries there's high ground that you can take reference points off, there are roads, or there are markers, and it's all quite easy. In the jungle, too, it's simple, because you've got lots of rivers and you can use contour lines. But here in the middle of the desert there was absolutely bugger all, so it was all down to bearings and pacing again, backed up by Magellan.

We found a suitable marker, a large rock, and started heading west on our anticlockwise loop. Within minutes we spotted our first location of the night and immediately heard a dog. Bedu throw their hand in at night; when the sun's down, they go to bed. So if a dog barks, they know there must be something afoot. Within seconds, this one had been joined by two others.

I had been the first to hear the low growling. It reminded me of patrolling in Northern Ireland. You stop and assess what's happening. Nine times out of ten you're intruding on a dog's territory, and if you back off, sit down, and just wait for everything to settle down, it will. Our problem was that we had to recce the location properly. The dogs could be part of a Scud site for all we knew.

As we sat down we pulled our fighting knives from their sheaths. They would be called upon to do the business if the dogs came to investigate and either started barking in earnest or decided to attack. Either way, we'd kill them. We'd take the bodies with us, so that in the morning the owners would assume that their animals had run away or wandered off. They would find it strange, but that would be the best we could make of a bad situation.

We listened, waiting for lights as people came to see what the dogs were barking at. Nothing happened. We started to box around the position, circumnavigating to see if we could get in another way to confirm what it was. We got around the other side and found it was just some local population. There were tents, mud huts, Land Cruisers, and a hash mash of other vehicles, but no military indication. We got a fix on it with Magellan so that when we returned to the LUP we could inform the others, then headed off northwest using the ground. We wanted to avoid until later the plantation that we knew to be to our north.

I was leading when I saw something ahead. I stopped, looked, listened, then slowly moved closer.

Four tents and vehicles were parked next to two S60 antiaircraft guns, indicating a setup of about platoon strength. All was quiet, and there didn't seem to be any stags. Mark and I moved slowly forward. Again, we stopped, looked, listened. We didn't want to get right on top of the position, just close enough to learn as much about it as we could. Nobody was sleeping on the guns or in the vehicles. The whole platoon must have been in the tents. We heard men coughing. The location wasn't an immediate danger to us, but what worried me was that antiaircraft guns are sited to guard something. If it was just the MSR that would be no problem. The danger was that it could be part of an armored battle group or whatever. Mark fixed the position with Magellan, and we headed north.

We went for 2 miles without encountering anything, and came to the conclusion that what we had crossed earlier must indeed have been the MSR. Magellan gave our LUP position as a half mile north of where the map said the MSR was, which was nothing to worry about. The map stated that roads, pylons, and pipelines were only of approximate alignment.

We now knew for sure that we had correctly found the bend in the MSR, but unfortunately we also knew that the area was full of population: we had plantations north and south of us, the civilians further down the road, and an S60 site to the northwest of our LUP. From a tactical point of view, we might as well have sited our LUP in the middle of Piccadilly Circus. Still, nobody said it would be easy.

We moved back to look around the buildings at the plantation to the north of the LUP. I had planned to look at this last as it was the most dangerous location we knew about prior to the recce. We had a bit of a mince around the plantation and found that it consisted of just a water tower and an unoccupied building that sounded as if it housed an irrigation pump. There were no vehicles, no lights, no signs of life, so we were fairly pleased. It was clearly something that was tended rather than lived around.

As we moved back to the LUP, we witnessed another Scud launch to our northwest, about 3 miles away. We seemed to be in the middle of a megalaunch area. We were going to have a fluffy old time of it. Again, we got a fix.

We patrolled back towards the LUP, found the marker, and walked due south towards the wadi. I approached, arms out in the crucifix position, as I came up to the lip of the watershed.

Bob was on stag. I stood there and waited for him to come up. He grinned at me, and I went back and got the rest of the blokes. I checked my watch. The patrol had lasted five hours.

It wasn't worth briefing the blokes at this moment because those not on stag had got their heads down, and to brief everybody at night just generates noise. It was important, however, that everybody knew what we had seen. Everything we had done and seen, everybody else had to know about. I decided to wait until first light.

The stag stood us to, and we covered our arcs as first light came. After that, and before I did the brief, I wanted to check the dead ground again, even though we'd covered it last night. I knew we were definitely on the MSR, but I wanted to look for any form of identification which would give us the landlines. It was also a personal thing; I wanted to check that there had been no changes above us. Shielded from sound by the walls of the cave, we could have sat there with Genesis giving an open-air concert and we wouldn't have heard a thing.

Chris covered me while I scrambled up the rocks and peered over the brim. It was the last time I'd risk doing this in daylight.

I looked northeast and there, just on the far edge of the MSR, were another two S60s. They must have arrived during the night. I could see two wagons, tents, blokes stretching and coughing—all just 1000 feet from our position. I couldn't believe it. This was getting unreal. Our recce patrol must have missed them by about 150 feet. I came down and told Chris, then went to brief the rest of the patrol. Mark went up and had a quick squint to confirm that I wasn't hallucinating.

I was not really impressed by this development. It was quite scary stuff, because these characters were right on top of us. They were going to inhibit us badly.

I spread out the map and showed all the locations we had discovered—including the new S60 sites. We spent the rest of the day trying to transmit our Sit Rep again. The new S60s were obviously there to protect the MSR. There was no reason, however, why they should send out clearing patrols. They were in their own country and they had mutual support. We reassured ourselves that we could only be compromised

from the opposite lip, and even then only if someone
was literally standing on it, looking down.

Again we all had a go with the radio, but to no avail.
Our lost comms contingency would have come into
effect by now, and the helicopter would have been
briefed to meet us the following morning at 0400.

There was no concern. We were in cover, and we
were an 8-man fighting patrol. When we met the aircraft we would get a one-for-one exchange, or get on
the aircraft and relocate.

In my mind I ran through the heli RV procedure
again. The pilot would be coming in on NVG *(night-
viewing goggles)*, watching for a signal from my infrared torch. I would flash the letter Bravo as a recognition signal. He would land 15 feet to my right, using
the light as his reference point. The loadmaster's door
was just behind the pilot, and all I would have to do
was walk up to it, put the radio in, and receive the
new radio that was handed to me. If there was any
message for us, he would grab hold of my arm and
hand me the written message. Or, if a longer message
was involved, the ramp would come down and the
loadie would come and drag me round to the back.
The rest of the patrol would be out in all-round defense. If I had to go and get them in, they knew the
drills. If I wanted to get us relocated, I would grab
hold of the loadie and point to the rear of the ramp.
The ramp would then come down, and we'd all get on.

And that was the plan. No drama. We would move
back that night and relocate.

6

We'd been listening to vehicles bumbling up and down the MSR all day. They posed no threat.

Around mid-afternoon, however, we heard a young voice shout from no more than 150 feet away. The child hollered and yelled again; then we heard the clatter of goats and the tinkle of a bell.

It wasn't a problem. We couldn't be compromised unless we could see the person on the other side of the lip. There was no other way that we could be seen. I felt confident.

The goats came closer. We were on hard routine, and everybody had their belt kit on and their weapons in their hands. It wasn't as if we'd been startled in our sleeping bags or caught sunbathing. Just the same, I felt my thumb creep towards the safety catch of my 203.

The bell tinkled right above us. I looked up just as the head of a goat appeared on the other side. I felt my jaw tighten with apprehension. Everybody was rock still. Only our eyes were moving.

More goats wandered onto the lip. Was the herder going to follow them?

The top of a young human head bobbed into view. It stopped and swiveled. Then it came forward. I saw

the profile of a small brown face. The boy seemed preoccupied with something behind him. He was half
looking over his shoulder as he shuffled forwards. His
neck and shoulders came into view, then his chest. He
can't have been more than a 3 feet from the edge of the
lip. He swung his head from side to side, shouting at
the goats and hitting them with a long stick.

I silently shouted at him not to look down.

We still had a chance, as long as he kept looking the
other way.

Please, no eye-to-eye, just look at what you're doing . . .

He turned his head and surveyed the scene.

I slowly mouthed the words: *Fuck . . . off!*

He looked down.

Bastard! Shit!

Our eyes met and held. I'd never seen such a look of
astonishment in a child's eyes.

Now what? He was rooted to the spot. The options
raced through my mind.

Do we top him? Too much noise. Anyway, what
was the point? I wouldn't want that on my conscience
for the rest of my life. Shit, I could have been an Iraqi
behind the lines in Britain, and that could have been
Katie up there.

The boy started to run. My eyes followed him, and I
made my move. Mark and Vince, too, were scrambling
like men possessed in an attempt to cut him off. Just to
get him, that had to be the first priority. We could
decide later what to do with him—to tie him up and
stuff his gob with chocolate, or whatever. But we
could only go so far without exposing ourselves to the
S60 sites, and the child had too much of a head start.
He was gone, fucking gone, hollering like a lunatic,
running towards the guns.

He could do a number of things. He might not tell
anybody because it would get him into trouble—
maybe he shouldn't have been in the area. He might
tell his family or friends, but only when he got home

later. Or he might keep running and shouting all the way to the guns. I had to assume the worst. So what? They might not believe him. They might come and see for themselves. Or they might wait for reinforcements. I had to take it that they would inform others and then come after us. So what? If they discovered us, there would be a contact before dark. If they didn't discover us, there would be a chance to evade under cover of darkness.

We had picked our LUP because it provided concealment from view—apart from the one place where the boy had gone and stood. We certainly hadn't picked it as a place to defend. It was an enclosed environment, at the top of a watershed, with nowhere to go.

There was no need to say anything: everybody knew we'd have to take it as a compromise. Everything happened in quick time. However, that wasn't to say we just got our kit on and ran, because that would have been totally counterproductive. It's worth taking those extra few minutes to get yourself squared away.

Everybody rammed chocolate down as well as water. We didn't know when we would next be able to eat. We checked that our pouches were done up, that the buttons were fastened on our map pockets so the map didn't fall out, that our magazines were on correctly. Check, check, check.

Vince put Stan and Bob out with the Minimis. As soon as two other men were ready, they'd swap places and let the two stags get themselves sorted out. Everybody else automatically carried out tasks that needed to be done. Vince went through the cached kit. He pulled out a jerrican of water and helped everybody fill their bottles. If we got into a contact, we were going to lose our bergens and all that they contained. People took great gulps to get as much water on board as they could, draining their bottles, then refilling. Even if there was no contact, we all knew we were in for a fearsome tab.

We checked our belt kit, making sure all pouches were done up so that we didn't lose anything as we ran. Mags on tight? Check them again. Safety catch on and weapon made ready? Of course they were but we checked them anyway. We closed down the two tubes of our 66s and slotted them together to make them easy to carry. We didn't bother to replace the end-caps or sling, just slipped the weapon between our webbing straps, ready for quick use.

We checked that spare magazines were ready to pull out. Pick them up the wrong way, and you waste a precious second or two turning them around. Put them in your belt kit with the curve the right way up, and they're ready to slap into place. A lot of people put a tab of masking tape on the mag to make it easier to pull out. When my mags were empty, I'd throw them down the front of my smock for refilling later. We could use the rounds from the belts of the Minimi.

All this took a couple of minutes, but it was time better spent than just getting up and running. They knew we were there, so why rush? The stags would tell us if they were coming.

Legs had got straight onto the radio. He went outrageous, running out all the antennas, trying different combinations that he hadn't been able to try while we were concealed. Now we were compromised, he could do anything he wanted. If the message got through, they could send some fast jets over. We could talk to the pilots on TACBE and get some fire down, which would all be rather pleasant.

Legs's water was done for him. While he was bent over, the radio blokes opened his belt kit, took the water bottles out, and let him drink before they filled them up again, and threw more food into his belt kit. When he sensed that we'd run out of time, he dismantled the kit and packed it at the top of his bergen.

"Instructions are in my right-hand map pocket in my trousers," he told everybody. "Radio's on top of my bergen." All of it was a well-established SOP so that if he went down we'd be able to retrieve the equipment quickly, but he was going by the book to ensure that everybody knew.

When he was ready, Legs replaced Bob on stag. There was an air of acceptance by everybody, the calm of well-practiced drills being followed to the letter. Bob, who'd done nothing but sleep since we'd arrived, was worried about having to move again so soon.

"We ought to have a union," he said. "These hours are scandalous."

"Food's fucking crap and all," said Mark.

The jokes were good to hear because they relaxed the situation.

Dinger got his fags out. "Fuck it, they know we're here. I might as well have a smoke. I could be dead in a minute."

"I'll put you on a fizzer!" Vince shouted as he went out and took over from Stan on the Minimi. It was a standard piss-taking joke, referring to a piece of army slang that people think is said but which in fact is never heard.

Everybody was ready to move if necessary. It had taken us a total of three minutes. There was about an hour and a half of daylight left. Our best weapon had been concealment, but the boy had disarmed us. Where we were, we couldn't fight. It was such a closed environment that it would take just one or two HE rounds to hose us down. The only option was to get out into the open and fight, or maybe get away. We were in the shit if we stayed where we were, and we were in the shit if we were out in the open because there was no cover. It was out of the frying pan into the fire, but at least in the fire we had a slim chance.

* * *

The rumble of the tracked vehicle came from the south. We couldn't get out of the wadi now; it was too late. Our only exit was blocked by this armored vehicle. We would just have to stand there and fight.

I couldn't understand why they were bringing an APC down in this small, confined space. Surely they would take it for granted that we'd have antiarmor weapons?

We snapped open our 66s and ran around to find a decent firing position. Chris pranced around with his old German Afrika Corps hat on, pointing at our 66s and talking to us like the world's most patient instructor. "Now boys, remember the backblast! Do, please, remember the backblast! This face has got to go downtown on a Saturday night. The last thing it needs is a peppering!"

Stan stared down the sights of his cocked Minimi at the line of the watershed, towards the sound of the tracked vehicle. It trundled closer. There was a glint of metal as it came into view. What in hell's name was it? It didn't look like the APC I had been expecting.

Stan shouted: "Bulldozer!"

Unbelievable. A major drama was about to erupt and this idiot was pottering about with a digger. It came to within 500 feet of our position, but the driver never saw us. He was dressed in civilian clothes. He must have been there quite innocently.

"Don't fire," I said. "We've got to take it as a compromise, but what sort of compromise we don't know yet."

The driver's attention seemed focused on finding a way out of the wadi. He maneuvred this way and that for what seemed an eternity.

"Fuck it," I said to Vince, "we need to go. We just can't sit here."

The ideal would have been to wait for last light, but I sensed that the situation was going to get out of hand.

The bulldozer disappeared suddenly, and the engine noise faded. The driver must have found the gap he was looking for.

It was time to go. I told Stan to bring in the blokes on the Minimis so everybody could hear what I was going to say.

We huddled around with our belt kit on and our bergens at our feet. It was a vulnerable time because everybody was so close together, but it had to be done: everybody had to know what was going on.

I started by stating the obvious. "We're going to move from here," I said. "We're going to go west, try to avoid the AA guns, and then head south and go for the RV with the helicopter. The helicopter RV will be at 0400 tomorrow."

"See you in the Pudding Club," Chris said.

"Fuck that," Dinger said in his terrible W. C. Fields voice. "Go west, young man, go west."

We shouldered our bergens and rechecked our belt kit. The rest of it was left behind. Even the claymores remained because we didn't have time to pick them up.

Because of the S60 sites, there was only one way out. West, then south, using dips in the ground as much as we could. But we wouldn't rush it. We didn't want to make mistakes. We had loads of time to make the heli RV, if we could only get out of this shit and get under cover of darkness.

I was feeling apprehensive but comfortable. We deserved better after all the hard work of planning, tabbing in, locating and confirming the MSR, and just the bad luck of lost comms. I'd thought we'd cracked it: we only had to wait until 0400 the next morning and we'd be back in business. But at the end of the day, we were an 8-man fighting patrol, we had guns, we had bullets, we had 66s. What more could a man ask for?

"Come on," said Mark, "let's make like rag heads."

We pulled our shamags over our faces. The sun was

in our eyes as I led us out in single file. We patrolled properly, taking our time, observing the ground.

The wadi petered out and became flat plain. We came out west, using the lie of the ground, then turned left, heading south.

I kept checking to the north because I didn't want us to get in line with the antiaircraft guns. With every step I expected to hear a 57mm round zinging past my head. What was keeping them? Didn't they believe the boy? Were they waiting for reinforcements? Or just waiting to get up the bottle to attack?

We patrolled further west for another five minutes, keeping distance between each man to minimize casualties in the event of a major drama. It was the correct thing to do, but if a contact happened up front, the man at the rear would have to run maybe 200 feet to catch up if required, depending on the action taken.

As we turned south there was a touch of high ground on the left-hand side that went up to the MSR. We were still in dead ground from the guns, which were further up the other side. As we started heading south, we couldn't believe our luck. Nothing happened. Then from the east, our left-hand side, we heard the sound of tracked vehicles.

Adrenaline rushed, blood pumped. We stopped. We couldn't go forwards, we couldn't go back. Where else was there to go? We knew it was going to happen.

I could see everybody preparing. They knew what to do. Bergens came off, and men checked that all pouches were closed. It's no good running to attack and finding out when you get there that you have no magazines because they've all fallen out. They checked their weapons and carried out the drills that were second nature. We were probably no more than seconds away from contact. I looked around for a deeper depression in the ground than the shallow scrape I was in.

The darkest minute is just before the firefight starts.

You can't see a thing. All you can do is listen, and think. How many of these things are going to come? Are they going to trundle straight up onto you—which is what they'll do if they've got any sense—and just turn the machine guns on you like a hose? There was nowhere to run. We'd just have to fight. The screech of armored tracks and the scream of the engines' high revs rolled around us. We still didn't know where they were.

"Fucking let's do it! Let's do it!" Chris screamed.

I was overwhelmed by a sudden feeling of togetherness, of all being in this shit together. I had no thought of dying. Just of: Let's get through this.

People have survived ambushes through pure aggression. This was going to be the same. I pulled apart the tubes of my 66 and made sure the sights had popped up. I put it beside me. I checked that my mag was on tight, checked that my 203 had a bomb in it. I knew it was there, but I couldn't help checking. It made me feel that bit more secure.

Basic instinct makes you want to keep as low as possible, but you have to look up and around. I raised myself into a semisquat. Each bloke was bobbing and moving around within his own 30-feet square trying to get a better vantage point and see what was coming. The earlier you can see it the better: then the awful dread of the unknown evaporates. This can work against you. You might see it's much worse than you anticipated, but it's got to be done.

I heard myself shouting: "Shit! Shit! Shit!"

There were shouts all along the line.

"See anything your end yet?"

"No, can't see jack shit."

"Fuck it! Fuck it!"

"Come on, come on, let's get this done!"

"Are they here yet?"

"No, fuck it."

"Fucking rag heads."

Everyone was concentrating, listening hard to locate the vehicles.

Whoof!

Everyone at my end ducked.

"For fuck's sake, what was that?"

In answer, right at the other end of the patrol, Legs or Vince fired off another 66.

Whoof!

Even if the Iraqis hadn't known we were there, they did now. But the boys wouldn't have fired without good reason. I strained my neck and saw that on the far left-hand side an APC with a 7.62 machine gun had come down a small depression that was out of sight of our end. Vince and Legs had the vehicle coming at them head-on.

"Fucking let's do it! Let's do it! Let's do it!" I screamed at the top of my voice.

It felt good all of a sudden to have got off the first round. I didn't know if I was shouting at them or at myself. A bit of both, most likely.

"Come on! Come on!"

A second APC with a turret-mounted gun opened fire all along the area. It's not nice to know you're up against armor and vehicles with infantry on board. All you are is a foot patrol, and these anonymous things are crushing relentlessly towards you. You know they carry infantry, you know all the details about them. You know the driver's in front and the gunner's up top, and he's trying to look through his prism, and it's difficult for him and he's sweating away up there, getting thrown about trying to aim. But all you can see is this thing coming screaming towards you, and it looks so anonymous and monsterlike, magnified ten times suddenly because you realize it's aiming at you. They look so impersonal. They leave destruction in their wake. It's you against them. You're an ant and you're scared.

The APC nearest me cracked off more rounds, firing

wildly. One burst stitched the ground about 30 feet in front of me.

In the British army you are taught how to react when the enemy opens fire: you dash to make yourself a hard target, you get down, you crawl into a fire position, find the enemy, set your sights at the range, and fire. "Reaction to Effective Enemy Fire," it's called. That all goes to rat shit when you're actually under fire. It always has done for me. As soon as the rounds come down, you're on the floor, and you want to make the biggest hole possible to hide in. You'd get your spoon out and start digging if it would help. It's a natural physical reaction. Your instincts compel you to get down and make yourself as small as possible and wait for it all to end. The rational side of your brain is telling you what you should be doing, which is getting up and looking to see what's going on so you can start fighting—there's no point just lying there because you're going to die anyway. The emotional side is saying, Sod that, stay there, maybe it'll all go away. But you know it's not going to and that something has to be done.

There was another sustained burst from the machine gun. Rounds thumped into the ground, getting closer and closer to where I lay. I had to react. I took a deep breath and stuck my head up. A truck had stopped 300 feet away, and infantry were spilling out of the back in total confusion. They must have known we were there because they'd heard the 66s and the turret-mounted guns were in action, but the small-arms fire they put down was only in our general direction.

There seemed to be no communication between the APCs. Both were doing their own thing. Infantry jumped out of the back, shouting and firing. They weren't entirely sure where we were. But even so, there was enough incoming from their direction to keep our heads down. If you're hit, there's not a lot of difference between a confused round and one that was deliberately aimed.

There was more hollering and shouting, from us and them. The firefight had to be initiated. It's no good just lying there and hoping that they won't see you or go away, because they won't. What they'll probably do is start coming forward and looking for you, so you've got to get on with it. It takes maximum firepower, balanced with ammunition conservation, to win a firefight. It's a question of you getting more rounds down than them and killing more of them initially, so they either back off or dig their own little holes. But their firepower was far superior to ours.

The APC stopped. I couldn't believe my eyes. It was using the machine gun as a fire base instead of coming forward with the infantry and overwhelming us, which was wonderful.

Everybody was getting the rounds down. The Minimis were fired in bursts of 3–5 rounds. Ammunition had to be managed. Two 66s were fired at the truck and found their target. There was a massive shudder of high explosive. It must have been very demoralizing for them.

Decisions. After this initial contact, what are you going to do? Are you going to stay there all the time, are you going to move back, are you going to move forward? We'd have to do something, or we'd all just face each other firing—they'd take casualties, we'd take casualties, but we would come off worse simply because we had the least number of men. This might just be the first gang coming forward; there might be another rifle company coming up behind: we didn't know yet. The only thing to do is go forward, or you'll be sitting there in a standoff until you run out of ammunition.

I looked over at Chris. "Let's fucking do it! Are you ready? Are you ready?"

He shouted down the line, "We're going to do it! We're going to do it!"

Everybody knew what had to be done. We psyched ourselves up. It's so unnatural to go forward into something like that. It's not at all what your vulnerable flesh and bone wants to do. It just wants to close its eyes and open them again much later and find that everything is fine.

"Everything Okay?"

Whether people actually heard further down the line didn't matter: they knew something was going to happen, and they knew the chances were that we were going to go forward and attack this force that vastly outnumbered us.

Without thinking, I changed my magazine. I had no idea how many rounds I had left in it. It was still fairly heavy: I might have only fired two or three rounds out of it. I threw it down the front of my smock for later on.

Stan gave the thumbs up and stepped up the fire-rate on the Minimi to initiate the move.

I was on my hands and knees, looking up. I took deep breaths, and then up I got and ran forward.

"Fuck it! Fuck it!"

People put down a fearsome amount of covering fire. You don't fire on the move. It slows you up. All you have to do is get forward, get down, and get firing so that the others can move up. As soon as you get down on the ground, your lungs are heaving and your torso is moving up and down, you're looking around for the enemy, but you've got sweat in your eyes. You wipe it away: your rifle is moving up and down in your shoulder. You want to get down in a nice firing position like you do on the range, but it isn't happening that way. You're trying to calm yourself down to see what you're doing, but you want to do everything at once. You want to stop this heavy breathing so you can hold the weapon properly and bring it to bear. You want to get rid of the sweat so you can see your targets, but you don't want to move your arm to rub your eye because you've got it in the fire position and you want to be firing to cover the move of the others as they come forward.

I jumped up and ran forward another 50 feet—a far longer bound than the textbooks say you should. The longer you are up the longer you are a target. However, it is quite hard to hit a fast-moving man, and we were pumped up on adrenaline.

You're immersed in your own little world. Me and Chris running forward, Stan and Mark backing us up with the Minimi. Fire and maneuver. The others were doing the same, legging it forward. The rag heads must have thought we were crazy, but they had put us in the situation, and this was the only way out.

You could watch the tracer coming at you. You heard the burning, hissing sound as the rounds shot past or hit the ground and spun off into the air. It was scary stuff. There's nothing you can do but jump up, run, get down; jump up, run, get down. Then lie there panting, sweating, fighting for breath, firing, looking for new targets, trying to save ammo.

Once I had moved forward and started firing, the Minimis stopped and they, too, bounded forward. The sooner they were up ahead the better, because of their superior firepower.

The closer we got the more the Iraqis were flapping. It must have been the last thing they expected us to do. They probably didn't realize it was the last thing we wanted to do.

You're supposed to count your rounds as you're firing, but in practice it's hard to do. At any moment when you need to fire, you should know how many are left and change mags if you have to. Lose count and you'll hear a "dead man click." You pull the trigger, and the firing pin goes forward, but nothing happens. In practice, counting to thirty is unrealistic. What you actually do is wait for your weapon to stop firing, then press the button and let the mag fall, slap another straight on, and off you go. If you are well drilled in this, it's second nature and requires no mental action. It just happens. The Armalite is designed so that when you've stopped firing, the working parts are to the rear, so you can slap another mag on and let the working parts go forward so that a round is taken into the breech. Then you fire again, at anything that moves.

We had got up to within 150 feet of them. The APC nearest me started to retreat, gun still firing. Our rate of fire slowed. We had to husband the rounds.

The truck was on fire. I didn't know if any of us was hit. There wouldn't have been a lot we could do about it anyway.

I couldn't believe that the APC was backing off. Obviously it was worried about the antiarmor rockets and knew the other one had been hit, but for it to withdraw was absolutely incredible. Some of the infantry ran with it, jumping into the back. They were running, turning, giving it good bursts, but it was a splendid sight. I fancied a cabby myself with my 66, and discovered that in the adrenaline rush I'd left it with my bergen. Wanker!

At the other end, Vince was up with Legs and still going forward. They were shouting to psych each other up. The rest of us put down covering fire.

Mark and Dinger stood up and ran forwards. They were concentrating on the APC ahead of them that they had hit with their 66s. They'd scored a "mobility kill"—its tracks couldn't move, though it could still use its gun. They were putting in rounds hoping to shatter the gunner's prism. If I'd been in his boots, I would have got out of the wagon and legged it, but then, he didn't know who he had pursuing him. They got up to the APC and found the rear doors still open. The jundies hadn't battened themselves down. An L2 grenade was lobbed in and exploded with its characteristic dull thud. The occupants were killed instantly.

We kept going forwards into the area of the trucks in

four groups of two, each involved in its own little drama. Everybody was bobbing and moving with Sebastian Coe legs on. We'd fire a couple of rounds, then dash and get out of the way, then start again. We tried to fire aimed shots. You pick on one body and fire until he drops. Sometimes it can take as many as ten rounds.

There is a set of sights on the 203, but you don't always have time to set it up and fire. It was a case of just take a quick aim and get it off. The weapon "pops" as it fires. I watched the bomb going through the air. There was a loud bang and showers of dirt. I heard screaming. Good. It meant they were bleeding, not shooting—and they'd become casualties that others now had to attend to.

We found ourselves on top of the position. Everybody who could do so had run away. A truck was blazing furiously ahead of us. A burnt-out APC smoked at the far-left extreme. Bodies were scattered over a wide area. Fifteen dead maybe, many more wounded. We disregarded them and carried on through. I felt an enormous sense of relief at getting the contact over with, but was still scared. There would be more to come. Anybody who says he's not scared is either a liar or mentally deficient.

"This is fucking outrageous!" Dinger screamed.

I smelled petrol and smoke, and pork—the smell of burning bodies. One Iraqi lolled out of the passenger seat of the truck, his face black and peeling. Bodies writhed on the ground. I could tell the 203s had done their job by the number of fearsome leg injuries. When they go off, slivers of metal are blown in all directions.

All we wanted to do now was get away. We didn't know what might be in the next wave. As we started moving back to the bergens, rounds kicked into the ground behind us. The surviving APC, a half mile away and surrounded by bodies, was still firing, but ineffectively. There was no time to hang around.

7

Night would be our cover, and it would be dark soon. The APC had backed off but was moving forwards again. Infantry followed in its tracks, firing wildly.

We heaved the bergens onto our shoulders. There was no point going south because they would have guessed that was our direction of travel. The object of the exercise was to put as much distance between them and us as we could. The only way to go was west, which meant running the risk of coming into line of sight with the S60s.

We wouldn't be patrolling now. We would be moving as fast as we physically could with bergens on to get out of the contact area. It was an infantry maneuver known as getting the fuck out.

Two trucks with infantry turned up from our east, came over the brow, and spotted us. They braked, and soldiers spilled out of the back and started firing. There were maybe forty of them, which was a colossal amount of fire bearing down on us.

They started coming forward. We turned to the east, got rounds down at them, and moved backwards to the west, firing like maniacs. Fire and maneuver, fire and maneuver, but this time away from them: two

men turned round and ran, then turned to give covering fire for the other two.

We were going up a gradual slope. As we hit the
brow we came into line of sight of the AA guns on the
northwest position. They started firing with a deep,
booming bass sound. The 57mm rounds screamed past
us, all of them tracered. The shells thundered into the
ground, blasting rubble all around us.

Chris and I turned round together to fall back. He
was running 6 to 10 feet to my right when I heard
what sounded like a massive punch. I looked across
just as Chris went down. He'd been hit by an antiaircraft shell. I ran over to his body, ready to jab a Syrette
of morphine into what was left of him—if he wasn't
already dead.

He was wriggling, and for a split second I thought it
was death throes. But he was very much alive and
struggling with his bergen straps. He released himself
and staggered to his feet.

"Fuck that!" he said. His bergen smoldered where
the round had smashed into it.

We ran on a few strides and he stopped. "Forgot
something," he said.

He ran back to the shattered bergen and rummaged
in the top. He came back with a silver hipflask in his
hand.

"Christmas present from the wife," he grinned as he
caught up. "Couldn't leave it behind: she'd kill me."

The rest of the blokes were also binning their
bergens. I hoped that Legs had managed to retrieve
the patrol radio from his.

The APC was moving up quite aggressively, firing
sustained and accurate bursts. Two Land Cruisers full
of infantry had also joined the fray.

We stopped and got some fire down with the 203s.
The vehicles braked sharply as the 40mm bombs ex-

ploded in front of them. Jundies spilled out, firing in a frenzy.

Mark and Dinger got severely pinned down by the S60s. They threw out their white phos and thick dirty-white smoke billowed around them. The trouble with isolated smokescreens is that they immediately draw the enemy fire, but there was nothing else they could do. The Iraqis knew the blokes were covering their withdrawal, and they emptied their magazines into the cloud. A couple of 203 rounds into the Iraqi positions slowed their rate of fire. Mark and Dinger jumped to their feet and ran.

"Cor, good here, ain't it?" Dinger said in a pissed-off tone of voice as he rushed past me.

We kept moving back and back. It was getting to last light, and they finally lost contact with us in the gloom. We were well spread out, and as darkness fell there was a danger of the patrol getting split. As we ran, we scanned the ground for a suitable rally point. Anybody in the patrol could make the choice.

There was a loud shout 150 feet to my half-right. "Rally, rally, rally!"

Whoever it was, he'd found some cover where we could get down and consolidate ourselves. This was good news, because at the moment we were fragmented, all fighting our own little dramas to get back. A rally point is much the same as an ERV except that it's given there and then and not prearranged. Its purpose is to get everybody together as quickly as possible before moving off. If anybody didn't make it, we would have to confirm that he was dead, if we hadn't done so already. Otherwise we would have to get back the "man down."

I ran over and found Chris and Bob waiting in a dip in the ground. I immediately put on a fresh mag and prepared my weapon to carry on firing. The three of us waited in all-round defense, covering all the arcs, waiting for the others to come in on us.

I counted heads as they rushed past and took up a firing position. It was five or six minutes before the last man appeared. If anybody had been missing, I'd have had to ask: Who was the last one to see him? Where did you see him? Was he just down or dead? If not, we'd have had to go forward and try to find him.

The headlights of tracked vehicles were frantically crisscrossing in front of us, no more than 1000 feet away. Now and then in the distance there was a burst of gunfire and shouting. They must have been firing at rocks, and probably at themselves. There was total confusion, which chuffed us no end.

The eight of us were closed up in a small area of a couple of square feet. People quickly sorted themselves out, taking off their sweaters and tucking them into their belt kit or inside their smocks. Nobody had to be told what was required. They knew we were either going for the helicopter or we were going for Syria. Either way, we would be doing a fearsome amount of tabbing.

"Got the radio?" I asked Legs.

"There was no way I could get to it," he said. "The fire coming in was outrageous. I think it was wrecked anyway because my bergen got shot to fuck."

I knew he would have got it if he could. But it didn't really matter anyway. We had four TACBEs between us and could get in touch with AWACS within fifteen seconds.

I was still out of breath and thirsty, and took a few gulps of water from my bottle. I dug a couple of boiled sweets out of my pocket and shoved them in my mouth.

"I'd only just lit that fag," Dinger said ruefully. "If one of them bastards has picked it up, I hope he chokes."

Bob giggled, and suddenly we were all laughing like drains. It wasn't particularly what Dinger had said. We were all just so relieved to be unscathed and back together after such a major drama. We couldn't give a damn about anything else at this stage. It was great to be all in one piece.

We had used a quarter of our ammunition. We amalgamated it and put fresh mags on. I still had my 66—the only one left, because like a dickhead I had left it with my bergen.

I adjusted my clothes, pulling my trousers right up to prevent leg sores and doing up my belt again to make sure I was comfortable. It was starting to get cold. I'd been doing a fearsome amount of sweating and started to shiver in my wet shirt. We had to get moving.

"Let's get on the net now," Legs said. "They know we're here. We might as well use the TACBE."

"Yeah," said Vince, "let's get some fucking shit down."

He was right. I got out my TACBE, pulled the tab, and heard the *hish*. I pressed the transmit button and talked.

"Hello AWACS, this is Bravo Two Zero: we are a ground call sign and we're in the shit, over."

There was no reply.

I repeated the message.

Nothing.

"Hello any call sign," I said, "this is Bravo Two Zero."

Nothing.

I kept trying for thirty seconds without success.

Our only hope now was to get a fast jet overfly so we could contact them by TACBE on the emergency frequency. It was very unlikely, however, that jets would be going over, unless one of Legs's signals had got through during the compromise phase and the FOB had scrambled some support aircraft. There certainly hadn't been an autoacknowledgment. Maybe they knew we were in the shit, maybe they didn't. There wasn't a lot we could do about it.

I did a quick appreciation. We could either tab 200 miles south to Saudi, head north towards Turkey, which meant crossing the Euphrates, or go just 100 miles west to Syria. There were infantry and armor in the immediate area. We were compromised and they were looking for us. They would naturally think that we were heading south towards Saudi. Even if we could make the heli RV, there was a chance of us being followed—and that could mean enemy activity in the area while the Chinook came in.

I decided that we had no choice but to head for Syria. We would initially move south as part of the deception plan, because that was the presumed way to go; then we'd head west to box around the area, and finally turn generally northwest. We would try to be on the other side of the MSR before first light because this would probably be the psychological perimeter of their search south. Then we could start heading for the border.

"Is everybody ready?" I said.

We started south in a single file. Vehicles were zooming backwards and forwards around us about a quarter of a mile away. We'd only gone a few hundred meters when one of them, a Land Cruiser, headed straight at us, its headlights blazing. We hit the ground, but we were out in the open. We turned our faces away to prevent the reflection and to save our night vision. The vehicle was 650 feet away and closing. If it came any nearer, we would be seen. I braced myself for another major drama. There was a shout. I flicked my head up and saw another vehicle flashing its lights about 1000 feet to our left. The Land Cruiser changed direction and sped off towards it.

We carried on at a brisk pace. Several times we had to stop and get down as vehicles came near. It was annoying: not only did we want to get out of the area quickly, but we also needed to keep going to keep warm. We only had smocks on over our shirts because we didn't want to sweat too much, and the temperature seemed to be dropping all the time now.

I was severely pissed off about AWACS not responding to our signal, and the thought of having to cover more than 100 miles to get to Syria didn't do much to lift my spirits.

After what seemed like a lifetime of tabbing, we looked back and saw that the headlight activity was focused in the distance. We were out of the immediate danger area, with a bit of cover from a dip in the ground. If we wanted to try TACBE again, it would have to be on this southern leg. Bob and Dinger immediately moved back onto the lip of the depression with their Minimis to cover the rear in case we had been followed. Everybody else was down in all-round defense. I got on my TACBE again, to no avail.

Everybody with a TACBE had a go. It was unbelievable that all four radios were playing up, but that seemed to be what was happening.

Mark made a nav check with the Magellan and worked out that we'd tabbed 15 miles. We'd covered it so quickly that with luck the Iraqis wouldn't believe it possible and would have been thrown off the scent.

"We'll head west now to get well clear of the area," I said. "Then we'll start heading north to get over the MSR before first light."

All I heard was abuse directed at the manufacturers of TACBE. We would not use it again now unless we got a fast jet flying over. We didn't know whether the Iraqis had aircraft up or not, but we'd just have to take the chance. We were in the shit, and freezing cold shit it was, too.

We got Dinger and Bob back in, gave them the good news, and off we tabbed. We'd only stopped for a minute or two, but it was good to get moving again. It was bitterly cold, and a strong wind blasted the chill deep into our bones. There was dense cloud cover, and we were in pitch darkness. We couldn't see our footing correctly. The only plus was that at least it made it a lot harder for them to find us. There was still the odd vehicle, but in the far distance. We had left them well behind. I was almost feeling confident.

We pushed west for 10 miles, moving fast on a bearing. The ground was so flat that we'd be warned well in advance of any Iraqi presence. It was a balance between speed and observation.

We stopped every hour to rest for five minutes, which is the patrolling SOP. If you go on and on, all you do is run yourself down, and you'll end up not being able to achieve what you set out to do. So you stop, get down, get some rest, drink some water, sort yourself out, get yourself comfy again, and off you go. It was freezing cold, and I shivered uncontrollably when we stopped.

We had one of our five-minute rests at the 10 miles mark and did a Magellan check. I made the decision that because of the time factor, we'd have to turn north now to get over the MSR before first light.

"Let's just get over that road," I said, "then we can go northwest to Syria."

We'd gone about another 6 miles when I noticed gaps appearing in the line. We were definitely moving more slowly than we had in the beginning. There was a problem. I stopped the patrol, and everybody closed up.

Vince was limping.

"You all right, mate?" I said.

"Yeah, I hurt my leg on the way out in that contact, and it's really fucking starting to give me gyp."

The whole aim of the game was to get everybody over the border. Vince clearly had an injury. We'd have to do all our planning and considerations around the fact that he was in trouble. None of this "No, it's Okay, skipper, I can go on" bollocks, because if you try to play the he-man and don't inform people of your injuries, you're endangering the whole patrol. If they're not aware of your problem, they can't adjust the plan or cater for future eventualities. If you make sure people know that you're injured, they can plan around it.

"What's the injury like?" Dinger said.

"It just fucking hurts. I don't think it's fractured. It's not bleeding or anything, but it's swollen. It's going to slow me down."

"Right, we'll stop here and sort ourselves out," I said.

I pulled my woolen bobble hat from my smock and put it on my head. I watched Vince massage his leg. He was clearly annoyed with himself for sustaining an injury.

"Stan's in shit state," Bob said to me.

Dinger and Mark had been helping him along. They laid him down on the ground. He was in a bad way. He knew it, and he was pissed off about it.

"What the hell's the matter?" I said, sticking my hat on his head.

"I'm on my chinstrap, mate. I'm just dying here."

Chris was the most experienced medic on the patrol. He examined Stan, and it was obvious to him that he was dangerously dehydrated.

"We've got to get some rehydrate down him, and quick."

Chris ripped open two sachets of electrolyte from Stan's belt kit and tipped them into his water bottle. Stan took several big gulps.

"Look, Stan," I said, "you realize that we've got to go on?"

"Yeah, I know that. Just give us a minute. Let's get some more of this shit down my neck, and I'll sort myself out. It's this fucking Helly Hansen underwear. I was sleeping with it on when we got compromised."

Dehydration is no respecter of climates. You can become dehydrated in the depths of an Arctic winter just the same as in the middle of the day in the Sahara.

Physical exertion produces sweat, even in the cold. And the vapor clouds we see when we exhale are yet more precious moisture leaking from our bodies. Thirst is an unreliable indicator of dehydration. The problem is that just a few sips of liquid might quench your thirst without improving your internal water deficit. Or you might not even notice your thirst because there is too much else going on that needs your attention. After losing 5 percent of your body weight through dehydration, you will be struck by waves of nausea. If you vomit, you'll lose even more precious fluid. Your movements will slow down dramatically, your speech will slur, and you'll become unable to walk. Dehydration to this degree can be fatal. Stan had been wearing his thermals ever since we left the LUP. He must have lost pints of sweat.

I started to shake.

"What do we do—take his kit off?" I asked Chris.

"No, it's all he's got on, apart from his trousers, shirt, and smock. If we take it off, he'll be in a worse state."

Stan got up and started moving around. We gave him another ten minutes to get himself organized; then it became too cold to stand still any longer and we had to get moving.

We had to do our planning around the two slowest and move at their speed. I changed the order of the march. I put Chris up front, with Stan and Vince behind him. I followed them, with the others behind me.

As scout, Chris moved on the compass bearing and used the night sight to make sure that we weren't going to walk into anything nasty. We stopped every half hour instead of every hour. Each time, we had to get more water into Stan. The situation was not desperate, but he did seem to be getting worse.

The weather had become diabolical. We weren't tabbing as hard as we had been because the cold was sapping our strength. The wind was driving into our faces and we were all moving with our heads turned at half cock to try and protect ourselves.

We pushed on, our pace dictated by the two injured men in front. At one stop Vince sat down and gripped his leg.

"It's getting worse, mate," he said. It was so out of character for him to complain. The injured leg must have been agony. He apologized for the hassle he was causing us.

We had two enemies now—time and the physical condition of the two slowest men. By now the rest of us were starting to feel the effects of the night's march as well. My feet and legs were aching, and I had to keep reminding myself that it was what I got paid for.

There was total cloud cover. It was jet-black. I checked the navigation, and the rest of the patrol covered the arcs to the sides and the rear. Chris was having trouble with the NVA because there was no ambient light. This was now slowing us down as much as the two injured men.

The wind bit into every inch of exposed skin. I kept my arms tight against my sides to preserve warmth. My head was down, my shoulders shrugged. If I had to move my head, I'd turn my whole body. I didn't want the slightest bit of wind down my neck.

We started to hear aircraft coming from the north. I couldn't see a thing because of the cloud cover, but I had to make a decision. Was I going to get on the TACBE, only to find they were Iraqi?

"Fucking yeah," Mark said, reading my thoughts. "Let's do it."

I put my hand on Vince's shoulder and said, "We're going to stop and try TACBE."

He nodded and said, "Yep, Okay, yep."

I tried to open my pouch. It was easier said than done. My hands were frozen and so numb that I couldn't get my fingers to work. Mark started fumbling with my belt kit as well, but he couldn't unclench his fingers enough to undo the pouch. Finally, somehow, I had the TACBE in my hand. The last couple of jets were still going over.

"Hello any call sign, this is Bravo Two Zero, Bravo Two Zero. We are a ground call sign and we're in the shit. Over."

Nothing. I called again. And again.

"Hello any call sign, this is Bravo Two Zero, Bravo Two Zero. We are a ground call sign and we're in the shit. We have a fix for you. Over."

If they did nothing else other than inform somebody of our position, we'd be laughing. Mark got out Magellan and pressed the fix button to give us longitude and latitude.

It was then that I heard the wonderful sound of an American voice, and it suddenly registered with me that these would be jets coming from Turkey to do raids around Baghdad.

"Say again, Bravo Two Zero, Bravo Two Zero. You're very weak. Try again."

The signal was weak because he was screaming out of range.

"Turn back north," I said. "Turn back north. Over."

No reply.

"Hello any call sign, this is Bravo Two Zero. Over."

Nothing.

They'd gone. They wouldn't come back. Bastards!

Five minutes later, the horizon was lit by bright flashes and tracer. The jets were obviously hosing something down near Baghdad. Their run-ins are crucial, timed to the split second. They couldn't have turned back for us even if they'd wanted to. At least he had repeated our call sign. Presumably this would get filtered through the system, and the FOB would know we were still on the ground, but in the shit—or at least, that one of us with a TACBE was.

It was all over within twenty or thirty seconds. I

hunched with my back to the wind as I replaced the TACBE in my pouch. I looked at Legs and he shrugged. He was right—so what? We'd made the contact.

"Maybe they'll fly back this way and things will be good," I said to Bob.

"Let's hope."

I turned into the wind to tell Chris and the other two that we'd better press on.

"For fuck's sake," I whispered, "where's everybody else gone?"

I had told Vince we were going to try TACBE. The correct response is for the message to get passed along the line, but it can't have registered in his numbed brain. He must have just kept on walking without telling Chris and Stan.

It's each man's responsibility in the line to make sure that messages go up or down, and if you stop, you make sure that the bloke in front knows that you've stopped. You should know who's in front of you and who's behind you. It's your responsibility to make sure they're always there. So it was my fault and Vince's that they didn't stop. We both failed in our responsibilities—Vince in not passing it on, me in not making sure that he stopped.

We couldn't do anything about it. We couldn't do a visual search because Chris was the only person with a night-viewing aid. We couldn't shout because we didn't know what was ahead of us or to either side. And we couldn't use white light—that's a big no-no. So we'd just have to keep on the bearing and hope that they'd stop at some stage and wait for us. There was a good chance that we'd meet up.

I felt terrible. We had failed, more or less, in our contact with the aircraft. And now, even worse, we'd lost three members of the patrol—two of whom were injured. I was annoyed with myself, and annoyed with the situation. How the hell had I allowed it to happen?

Bob must have guessed what I was thinking because he said, "It's done now: let's just carry on. Hopefully we'll RV."

That helped me a lot. He was right. At the end of the day they were big boys: they could sort themselves out.

We headed north again on the bearing. The freezing wind pierced our flimsy desert camouflage. After two hours of hard tabbing we came to our MSR and crossed over. The next objective now was a metaled road further to the north.

We encountered a couple of inhabited areas, but boxed around without incident. Soon after midnight we heard noise in the distance. We started our routine to box around whatever it was and came across some armored vehicles, laagered up, then a forest of antennas. The face of a squaddy was briefly illuminated as he lit a cigarette. He probably should have been on stag, but he was dossing in the cab of a truck. It was either a military installation or a temporary position. Whatever, we had to box around again.

Chris and the others can't have gone into it, or we would have heard the contact.

We carried on for about twenty minutes. All of us were on our chinstraps. We'd had eight hours of head down and go for it. The stress on the legs had been immense. My feet hurt. I felt completely knackered.

I had been thinking about the aircraft. It was hours ago that we'd heard them, so the pilots would be back in their hotels now enjoying their coffee and doughnuts while the engineers sorted their aircraft out. Such a lovely way to go to war. They climb into their nice, warm cockpits and ride over to their target. Down below, as far as they are concerned, is jet-black nothingness. Then what should they hear but the old Brit voice gobbing off, moaning about being in the shit. It must have been a bit of a surprise. I hoped so much that they were concerned for us and were doing something. I wondered if they would have reported the incident by radio as soon as it had happened, or if they'd wait until they returned to base. Probably the latter. Hours ago, and no other fast jets had come over. I didn't know what the American system was for initiating a search and rescue package. I just hoped they knew that it was really important.

I blamed myself for the split. I felt a complete knobber and wondered if everybody else held the same opinion. I remembered a speech I had read by Field Marshal Slim. Talking about leadership, he had said something to the effect of, "When I'm in charge of a battle and everything's going well and to plan and I'm winning—I'm a great leader, a real good lad. But you find out whether you can really lead or not when everything's going to rat shit and you are to blame." I knew exactly how he felt. I could have kicked myself for not confirming that Vince had registered that we were stopping. In my mind, everything was my fault. As we tabbed north I kept thinking, what the hell did I do wrong? The E&E must go right from here on. I mustn't make any more mistakes.

It was time to think about finding somewhere to hide. We'd been going over shale and rock, and had come to an area of solid sand. Our boots were hardly making any imprint. This was fine from the point of view of leaving sign, but the ground was so hard there was no way we could scrape a hiding place. It was nearly first light, and we were still running around. Things were just starting to look a bit wriggly when Legs spotted some sand dunes a half mile to our west. We found ourselves in an area where the constant wind had made ripples and small mounds about 15–30 feet high. We looked for the tallest one. We wanted to be above eye level.

We did what we should never do by going for isolated cover. But there was only this small knoll on an otherwise flat surface. On top of it was a small cairn of stones. Maybe somebody was buried there.

There was a small stone wall about a foot high around the cairn. We built it up slightly and lay down behind. It was icy cold as the wind whistled through the gaps in the stones, but at least it was a relief to stop tabbing. In the course of the last twelve hours, in total darkness and atrocious weather conditions, we had traveled 50 miles, the length of two marathons. My legs were aching. Lying down and being still was wonderful, but then cramp would start. As you moved, other areas were exposed to the cold. It was incredibly uncomfortable.

Looking to our south, we saw pylons running east–west. We used them to fix our position on the map. If we followed them, we would eventually hit the border. But if we used the pylons for navigation, who was to say that other people wouldn't as well?

We lay there for about half an hour, getting more and more uncomfortable. To our east about a mile away was a corrugated iron building which was probably a water-boring station. It looked very inviting, but it was even worse isolated cover. There was nothing to the north. There was no alternative but to stay where we were.

We had to keep really low. We cuddled up and tried to share body warmth. Dark clouds raced across the sky. The wind howled through the stones; I could feel it bite into me. I had known cold before, in the Arctic, but nothing like this. This was lying in a freezer cabinet, feeling your body heat slowly slip away. And we would have to stay there for the rest of the day, restricting our movement to what was possible below the height of the wall. When we got cramp, a common problem after a major tab, we had to help each other.

Legs got out the signals info from his map pocket and destroyed all the sensitive codes and other odds and bods. We lit the code sheets and burnt them one at a time to ensure that everything was destroyed, then crushed the ashes and spread them into the ground.

"I'll have a fag on while you've got your bonfire going," said Dinger. "Got to have a gasper before the fun starts."

We resterilized ourselves, going through all our pockets to make doubly sure we had nothing left on us that would compromise the mission, ourselves, or anybody else. You might have something on you that would mean nothing to them unless you told them, but it could be something they could use as a starting point for the interrogation. "What is this? What does it do?" You can go through a lot of pain for something that's totally irrelevant.

There were vehicle sounds in the distance. Two APCs were about a half mile to the south, too far away to be an immediate danger. I hoped they didn't take it into their heads to start looking in places of obvious cover.

At about 0700 it started to rain. We couldn't believe it. We were in the middle of the desert. The last time I saw rain in the desert was in 1985 in Oman. We were drenched, and within ten minutes the rain had turned to sleet. We looked at one another in total amazement. Then it started to snow.

Bob sang, "I'm dreaming of a white Christmas."

We might as well have been on an exposed mountainside in winter. This could get serious. We cuddled up more. Not a single therm of body heat could be wasted now. We got out our map covers and tried to improvise little shelters. Our main concern was to conserve heat at the core of our bodies, the trunk.

Man is a "homeotherm"—that is, our bodies try to maintain a constant body temperature irrespective of the temperature of their surroundings. The body consists of an inner hot core, surrounded by a cooler outer shell. The core consists of the brain and other vital organs contained within the skull, chest, and abdomen. The shell is what is left: the skin, fat, muscle, and limbs. It is in effect a buffer zone between the core and the outside world, protecting the organs from any catastrophic change in temperature.

The maintenance of proper internal body temperature is the most important factor in determining your survival. Even in extreme cold or heat, your core temperature will seldom vary more than two degrees either side of 98.4° F (36.8° C), with the shell just a few degrees cooler. If your core temperature rises above 109° F (42.7° C) or falls below 84° F (28.8° C), you will die. Your body generates both energy and heat as it burns fuel. When you start to shiver, your body is telling you that it is losing heat faster than it is being replaced. The shivering reflex exercises many muscles, increasing heat production by burning more fuel. If the temperature at the core of your body drops even a few degrees, you're in trouble. Shivering will not be enough to warm you again.

The body has a thermostat, located in a small piece of nerve tissue at the base of the brain, which controls the production or dissipation of heat and monitors all parts of the body in order to maintain a constant temperature. When the body starts to go into hypothermia, the body thermostat responds by ordering heat to be drawn from the extremities into the core. Your hands and feet will start to stiffen. As the core temperature drops, the body also draws heat from the head. When this happens, circulation slows down, and the victim doesn't get the oxygen or sugar the brain needs: the sugar the brain ordinarily feeds on is being burned to produce heat. As the brain begins to slow down, the body stops shivering, and irrational behavior begins. That is a sure danger sign, but one it is hard to recognize in yourself because one of the first things hypothermia does is take away your will to help yourself. You stop shivering and you stop worrying. You are dying, in fact, and you couldn't care less. At this point, your body loses its ability to reheat itself. Even if you have a sleeping bag to crawl into, you will continue to cool off. Your pulse will get irregular; drowsiness will become semi-consciousness, which will become unconsciousness. Your only hope is to add heat from an external source—a fire, hot drinks, another body. Indeed, one of the most effective ways of rewarming a hypothermia victim is to put them in a sleeping bag with another person whose body temperature is still normal.

I was feeling quite secure, which was silly because our situation was far from secure. We were on a barren landscape and occupying one of the two pieces of obvious cover for miles around. I was happy that we'd stopped because we could rest, but unhappy because our bodies wanted to keep on moving to keep warm. But there was nothing we could do except lie there and exchange body heat and wait for dark.

The compacted sand was like hard mud. It had looked alien before; now that it was covered in snow it looked like the moon. The snowfall turned into a blizzard. I tried to look on the bright side: at least it cut visibility down to about 150 feet.

Vehicles moved up and down all day, moving east and west as they followed the line of the pylons—civilian trucks, water bowsers, Land Cruisers, and armored, wheeled vehicles. The last two vehicles got us flapping because they came to within 600 feet of our position. Were they coming for us? Not that we could do much about it; we could hardly get up and run because there was nowhere to run to.

There were more vehicles than we were expecting, much more military activity, but that was not the major consideration now. Lying in the snow, lashed by a wicked wind, we were more concerned about keeping warm and keeping alive. We were physically exhausted and exposed to the wind. All the potential was here for a major drama. An already cold air temperature, combined with a strong wind, can produce an equivalent windchill temperature that can kill. In a 30 mph wind, exposed flesh freezes in sixty seconds or less at just −9° C. It was only much later that we learned that these were the worst weather conditions the region had experienced for thirty years. Diesel was freezing in vehicles.

From feeling secure I started to become seriously concerned. I'd seen people die in this sort of stuff. What a way to go, I thought, for the patrol to die of exposure rather than getting shot. I didn't think I'd be able to bear the slagging.

We couldn't sit up, because we would be silhouetted against the skyline. We were depending for concealment on the level of view: because they would have to look up, our hope was that the small wall would afford us cover as long as we kept still and kept down.

By 1100 the situation was getting out of control. We were huddled up, cuddling one another, shivering convulsively, muttering words of encouragement, making stupid irrelevant jokes. My hands were numb, frozen, and very painful. We had a mound of snow over us. It was a case now of sod the tactics, let's try to survive. The balance was between breaking SOPs and therefore being compromised, and getting into such a bad condition that we would just die anyway. I decided that we'd have to break SOPs and get a brew on.

I scraped a small hole and lit a hexy block. I filled a mug with water and held it over the flame. The heat on my hands and face was wonderful. I waved my hand to disperse the steam. I added coffee granules, sugar, and milk to the hot water and passed it around.

I immediately put on another brew of hot chocolate.

"Look at all that bloody steam," said Dinger. "I might as well have a smoke."

It was pathetic to watch him trying to light the cigarette. His hands were shaking so badly that he couldn't get it in his mouth, and when he did it was soggy because his hands had been wet. He persisted, and five minutes later was inhaling contentedly, blowing the smoke into his smock to hide it.

By the time the hot chocolate came around everybody was shaking and gibbering again. The hot drink didn't move us too many notches up the temperature chart, but it was better than a kick in the tits. Without a doubt, it had made the difference between life and death.

Come midday, vehicles were still passing. We couldn't always see them but that didn't matter. We'd hear them if they stopped. We tried to change around so that people on the outside who were exposed to the wind and snow had the chance to be surrounded by the others and get some body warmth. As our body-core temperatures continued to drop, I realized that my speech was slurring and I was feeling very light-headed. I was suffering from the first stages of hypothermia.

At about 1400 Mark realized that he was in deep trouble. "We'll have to get going in a minute," he blurted. "I'm starting to go down here."

He was wearing less than the rest of us. All he had on his chest was his smock, shirt, and jumper, and those were soaking wet. We got around him and tried to give him our body heat. A decision had to be made, and we all had to be in on it because it affected us all: did we move in daylight to help Mark survive but risk a compromise? There were hours of daylight and we didn't know what was out there. Or did we wait until the very last moment, when he thought he simply couldn't take any more?

I tried to encourage him to hold on. "If we've got to move in half an hour, fine, but let's try and stay here as long as we can."

If he had shaken his head and said he needed to

move, I would have got up without a murmur, but he nodded his assent.

By the time another two hours had elapsed it wasn't just Mark who needed help. All of us were in a desperate state. If we stayed static, we'd be dead by the evening.

I peered over the wall. There was only about an hour and a half of daylight left; the cloud cover and snow would make it dark earlier. It was still snowing hard. I couldn't see or hear anything, apart from the sight of a typically arid desert scene, covered in a blanket of thick snow.

"Let's go," I said.

We put in a deception plan because we would be leaving a lot of sign in the snow, though hopefully it would snow or rain during the night and destroy our trail. We headed east, then did a loop to end up going towards the northwest. The deception plan proved to be a good move because we were no more than a half mile off the position when we heard hooting and hollering behind us. We turned and saw lights. Vehicles were in and around our position.

"Shit!" Legs said. "All they've got to do now is follow the sign."

But it was starting to get dark, and the tracks and footprints of the Iraqis must have got mixed up with ours and confused them.

The plan had been to head northwest after crossing the metaled road, then take the shortest route to the Syrian border. If we'd started to head northwest this side of the road, the chances were that we'd be compromised because of the movement we had seen during the day.

But now the plan had to change. Water was going to be a problem soon. We'd filled up our bottles with snow, but even in the best of circumstances it takes a long time to melt and produces little water anyway. In our case, the weather was so cold that it stayed as snow and ice. You can't eat snow. Not only does it waste crucial body heat melting in your mouth, but it cools the body from the inside, chilling the vital organs in the body core. We didn't know where and when we'd be able to get water again. We had to get to the border as soon as possible.

The second, and more important, consideration behind our change of plan was the weather. We were on high ground, about 900 feet above sea level, and to the northwest it got higher still. The windchill factor in these conditions was horrendous. The temperature was low anyway, but the wind took it bitterly, freezingly lower. We needed to get out of the wind, and we needed to get off the snowline. However, the chances of getting out of the wind were slim because the ground afforded no cover.

Like all water systems the Euphrates follows the low ground. The river was 400 or 500 feet lower than we were, so if we headed north towards it we would not only come off the snowline but hopefully also find protection from the wind.

We headed north. We could worry about the west a bit later; it was just imperative that we got off this high ground or we'd die.

A mile and a half from our stone-wall LUP we came off the snowline. I was horrendously pissed off. If only we could have made the extra bit of distance that morning, we wouldn't have spent the entire day lying in snow. We still had a desperate problem with windchill. I had my shamag wrapped around my head and the compass in front of me as we marched on a bearing. My left hand was crooked with my thumb over the luminous part of the compass and my smock pulled over my hand as much as I could to keep out the cold. I cradled my weapon in my right arm. I looked down and saw that my smock had frozen solid. It was iced over like a pond. The shamag, too, was solid around my face. I wanted to adjust it, but it was as stiff as a board.

I daren't move my hands because that let the cold in. We had to move as fast as we could to generate body warmth. It was desolate, no ambient light, just the sound of the wind. It was as if we were on a different planet, and the only people on it.

We pressed northwards, heads down and faces blue with cold. Vehicle lights moved now and again in the distance, indicating the metaled road. The ground started to change again, from hard sand to bedrock with shale. All round the area there were tank berms where bulldozers had made trenches for tanks to get into the "hull down" position. They were filled with water and ice; they weren't new.

We'd dropped about 200 feet in elevation. All of us were suffering badly. I looked out from behind my shamag and thought: If the weather doesn't improve soon, we're going to die.

We had marched about a mile and a half over the road when I decided we should turn back. Windchill was going to kill us. We were stumbling, shivering violently, starting to switch off, our minds wandering. If we didn't act now, they were the last symptoms that we would recognize. The next stage was coma. We'd get back across the metaled road and retreat for another mile to a dried-up riverbed I remembered which ran more or less parallel with the road. It was the only place we had found that night that was out of the wind. If we didn't get back there and sort ourselves out, there'd be no selves to sort out.

We turned back, tactics thrown literally to the wind. Stealth was irrelevant now. All we wanted to do now was save our lives. We stumbled into the ditch and huddled together. Mark was the worst affected, but we all needed help. Bob and I jumped on top of him and gave him body heat. Dinger and Legs did the same together and got a brew on. It's an outrageous big no-no, making brews at night, but so what? If you're dead, that's it. Better to take the chance and live to fight another day. If we didn't get compromised, we would hopefully start to recover. If we did, we would either get away with it or die. If we didn't do it, we could die anyway.

They got two brews on, one after the other, and passed them around. We got some hot food down Mark. He was slurring his words good style, definitely on his way out. I seriously thought we were all going to die.

We were there a couple of hours, just trying to get warm in a big huddle. We got a slight improvement. I didn't really want to make a move because we were still freezing and soaking. But we all knew we had to get going or we were never going to make any headway. After all, the aim was to evade capture.

We had three factors to worry about: the weather, our physical condition, and the enemy. Because of the terrain it was very unlikely that we would avoid the wind that was giving us so much trouble. No matter where we went or what we did it would be there. Our physical condition could have been worse, but not much. The ideal would have been to stay there out of the wind until it stopped or the weather improved. But how long would that be? Water would be of concern sooner or later as well. The longer we went without it, the greater the problem would become.

There were far more enemy in the area than we had been told. Something was wrong somewhere. If we were compromised, action could be taken quicker because the troops were there on the ground. Would they now know that we were in the area after moving onto our LUP?

We had to move, but in which direction? In favor of going north then west was the fact that we would keep off the snowline. Against, that we would be exposed to the wind for longer and closer to the river, closer to habitation, and concealment would be difficult. Heading northwest would take us back on to the snowline, but it would be quicker, and the chances of concealment would be better. The height was approximately 1,100–1,200 feet, but once we were over that we would be down to around 600 feet all the way to the border. We could also do it in one night as long as our physical condition didn't get any worse.

Whatever direction we went, the wind was going to get us. So it was best not to waste time. If we couldn't make it, we would just have to come down again and rethink. It got to the stage where, if we didn't move now, there wouldn't be enough time. The longer we left it, the less darkness we had to get over this high ground. We would have to cover a good 12–15 miles, so we needed to get our arses into gear and get away.

The riverbed ran northwest, and we decided to make use of it for two reasons. One, it gave us tactical cover; two, it gave us a certain amount of protection from the wind. The only disadvantage was if we were approaching any military installations. The ditch was a good approach route if anybody was going to attack, so the chances were that it would be covered by fire and observation. However, we would take the chance.

It was about midnight, and we'd been moving for about two hours, patrolling tactically because of the amount of vehicles we'd seen coming from this direction. Moving so slowly is bad because you can't keep as warm as you'd like to; however, it prevents you stumbling into something you may not be able to get out of.

Legs was in front as scout. I was behind him, then Bob, Mark, and Dinger. As we moved along the riverbed, I checked our navigation with the compass to make sure the ditch was leading us in more or less the right direction. The rest of the lads were covering the arcs. It was still freezing, but because we were moving tactically, we had something else to think about.

The ground started to change back to bedrock with shale. That was an added pain in the arse because of the noise, but for once the howling wind worked in our favor. It was a clear sky, with a three-quarter moon set in the west, a plus for navigation but not for concealment. The clouds were now gone, but this only made it colder.

The landscape was starting to change. The area had been generally flat, but from time to time now the ground gently rolled up into a mound which lasted for 1,000–1,250 feet. Undulating ground is good for concealment, and we started to feel better about our predicament. At last this desolate flatness was changing in our favor as the high ground started.

The distance between patrol members was dictated by the light. Ideally you want as much distance as possible so that if you come under fire, not everybody is caught in the same area and hosed down all at once. But it's a compromise between that and actually seeing what's going on with the bloke in front. We were patrolling with about four meters between each man.

There was no talking. You communicate by hand signal or by duplicating the scout's movements. If the scout stops, the bloke behind him does the same, and it reverberates all the way down. If the scout kneels down, you all kneel down. Everything's done very slowly and very deliberately, or you create movement, you create noise.

Legs suddenly froze.

Everybody behind him froze too. We all covered our arcs, looked around, waiting to see what he had seen. There was a plantation to our right—we could just see the tips of the trees. There were no lights or movement. There was high ground forward to the left, less than 350 feet away. Slowly coming into view as they got to the top of the hill were the silhouettes of two men. Both had "longs"—long weapons.

Legs started to kneel down very slowly, to get into the lip of the riverbed itself. We had the cover of the wind and the cover of them making noise. But spotting two men didn't mean there weren't two hundred about. We just didn't know. Slowly and deliberately we started to get into cover.

Could it be two of our missing patrol members? The wind carried brief bits of chat in our direction, and I tried hard to hear a voice or word I recognized. But surely Vince, Stan, or Chris would never let themselves be skylined like that, let alone walk around chatting? It was very frustrating. I was hoping so much that it was them and we'd be able to grab hold of them in some way.

They stopped and looked all around. I hoped they didn't have night-viewing aids. If they did, we'd have to go for it good style if they saw us from such a distance. Then I had the mad thought: Chris has got our set of NVG; if we show ourselves, he'll be able to see us. No, I really wasn't going to do that. He'd look and just see bodies: he wouldn't be able to identify us. In reality, the chances of us making a union were going to be quite slim.

They were still too far away for us to ID them. They started moving again, and I watched as they came down from the high ground and walked across in front of us. We got right down, moving very slowly, very deliberately. Even if one of the blokes at the back of the patrol hadn't seen the two figures on the sky-line, he'd have known there was a drama. It would be tactically imprudent to tell him what was happening because that would involve movement and speech.

We were there for what seemed an eternity, just staring at these characters and looking around to see if there was anybody else. They got to our riverbed and started walking along the edge towards us. This was a

severe drama. We were going to get compromised by
these dickheads. We would have to keep covert as
long as possible, but then go overt the moment they
saw us. Everybody had made the same appreciation. I
saw Legs rest his 203 very gently on the ground and
slowly, slowly reach for the fighting knife in its leather
sheath. The weapon is housed this way precisely so
that it makes no noise when extracted. They were very
slow, very deliberate movements. Bob was right up on
my shoulder by this stage, and he was very slowly
taking the sling of the Minimi off his shoulder. He
didn't have a fighting knife. He had an M16 bayonet,
which is stored in a plastic and metal sheath. The bayonet makes a scraping sound as it is pulled out, so Bob
just put his hand on the handle and pulled it out a
little way. He'd fully extract it at the last minute.

We couldn't take the risk of them shouting a warning. We'd have to kill them as soon as they came
within range. In films, the attacker puts his hand over
his target's mouth and with one smooth motion runs a
knife into his heart or along his neck and the boy just
drops. Unfortunately it doesn't work quite like that.
The chances of getting one smooth stab into the heart
are very remote and not even worth the effort. He
might have a greatcoat on, and there could be webbing
underneath. You'd do your neat stab, and he'd just
turn around and ask you not to. If you're 5'10" and
he's 6'5" and weighs seventeen stone, you're going to
be in the shit. Even if you cut the boy's jugular, you're
going to get a minute or so of screaming and shouting
out of him. In reality, you have to get hold of his head,
hoik it back as you would with a sheep, and just keep
on cutting until you've gone right through the wind-
pipe and the head has just about come away in your
hands. That way he's not going to breathe any more or
have any means of shouting out.

Legs and Bob were ready. The rest of us would be
up also to help with the killing by covering their

mouths to stop the screaming. They'd have to get out of the riverbed very swiftly and up and on top of them, check they weren't two of ours, and do the business. The ideal would have been to ID them before they could see us, but it was all going to happen together. If the two characters were ours, there was a chance of them taking us for Iraqis in the sudden attack, and we'd have a nasty "blue on blue." It happened in the Falklands, when a Regiment patrol got into a contact with a Special Boat Squadron patrol.

They were within 60 feet of us. I crouched against the bank of the riverbed and looked up. Ten or fifteen more paces, I reckoned, and there would be an explosion of movement from in front of and behind me— and then, either a reunion with our lost blokes or two more statistics.

I held my breath. All thoughts of windchill and exposure were banished now. My mind was concentrated 100 percent on every single little movement that was going on. And these blokes didn't have a clue they were about to get their throats done.

They stopped.

Had they seen something? They were close enough for me to see that the longs were AKs. They jumped down into the riverbed no more than 20–25 feet in front of us and ambled across to the other side. They scrambled up the other side and walked off towards the plantation, the two luckiest men in Iraq. I almost laughed. I would have enjoyed seeing Bob leap up and do the business, little midget that he was.

We stayed where we were for about a quarter of an hour, tuning in all over again. We were all right, we were in cover, we weren't making any noise. All we had to do was take our time and make sure we weren't going to blunder into anything.

We "closed in."

We didn't know what was on the other side of the

high ground that the two Iraqis had come from. They might just have been two blokes who lived at the plantation, or we might be walking into a major drama. Better to stop, take our time, use concealment.

"We'll head south and box it," I said into Bob's ear, and he passed the message down the line.

We patrolled as before with Legs as scout. We had gone about a mile when we came to a mound of high ground to our front. We chose to go through a saddle, and as we moved towards it, Legs stopped. He got on his knees and lay down. We were right out in the open.

I got on my belly beside him, slowly and deliberately. He pointed up. There was a head on the ridge line about 150 feet away. We watched him as he shuffled around, but I couldn't see any others. I indicated to the patrol by pointing east that we'd have to box around the position. We circumnavigated the high ground for about 1,200 feet and headed west.

We encountered static interior vehicle lights on the other side of the high ground. We had walked into a laager of vehicles parked up for the night. Again we had to back out, head south, then try again heading west. We came across more troops and tents. We turned south again for a half mile, then west again, and at last were in the clear. These encounters had cost us a good two hours, and we didn't have time to spare.

We pressed on towards Syria along the higher ground. By now we were at an altitude of over 1,000 feet, and it was colder than we could have imagined. The area looked like a NASA photograph of the moon, bleak and white, with random outcrops of higher ground. The hills funneled the wind towards us. We had to lean hard into it as we pushed into the gaps. We came to an area of scorched earth that was broken by craters and tank berms. It could have been an old launch site or the scene of a battle. The craters were full of water, snow, and ice, and reminded me of photographs of the Somme.

We had agreed that if anybody started to suffer from exposure, they were to say so at once and not play the hard man. At anybody's request we would come down as fast as we could or find some area out of the wind. If we had to stay up there for the following day, we'd die. We were still soaked and frozen.

In the early hours, Mark started going down. "We've got to get off the high ground because I'm suffering severely here."

We stopped and I tried to think. It wasn't easy to concentrate. Icy rain was now driving horizontally into my face. My mind was a blur of wet and cold, and it was hard to shut out the pain for long enough to think. Did we go forward west and try to get over the high ground and hopefully find some cover? Or did we go back to where we knew we would be out of the wind? I decided we must come off the high ground for Mark to have any chance of survival.

The only place we knew for sure was out of the wind was back at the area of the riverbed near the metaled road. We came down more or less parallel with the road but about 600 feet away from any possible headlights. We couldn't be arsed with navigating: there was not enough time—we needed to get back and recover, and we didn't want to be out in the open at first light. It was a really bad two hours as we made our way down. We tabbed as fast as we could, and just before first light we found a position, a depression in the ground, a compromise between concealment and keeping out of the elements. We would try again tomorrow.

It was a dip no more than three feet deep. We got in and cuddled up. It was heartbreaking. We had traveled a horrendous number of kilometers just to make less than 6 miles northwest. But it was better to lose a night's distance than to lose a man. We could see the metaled road about a mile to the north. The depression ran along the line of the wind, but we were out of the worst of it. We cuddled up and kept our eyes open.

At first light on the 26th we checked that we weren't sitting on top of an enemy position. There was only one piece of ground that overlooked us, and as we were huddled up against one edge of the depression, it cut the chances of anybody seeing us.

The weather had changed. There wasn't a cloud in the sky, and when the sun came out, it was quite comforting, psychologically, though it was still very cold. The wind was still biting and we were soaking wet.

I had a pair of small binoculars, an excellent bit of kit that I'd bought at a jeweler's in Hereford. I looked north at the road that went up to a pumping station. There was a steady stream of vehicles, one every few minutes: oil convoys, water bowsers, civilian Land Cruisers with the husband driving and the wife all in her black kit sitting in the back. The vehicles normally came in groups of three or four. There were also lots of military convoys, consisting of armored vehicles and trucks.

Looking south I saw pylons a mile or so away that ran southeast–northwest, parallel to the road. Three or four vehicles also headed southeast along the line of the pylons as if following them as a navigational aid. We were sandwiched between the two.

We cuddled each other for warmth, trying to keep our eyes open but frequently dozing off and waking up with a start. We had survived the night, and now I just hoped that we could hold out until last light again.

We sorted our feet out. This is done in such a way that at any one time only one person has one boot off. We were well used to harsh tabbing in tough conditions, but last night's efforts had taken the biscuit. We had tabbed for twelve hours, covering well over 30 miles, in the worst weather conditions any of us had seen for a very long time. Our feet had taken a fearsome pounding.

Dinger remembered that Chris had been wearing a pair of GoreTex go-fasters that had set him back a hundred quid. "If he's still running around, I bet his feet are Okay in them Gucci boots," he said, massaging his sore toes.

We got some cold scoff down us. We wouldn't cook because the ground was too open. We had enough sachets of food to last a few days yet; water was the more pressing concern.

We rested and plotted. The big plan now was to take the high ground tonight, get over it, then hit the low ground, which according to the map was flat gravel plain that would take us into the border. In theory we could get over the border that night if we really went for it. All it would take was another twelve hours all-out tabbing. On the positive side, we weren't carrying much weight because all we had was our belt kit and our weapons. And we had the incentive, which was to get out of Iraq and into Syria. We had no idea what the border was going to be like; we'd just have to find out when we got there.

We did our map studies again to make sure we all knew where we were, where we were going, and what we were likely to see on the way—which wasn't a lot because we were working with air maps. The alignment of pylons and so forth is approximate on these maps, but we did know that we'd have a major built-up area about three hours north of us to our right. That seemed to be the only fixed obstacle.

We were all recovering quite well now. We whispered bad jokes to each other as the hours passed, trying to keep up morale. Everything was beginning to feel all right again. We were still cold, but we had it under control. At least it wasn't snowing or raining any more. I was confident that we would be able to do it in one last big effort.

It was at 1530 that we heard it.

Ding ding, baa baaa.

We really don't need this, I said to myself.

I had a quick scan but couldn't see anything. We hugged the ground. There was no hollering or shouting as there was before in the last compromise, just the sound of chuntering and a solitary bell. It got closer and closer. I looked up, and there was the head goat with a bell around his neck. Wherever he went, it seemed, the other goats followed, because his entourage came and joined him one by one. Soon there were ten of them standing gawping over the edge of the dip. They looked at us and we looked at them. I lobbed a couple of small pebbles at the head boy to try and shoo him away.

His response was to come forward even more, and the rest of the goats followed. They put their heads down and started chewing, and there were five sighs of relief. They were a bit premature. A few seconds later the old goatherd turned up. He must have been 70 if he was a day. He had a big woolly dish-dash on, with a baggy old cardigan over the top. His head was swathed in a shamag. Over his shoulder was a tatty leather satchel. He had beads in his hands and muttered "Allah" as he pushed them through his fingers.

He looked at us and didn't miss a beat. No surprise, no fright, no nothing.

I smiled at him, as one does.

Totally nonchalantly, as if it was an everyday occurrence to find five foreigners huddling in a dip in the ground in the middle of nowhere, he squatted down beside us and started gobbing off. I didn't have a clue what he was saying.

We gave him the greeting, "As salaam alaikum."

He replied, "Wa alaikum as salaam."

We shook his hand. This was bizarre. He was so friendly. I wondered if he even knew there was a war on. Within seconds we were all best mates.

I wanted to keep the conversation going, but our Arabic wasn't quite up to it. Even as I spoke, I couldn't believe what I heard myself saying next.

"Wayn al souk?" I asked.

Here we were, in the middle of nowhere, and I was asking him the way to the market.

He didn't bat an eyelid, just pointed south.

"Good one," Dinger said. "At least next time we're here we'll know the way to Sainsbury's."

Bob spotted a bottle in the old boy's satchel. "Halib?" he asked.

The goatherd nodded that yes, it was milk, and passed the bottle around. Then he got out some smelly, minging dates from the bag and a bit of old bread, and we sat down and played the white man.

Mark stayed on his feet, having a casual look around. "He's on his own," he said, all smiles.

The goatherd pointed south again and waved his hand. "Jaysh," he said, "jaysh."

I raised a quizzical eyebrow at Bob.

"Army," he translated. "Militia."

Bob asked: "Wayn? Wayn jaysh?"

The old boy pointed back the way we had come.

We couldn't understand if he meant: there's loads of soldiers down there; or there's loads of soldiers down there, and they're looking for you; or are you with the soldiers from the jaysh back there? None of us could remember the Arabic for distance. We tried to do signs for far away and close.

All in all it was quite funny. There we were, sitting having a cosy kefuddle in the middle of the desert, in weather that was so bad we had nearly frozen to death.

We carried on with this for about half an hour, but we were getting to the point where a decision had to be made. Did we kill him? Did we tie him up and keep him until we moved out? Or did we just let him go and do his own thing? The only benefit to be gained by killing him was that nobody else would then know what was going on. But if the countryside was littered with the corpses of elderly members of the indigenous population and we got caught—which we had to assume was likely—then we could hardly expect red-carpet treatment at the hands of our captors. If we tied him up to keep him out of play, he would be dead by first light anyway because of the cold. There was little doubt his body would be discovered. It looked as though every square foot of this country was patrolled by goats and herders.

If we let him go, who could he tell, what harm could he do? He had no transport, and as far as Mark could make out he was on his own. It was about 1600 hours now, and it would soon be last light. Even if he raised the alarm, by the time there was any reaction it would be dark and we'd be legging it towards the border. We might as well let him go. It was the SAS we were in, not the SS.

We made up our minds that when he decided to go, we'd watch him, wait until he got out of sight, then we'd put in a deception plan south.

Five minutes later he was giving his goodbyes, and off he shuffled with the goats, not a care in the world. We let him go for about a half mile until he disappeared into some dead ground, then we moved off. We went south for a few miles, then turned west.

We came into a small depression and stopped to take stock. There were several factors to discuss. First was our water supply. We had enough food to last us another couple of days, but we were almost out of water. Second, we had to assume that the enemy knew where our last LUP was from the night before, so they knew our direction of travel. Third, we'd had another compromise—I was already thinking that we should have kept him with us until last light before letting him go. We were still in bad physical shape, and the weather would get very bad up on the high ground. We had nearly died the night before, and I didn't want to take another chance. We had lost a night's march and didn't want to lose another. All in all, the situation was not very good, and we probably hadn't done ourselves any favors by letting the old boy go. But what was done was done.

We went through the options that we had left to us as a patrol. One, to keep west, hoping to find water on the way: the chances were good on the high ground due to the snow and ice. Two, to head north to the river and then head west, but we were a large number and concealment would be a problem because the closer we got to the border, the more habitation there was going to be. Three, to hijack a vehicle and drive for the border that night. It was 1715 and starting to get dark. Given the amount of enemy activity and our physical condition, we decided to go for the vehicle hijack, any time after last light. The sooner the better.

We were going to have some major drama tonight, one way or another. Before moving down towards the road we carried out a weapon check. One man at a time, we pulled the working parts out, slapped on some oil, and made sure everything was ready.

I scanned the road through my binos. We wanted to have an area where we could come out and be more or less straight on top of them, so they couldn't see us coming. I spotted a small mound on a patch of high ground that would do the trick.

The plan was that Bob would play the cripple, leaning on my shoulder, and I'd wave down a good Samaritan. To make us look even more harmless we'd leave our weapons and webbing with the others. They would come out, do the hijack, and away we'd go. We'd been looking at nothing but lorries and Land Cruisers for six hours. Depending on the type of vehicle, we could go cross-country—heading south until we hit the pylons and then following them west—or take our chances on the road.

The road was half an hour's tab away. We got to the highish ground just on last light. Legs found a purpose-made ditch in the area to the right of the road, and we all piled in. We had a good view to the southeast because the road was long and straight for a number of miles and we were on high ground looking down. To the northwest, however, there was a small crest about 900 feet down the road. We wouldn't have much time in which to react if the vehicle came from that direction. Bob and I would try to stop it right opposite the ditch so the lads could just jump up and give them the good news.

We sat there with the binos out, looking to the east. Two trucks moved along the road and then went off in the general direction of our last LUP. Because of the low light I couldn't see whether people were getting out, but there appeared to be general activity on both sides of the road. They were obviously looking for something, and I took it to be us. After a while the vehicles came back onto the road and started to move towards us.

Fuck! Was this the follow-up from the night before? Either we were lucky that we had moved, or unlucky that we hadn't held the old boy and had let him go and bubble. But he had gone in totally the opposite direction to the one these troops were coming from. It didn't make sense.

We watched the lights coming nearer, and then we could hear the engine grinding up the hill. We got our heads down, just hoping that the elevation of the trucks would not give any blokes in the back the chance to see down into the dip.

We waited. As soon as we heard the trucks stop opposite us, we'd be up and firing. We had nothing to lose.

They drove straight past. Big grins all round.

Bob and I moved up onto the road and sat watching in both directions. After about twenty minutes, vehicle lights came over the small crest and drove towards us. Satisfied that it was not a troop truck, we stood up. The vehicle caught us in its headlights and slowed down to a halt about 10 feet down the road. I kept my head down to protect my eyes and to hide my face from the driver. Bob and I hobbled towards it.

"Oh shit," I muttered into Bob's ear.

Of all the vehicles in Iraq that could have come our way that night, the one we had chosen to hijack and speed us to our freedom was a 1950s New York yellow cab. I couldn't believe it. Chrome bumpers, whitewall tires, the lot.

We were committed. Bob was in my arms giving it the wounded soldier. The blokes were straight up from the ditch.

"What the fuck have we got here?" Mark shouted in disbelief. "This is the story of our lives, this is! Why can't it be a fucking Land Cruiser?"

The driver panicked and stalled the engine. He and the two passengers in the back sat staring open-mouthed at the muzzles of Minimis and 203s.

The cab was an old rust bucket with typical Arab decoration—tassels and gaudy religious emblems dangling from every available point. A couple of old blankets were thrown over as seat covers. The driver was beside himself with hysteria. The two men on the back seat were a picture, both dressed in neatly pressed green militia fatigues and berets, with little weekend bags on their laps. As the younger of the two explained that they were father and son, we had a quick rummage through their effects to see if there was anything worth having.

We had to move quickly because we couldn't guarantee that there wouldn't be other vehicles coming over. We tried to shepherd them to the side of the road, but the father was on his knees. He thought he was going to get slotted.

"Christian! Christian!" he screamed as he scrabbled in his pocket and pulled out a keyring with the Madonna dangling from it. "Muslim!" he said, pointing at the taxi driver and trying to drop him in it.

Now the driver sank to his knees, bowing and praying. We had to prod him with rifle barrels to get him to move.

"Cigarettes?" Dinger enquired.

The son obliged with a couple of packs.

The father got up and started kissing Mark, apparently thanking him for not killing him. The driver kept praying and hollering. It was a farce.

"What's his problem?" I said.

"This car is his occupation," the son said in good English. "He has to feed his children."

Bob came storming over and said, "I've fucking had enough of this." Sticking the end of his bayonet up one of the driver's nostrils, he walked him over to the ditch.

We left them all there. We had no time to tie them up; we just wanted to get going. We needed to put in some miles.

"I'll drive," I said. "I saw Robert De Niro in *Taxi Driver*."

It was an old column gearshift, and I couldn't work it. To the accompaniment of jeers and much slagging, I did a six-point turn to get us facing west, and off we lurched. Legs was in the front to do the compass bearings; the other three were crammed into the back. The way our luck had been going I fully expected the compass to pack in and the next sign we saw to be "Baghdad Welcomes Safe Drivers."

We had no shorts *(pistols)*; they were all longs, and it was going to be almost impossible to bear them if we were compromised. Nevertheless we were happy as

Larry. This was make-or-break time. We'd either make it tonight or we'd be dead.

It was unfortunate that we were committed to going on roads but we'd just have to make the most of it. We had just over half a tank of fuel, which was plenty for the distance we had to cover. We were going at quite a fuel-efficient pace anyway because we didn't want to look conspicuous or get involved in the slightest accident. We'd just drive as far as we could, dump the vehicle, and go over the border on foot.

We tried to make up game plans for what we would do if we got caught in a VCP *(Vehicle Checkpoint)*. We didn't know what we'd do. We couldn't try to barge through a checkpoint barrier on the road. That might happen in films but it's fantasy stuff; permanent VCPs are made to stop that sort of thing. The vehicle draws fire every time, and we'd end up as perforated as Tetley teabags. I'd probably just have to brake as fast as I could, and we'd pile out and do a runner.

Unfortunately, we were reading air charts, not an AA road atlas. The roads were very confusing. Legs directed me to take junctions that went generally west, and I constantly checked the mileometer to see how far we'd gone.

The first major location we came to was the pumping station area. There were military vehicles and blokes milling around, but no checkpoint. Nobody took a blind bit of notice of us as the cab chugged past.

We had to look as though we knew where we were going. If we looked lost it would arouse suspicion, and people might even come over and offer to help.

We came to yet another set of junctions. There was nothing going west and the best we could do was to turn north. It was a normal two-way road instead of the single-track ones we had been moving on. It was busy with convoys of oil tankers. We pulled out to overtake, but military vehicles were coming the other way. Nobody else was doing it so we had to play the game to blend in. At least we were moving, and the heater was going full blast. It was blissfully warm.

The convoy stopped.

We couldn't see why. Traffic lights? A broken-down vehicle? A VCP?

Legs jumped out and had a quick look but could see nothing in the darkness. We started inching forward. We stopped again and Legs got out.

"Military vehicles at the front of the convoy," he muttered. "One of them has crashed or broken down."

Squaddies were hanging around on foot and in Land Cruisers, and cars and trucks were maneuvering around them. We started to drive past, and I held my breath. One of the blokes directing the traffic spotted us and started to wave us on. Mark, Bob, and Dinger pretended to be asleep on the back seat; Legs and I grinned like idiots inside our shamags and waved back. As they disappeared in the rearview mirror, we laughed ourselves silly.

We hit a built-up area. Statues of Saddam stood outside public buildings and pictures of him were plastered on every available space. We drove past café bars with people milling around outside. We passed civilian cars, armored cars, and APCs. Nobody turned a hair.

Sometimes the roads and junctions funneled us in totally the wrong direction. We did a touch of north, then east, then south, then west, but ensured we were generally keeping west. Mark had the Magellan on his lap in the back and was making attempts to get a fix so that if the shit hit the fan, we would each have the information we needed to get us over the border.

Dinger was smoking like a condemned man enjoying his last request. I was considering whether to join him. I'd never had a cigarette in my life, and I thought: By tonight I could be dead, so why not try one while I have the chance?

"What's the score on these fags?" I asked Dinger.

"Do you drag all the smoke down, or what do you do?"

"You've had one before, have you?"

"No, mate—never smoked in my life."

"Well, you ain't going to start now, you wanker. You'll flake out and crash the car. Anyway, do you have any idea how many people die of lung cancer each year? I can't possibly expose you to that sort of risk. Tell you what, though—you can have a bit of passive."

He blew a lungful of smoke in my direction. I hated it, as he knew I would. When we were on the Counter Terrorist team together, Dinger used to drive one of the Range Rovers. He knew I loathed cigarettes so he'd be at it all the time, keeping the windows wound up. I'd go berserk and open them all, and he'd be laughing his cock off. Then the windows would go up and he'd do it again. He had a tape called something like "Elvis—The First Twenty Years." He knew I hated it so he'd put it on at every opportunity. We were driving along the M4 one time, and I'd wound down the window because he was smoking. Dinger put the cassette on and grinned. I pressed Eject, grabbed the cassette, and chucked it out of the window. War was declared.

I had my own tapes which I took with us on long drives, but the difference was that it was good music—Madness, usually, or The Jam. One night, many weeks later, I put one of them on and closed my eyes as I complained about his smoking and farting. Before I realized what he was doing, he ejected the tape and sent it the way of Elvis.

I waved away the cloud of Iraqi cigarette smoke.

"I hate it when you do that," I said. "Do you know, for every nine cigarettes you smoke, I'm smoking three of them?"

"You shouldn't honk," he said. "It's cheap. You're not paying, I am."

* * *

The road signs were in English as well as Arabic, and the blokes in the back had a map spread out on their laps, trying to work out where we were. Nothing actually registered. The built-up area stretched all along the Euphrates, and there were no place-names.

All things considered, we were doing rather well. The mood was quietly confident but apprehensive. They must have found the people at the hijack site by now and would be on the lookout for the yellow cab. Compared with what we'd been through in the last few days, it was quite a funny time, and at least it was warm. The car fugged up, and our clothes started to dry.

There were more convoys, consisting of about twenty vehicles at a time. We tagged on behind. There were civilian cars everywhere. There was no street lighting, which was rather good. We tried our best to hide our weapons, but there had to be a compromise between concealment and being able to get the weapons up to bear in the event of a drama.

We rounded a corner on the open road and got into another slowly moving jam. Vehicles had come up behind us, and we were stuck. This time Legs couldn't get out or he'd be seen by the people behind. We'd just have to bluff it out.

A soldier with his weapon slung over his shoulder was coming down the queue on the driver's side, the left-hand side as we were looking. People were talking to him from their cars and trucks. There were two more squaddies on the right-hand side. They were mooching along more slowly than their mate, weapons over their shoulders, smoking and chatting.

We knew we were going to get compromised. The moment the jundie stuck his head inside and had a look at us, he'd see we were white eyes. There was no more than a 1 percent chance of us getting away with it.

Big decision: What did we do now? Did we get out straightaway and go for it, or did we wait?

"Wait," I said. "You never know."

Very slowly we tried to get our weapons up to bear. If we had a drama, we would have to get out of the car. Every handle had a hand on it, ready for the off.

Mark quietly said, "See you in Syria."

We'd try to keep together as much as possible, but there was a strong chance we'd get split. It would be every man for himself.

We waited and waited, watching these people slowly working their way down the line. They didn't look particularly switched on: they were just killing time. Mark tried to get a fix on the Magellan to find out how far we were from the border, but he ran out of time.

"Let's just go south, and then west," I said.

That meant jumping out on the left-hand side of the road, firing off some rounds to get their heads down, and running like mad. As far as I was concerned, this was our most dangerous moment since leaving Saudi.

The blokes at the back had got their weapons up. Legs had his 203 across him with the barrel resting on my lap.

"If he comes up and puts his head through, as soon as he ID's us, I'll slot him," he said.

All I needed to do was keep my head out of the way. Legs would just bring the barrel up and do the business.

"We'll take the other two," Bob said.

I leaned forward to hide Legs's weapon.

The jundie got to the vehicle in front of us. He leaned down to speak to the driver, laughing and gobbing off, not a care in the world. He waved his hands as he spoke, probably moaning about the weather. With our Arabic we wouldn't have much to talk about when he got to our car. I could ask him the way to the market, but that was about it.

He said his goodbyes to the vehicle in front and sauntered towards our cab. I leant forward and fiddled with the dashboard controls.

He did one tap on the window. I put my head right back and in the same motion pushed my legs out and pressed my body against the seat. The squaddy's face was pressed expectantly against the window. Legs lifted the barrel of the 203. One round was all it took. There was an explosion of shattered glass, and the car doors flew open. We were out and running before the body had even hit the ground.

The two other squaddies started running for cover, but the Minimis took them down before they'd taken half a dozen paces. The civvies were straight down into the footwells of their vehicles and quite rightly so.

We ran at right angles to the column of cars until we came into line of sight of the VCP and were illuminated by the spill from headlights. They opened up, and we returned a massive amount of rounds. They must have been wondering what the hell was going on. All they would have heard was one round, then a couple of short bursts, followed by the sight of five dickheads in shamags legging it into the desert.

The first people over the road put covering fire down on the VCP until the others got across. Once there, we all moved. The whole contact lasted no more than thirty seconds.

We ran south for several more minutes. I stopped and shouted, "On me! On me! On me!"

Heads dashed past me, and I put my hand on them and counted one, two, three, four.

"Everybody's here. Okay, let's go!"

We ran and ran, making the best of the confusion we'd created behind us. To my right, I heard the sound of Dinger laughing as he ran, and before long we'd all joined in. It was sheer bloody relief. None of us could believe we'd got out of it.

We headed west. From Mark's last fix on the Magellan we estimated we had maybe 8 miles to the border. Eight miles in over nine hours of darkness—a piece of cake. All we had to do was take our time and make sure we got there tonight. There was no way a group this big could lie up the next day.

We came to an inhabited area. There were pylons, old cars, rubbish tips, dogs howling, the lights of a house. Sometimes we had to get over fences. There were vehicle headlights on roads. Behind us in the area of the VCP there was still an incredible amount of noise. People were still hollering, and there were sporadic bursts of small-arms fire. Tracked vehicles screamed up and down the road. It was just a race now, a matter of the hares keeping in front of the hounds.

The moon started to come out. A full moon, in the west. It couldn't have been worse. The only good thing was that we, too, could see more and move faster.

We landed up paralleling another road. We couldn't avoid it. We had a built-up area to our left and the road to our right. We didn't have time to fart-arse around. We were going for it big style. We had to hit the border before their initial confusion died down and reinforcements arrived.

Every time a car came from either direction we had to take cover. We were climbing fences, avoiding dogs, avoiding buildings. There were houses everywhere now, lights on, generators going. We picked our way through without incident.

Vehicles started to move along the road without their lights, presumably hoping to catch us out. There was still shooting way off in the distance. In our desert camouflage, against an almost European background of plantations and lush arable land, we glowed like ghosts in the moonlight.

We were spotted from the road. Three or four vehicles came screaming along, and blokes jumped out firing. We were down to a few mags each by now, and there was bound to be lots more drama before the night was over. All we could do was run. There was no cover. They kept on firing and we kept on running, the rounds zinging past us and into the built-up area.

We sprinted for 1,200 feet. We passed through little clusters of houses, expecting at any moment to be slotted by people coming out, but the local population kept themselves to themselves, bless their cotton socks. I was sweating buckets, panting for breath. Adrenaline gets hold of you and you clock Olympic times, but you can't sustain it. Then the firing sparks up again and you find a bit more.

We started to move over a crest. We looked down on the lights of Abu Kamal and Krabilah, the two built-up areas that straddled the border. It was just a sea of light, as if we'd run on to the filmset of *Close Encounters.* And there were the masts, the taller one on the Iraqi side. The boys in pursuit kept firing.

"Fucking hell," Bob shouted, "look at this, this is good news! We're nearly there!"

Like a prat, I said "Shut the fuck up!" as if he was a naughty schoolboy. I regretted it as soon as I said it. I was thinking exactly the same thing myself. Those lights, Abu Kamal, that tower—they weren't in Iraq, they were in Syria. I could almost taste the place. I was as sparked up as Bob was.

We ran over the crest. But the moment we came down from the higher ground we were skylined to some boys stationed below. They turned out to be antiaircraft battery. They greeted us with small-arms fire, and then opened up with triple A.

We ducked north to get across the road, committing ourselves to going through the built-up area that lay between us and the river. Vehicles were revving up near the AAA battery, and to top it all some jets screamed over. They must have been ours because the S60s diverted their fire. In the chaos we slipped away.

There was firing left, right, and behind us, but we

just kept going, heads down. Heavy tracer went up vertical, then horizontal where the Iraqis were just firing at anything that was moving. It was outrageous of them because there were civilian buildings all about. We were deafened by AAA gunfire. We had to scream our instructions and warnings to each other.

We got up to a road, made a quick check, and were straight over. We stopped on the other side and took a deep breath to sort ourselves out. Going into a built-up area is a totally different ballgame; it's something you always try to avoid, but we had no choice. There was a plantation to the right, but it was protected by a high fence.

There was about 900–1,200 feet meters of habitation to get through, a big amalgamation of houses with perimeter walls. Two-inch plastic irrigation pipes ran along the ground from the houses to the plantation. We moved down, trying to use the shadows as much as possible, walking with our weapons facing out, safety catches off, fingers on the trigger. We were moving north, and the moon was in the west. I was in front. If anybody appeared I'd give it to him with my 203, and Mark would come out two or three steps and give it a burst with his Minimi. Then we'd withdraw around the first corner and reorganize ourselves, or move forward, depending on what we had been firing at.

People were shouting their heads off in the houses, lights were going off, doors being slammed. We walked: we couldn't be arsed to run. If it was going to happen there was nothing we were going to achieve by running.

From the end of the buildings there were pathways and large pipes running down to the Euphrates about 450 feet away. Diesel pumps chugged. There was mud and shit all over the place which had iced over. We got into the corner of a plantation for a bit of cover and stopped.

The first priority was to fill up our water bottles.
Two of the lads went down to the river's edge while
Mark got a fix on the Magellan. "Exactly 10Ks from
the border," he whispered.

All the chaos was over the other side of the road.
Tracked vehicles were maneuvering and firing, and
the AAA guns were still pumping away. In the middle
and far distance there were bursts of small-arms fire.
They must have been shooting at dogs and anything
else that moved—including each other. We were almost past caring. There were six miles to go, and we
would have to fight for every mile.

We sat with our backs against the trees, watching
the two lads filling the bottles.

"Ten Ks," Dinger said. "Fucking hell, we could run
that in thirty minutes."

"Pity about the full moon," Bob said.

"And the desert camouflage," Dinger said. "And
the fact that every man and his dog is out looking for
us."

When Mark and Legs came back with our bottles we
considered the options. There seemed to be four. We
could cross the river; move east to avoid the border
and attempt to cross on the following night; keep going west; or split up and try any of the three as individuals.

The river was a fearsome sight. It must have been
about 1,600 feet across, and after the torrential rainfall
it was in full flood, flowing fast and furious. The water
would be freezing. We were weakened by the long tab
and lack of sleep, food, and water. We couldn't see any
boats, but if we found one it would become an option.
That left swimming, and I doubted we'd last more
than ten minutes. And who was to say there wouldn't
be troops waiting on the other side?

We ruled out moving east because there was too
much habitation for us to conceal ourselves in daylight. Moving west seemed the best option: they knew

we were in the area, so why not just keep going? But should we do it as a patrol or as individuals? Going it alone would certainly create five lots of chaos for our pursuers, but at the end of the day we were a patrol.

"We'll go west as a patrol and cross the border tonight," I said. "There must be some follow-up in the morning."

It was about 2200 and bitterly cold. Everybody was shivering. We had been sweating and the adrenaline had been flowing. In these conditions your body starts to seize up as soon as you take a rest.

Looking west along the Euphrates, we saw headlights crossing a bridge a mile or so down. There wasn't a lot we could do. We couldn't waste time boxing around it. It was too late for anything fancy like that. We would have to take our chances.

"Let's just take our time and patrol," Bob said. "We've got enough time."

The natural water courses ran into the Euphrates. Normally we would have kept to the high ground. It's easier to travel along, which saves time and makes less noise and movement. We were cross-graining them to stay parallel to the river, but not so close to the water that we left sign in the mud.

The ground was frozen mud and slush. Barbed wire fences cordoned off bits of land. We encountered small, rickety outbuildings, knolls of high ground, trees, old bottles that we tripped over, bits of frozen plastic that crushed noisily underfoot. It could have been wasteland in Northern Ireland.

The wind had stopped. The slightest sound traveled hundreds of feet. We were patrolling into the moon, our breath forming clouds in the freezing air. We took our time, stopping and starting every five minutes. Dogs barked. When we came to a building, somebody would go up and check; then we'd skirt around. When we came to a fence, the first man would test to see if it was going to make a noise; then he'd put his weapon on it to force the wire down and make it good and tense, and he'd keep it there while everybody stepped over.

We had to go round a three-sided hut. The owner was snoring by the embers of a fire but didn't stir as we tiptoed past. Forward of us was a road. If we looked to the left there was the road that ran into the frontier town of Krabilah. Lights were going on and off in buildings. Tracked vehicles trundled backwards and forwards, but far enough away not to worry us. There was still the odd shot or burst behind us. We'd been patrolling for about 2 miles. Four to go. It wasn't even midnight yet. Hours of darkness lay ahead. I was feeling quite good.

We followed the line of a hedgerow, then cut across left into a natural drainage ditch. It ran into a steep wadi, which in turn seemed to run into the Euphrates. The wadi was about 150–160 feet wide and 80 feet deep. Both sides were more or less sheer. The bottom was virtually flat, with a trickle of a stream. We couldn't box around it because we didn't know how far it went. It might have headed south, and there were roads to our south that we wanted to avoid. I then noticed that it went round to the west, which would be great. We could use the shadow that it created for as long as we could.

As I got to the edge of the wadi, I crawled over the lip to have a look inside. Mark was behind me. I started to move down, and as I did so, the horizon on the opposite side of the wadi was a lot easier to see. The first thing I saw on the skyline was the silhouette of a sentry.

He was walking up and down, stamping his feet and blowing into his cupped hands to keep warm. I looked around him, and I couldn't believe what I saw. It was a vast location—tents, buildings, vehicles, radio antennas. As my eyes focused, I started to notice people coming out of the tents. I heard bits of talking.

They had their backs to the moon, looking in our direction. I didn't move.

It was fifteen minutes before I could make my way back to Mark. I knew he would have seen the same as I had because he hadn't come to join me. He, too, was lying as still as a stone. This was scary stuff. We were terribly exposed.

I got back level with Mark. "Have you seen it?"

"Yes, this is outrageous," he said. "We need to get back and sort our shit out."

"No drama."

We'd crawl back to the others to regroup. From there we'd make our way back to the hedgerow, sort ourselves out, and find another route round. We had gone 100 feet to get out of the immediate area when we got up to a semicrouch position in the ditch.

Jittery shouting and firing happened at the same time. All hell was let loose. Mark was down with the Minimi and stitched all along the hedgerows, wherever he saw muzzle flashes. The location on the other side of the wadi opened up. I was severely unimpressed because they were on higher ground.

I used the last of my 203 bombs; then it was time to run away gracefully. I wanted to get back to the riverbank because it would give us cover. There was shouting and firing all over the place as we legged it. The rest of the patrol was having contacts. There was major chaos going on all around the hedgerow. I assumed that Bob and the others were in a group of three.

The Iraqis on the other side of the wadi were firing in all directions. I heard 203 bombs, which had to be Legs because Dinger and Bob both had Minimis. It was very noisy. Everybody was involved in his own little world. I realized with a sinking heart that there was no chance of us getting together again. We were split now into another two groups, with only miles to go. What a pisser. I really thought we'd cracked it.

* * *

Mark and I were on the bank of the Euphrates, trying to make sense of what was happening. The waterline was 30–50 feet below the line of the ploughed land that we'd just come over, and in between lay a system of small plateaus. We were on the first one, in amongst the bushes.

We could hear the follow-ups from the opposite bank, working towards us with torches and shouting to one another. There was intermittent, nervous enemy fire from our side of the wadi, then contacts to our left and half left involving 203s and Minimis. Tracer was going horizontal and then vertical as it hit rocks and buildings.

We stuck our heads up like a couple of ferrets and looked around. It was hard to know what to do and where to go—whether to cross the river or go through the positions and risk getting killed or captured.

"No way the river," I whispered into Mark's ear.

I wasn't brave enough for that, so we decided to go through the positions. But when? There was so much confusion, it was difficult to say what was a good opportunity and what wasn't.

"Fuck it," Mark whispered, "we're in the shit, so what does it matter?"

If we got out, all well and good, but if we didn't, so what—I just hoped that it would be nice and quick. I was feeling quite dispassionate about the whole business.

We checked our stocks of ammunition. I had about one and a half mags; Mark had a hundred link for the Minimi. It was such a ridiculous situation we were in, with contacts and shouting and tracer all over the place, and there's us sitting in a bush trying to organize ourselves and look over the other side of the bank at the same time. My hands were freezing cold. The grass and leaves were brittle with frost. The river was shrouded with mist.

I looked at Mark and nearly laughed. He was wearing a long woolen scarf known as a cap comforter that can be folded into itself to make what looks like a Second World War commando hat. Mark had failed to tuck the top of his hat in, and he looked like Noddy. He was peering through the bushes with a serious expression on his face and he looked so comical.

"If we don't go now, mate, we never will," he said.

I nodded.

Still looking out as he spoke, he dug in his pocket for a boiled sweet and popped it into his mouth.

"It's my last one. I might as well have it now: it might be my last one ever."

All of mine had gone. I looked at him longingly.

"You ain't got none left, have you?" he smirked.

"No, fuck all left."

I looked at him like a puppy dog.

He took the sweet out of his mouth, bit it, and gave me half.

We lay there savoring the moment and psyching ourselves up to go.

In the end the decision was made for us. Four Iraqis came along the bank, and they appeared to be well trained and switched on. There was no shouting, and they were well spread out. They looked nervous though, as you do when you know there are people about who might fire weapons at you. If we moved they would see us. I signaled to Mark: if they don't see us, let them go on; if they do, they get it. But they got so close there was no way they were going to avoid us, so we dropped them.

Now we had to go, whether it was the right time or not. We legged it up the ploughed field, parallel to the river. Further up to the right we started to come over a gentle rise where the ground went down to the water. There was movement, and we went straight down.

The furrows were running north–south so we were in the dips. We started to belly crawl and worked our way the whole length up to the hedgerow. Orders were being barked, and squaddies were running around confused. They were no more than 80 feet away. We crawled for twenty minutes. The ground was icy cold, and it hurt to put your hands on the mud and pull yourself along. My clothing was drenched. Tiny puddles of water had frozen, and as we moved the ice cracked. The sound was magnified a thousand times in my head. Even the noise of my breathing sounded frighteningly loud. I just wanted to get through this shit and get to the treeline, and then it would be a totally different, brave new world.

There was still firing, shouting, and all sorts of confusion going on. How we were ever going to get out of it I had no idea. In situations like this you just have to keep on going and see what happens. It was so tempting just to get up and make a bolt for it.

The Iraqis were still down at the bottom of the field. Maybe—I hoped—they thought we'd gone further down the riverbed, heading east to get to the other lot. I didn't actually care what they were thinking, as long as they did it a good distance away. The one and only thought I had in my mind was that we needed to get over the border that night.

We got to the hedgerow. It was a purpose-built field division, small trees and bushes growing out of a two-foot mound of earth. Our initial plan was to cross the hedgerow that was running east–west, purely so that we didn't have to cross the south–north one as well. We heard noises to our right. Mark had a look. It was more enemy, behind the hedgerow. And beyond that, further south, there was yelling and shouting and a profusion of lights. Mark signaled me to stay this side of the hedgerow and move left.

We crawled along the line to get to the hedge that ran north–south. We tried to find a place where we could get through without making any noise. I started pushing through. My head emerged the other side, and I immediately got challenged.

As the boy shouted, Mark gave him the good news. His body disintegrated in front of my eyes. Mark gave it a severe stitching all the way along—from where we were, all the way along west. I scrambled out of the hedge line and carried on the fire while Mark came through. We moved east, stopped, put down a quick burst, ran, gave it another quick burst, and then just ran and ran.

There was high ground to our front. Below it were buildings with lights on and movement. We didn't want to cross the open ground, so we had no option but to use the obvious cover of a ditch. I had no idea what we'd got ahead of us.

The fence line was above us. Because the fields were irrigated, the roads and buildings were on built-up land to keep them above the waterline. We got into a little dip below the fence and moved south.

We started to slow down now that we seemed to be out of immediate trouble. We took the 6-foot chainlink fence to be the perimeter of a military installation. We got halfway along and stopped. We'd seen a road to our front, running east–west. Vehicles were driving up and down, fully lit. Other vehicles drove with their lights off.

There had to be a definite junction to the east of us. We could see vehicle lights heading up there and changing direction. There was a mass of activity. Every man and his dog seemed to be on alert. They must have thought the Israelis had turned up or the Syrians were invading. All I hoped was that in all this confusion a little gang of two and a little gang of three could work their way through.

We found ourselves opposite a large mosque on the other side of the fence. We stopped and observed the road. Closer now, we could see vehicles parked up along the side of the road as headlights swept past. Trucks, Land Cruisers, APCs. Where there are vehicles there are people. We could hear talking and the mush of radios. I couldn't tell how far the column extended, east or west. From the initial contact on the edge of the wadi to here had taken three hours. With only two and a half hours of darkness left I was flapping. We'd have to take a chance. There was no time left for boxing around.

We were lying in the dip, wet and freezing, trying to work out where we were going to go through the fence. Both of us were sweating and shivering. We were almost out of ammunition. We waited for lights to pass so we could get an idea of where all the vehicles were sited. We would cross in the biggest gap.

Two of the trucks were about 50 feet apart. If we could get through unchallenged, the border beckoned. We'd just have to brass it out. We started across the field, taking our time. Each time a vehicle passed we hit the ground. It was important to get as near to the parked convoy as we could before we made our dash. All we planned to do was run through them. Neither of us had a clue what was on the other side, but we didn't care—we'd sort that out when we came to it.

The vehicles were 3 feet above us on the raised road. At the top of the bank, we discovered, was a three-strand barbed wire fence, 3 feet high. We'd have to get over it before we could even start to dodge between the vehicles.

The gap was between two canvas-topped trucks. In one of them a radio hissed loudly. We were going to have to climb the mound, and would be committed from the moment we started moving.

I clambered over the fence and got down to give Mark cover. He cleared the fence, but the wire twanged as he removed his weight. A jundie started jabbering and stuck his head out of a truck window. He got it from me straightaway. I ran to the back. The tailboard was up, but there were two slots at floor level which would have served as footholds when it was down. I put my muzzle through and gave it a good burst. Mark went straight across the road and was down on the other side of the mound, firing along what to him was the right-hand side of the convoy. I didn't know if the other vehicle had characters aboard, so I threw in a grenade and legged it over the road to Mark. We fired until we ran out of ammunition, which was all of five seconds. We dropped our weapons and legged it. They were no use now. The Iraqis used 7.62 short, and we needed 5.56. Now the only weapon we had left was darkness.

We must have put down enough rounds to get them flapping because they didn't follow immediately. We ran for 900 feet. The sounds of screaming filled the night.

We stopped near a water tower. It wasn't that long now before first light. Looking straight ahead, we could see the road that we'd just crossed to our right-hand side, the mast on the Iraqi side, and another road that we'd have to cross to go west.

We looked at one another and I said, "Right, let's do it."

We scuttled on across the fields and stopped short of what we could see was a large depression. On the other side was a built-up area, unlit. The right-hand corner, the end of it, was more or less at a road junction.

The depression must have been used as a rubbish dump. Small fires smoldered in the darkness. We went down into the dip and stumbled over old tins and tires. The stench of rotting garbage was overpowering. We started to come back up the other side. About halfway up the rise we were opened up on by two AKs, from really close range. We hit the ground and I went right.

I ran for what I thought was enough distance to get me level with the junction, then turned left. I wanted to get over the road and carry on running. I ran around the side of a mound and thought I could get up the other side, but what I'd come into was a large water storage area. There were two big pools, oily and greasy. I was flapping, running around like the cornered rat that I was, trying to find a way out. The sides were sheer. I couldn't get up. I had to retrace my steps. I wasn't even looking now, I was just running. If they were behind me, knowing about it wasn't going to change anything.

I got out of the immediate area and stopped at the road. My chest heaved as I fought for breath. Fuck it, I thought, just go for it.

I got past the buildings. I was elated. I felt I'd cracked it. Just the border now. I didn't worry about Mark. I'd seen him go down. I didn't hear anything after that, and he didn't come with me. He was dead. At least it had been quick.

8

I felt it was all behind me. All I had in front of me was a quick tab to the border.

The mud built up around my boots. It was heavy going. My legs were burning. Physically I was wrecked. I stopped to get some scoff down my neck. It felt good. I drank some water and forced myself to calm down and take stock. Navigation was easy enough. The mast was right ahead of me. As I walked I tried to work out what had happened during the contacts. But there had been total confusion, and I couldn't make sense of it. There was still firing behind me.

It was the early hours of the 27th, and I had about 2–3 miles to go. In normal circumstances I could run that in less than twenty minutes with my equipment on. But there was no point just running blindly towards Syria with only an hour of darkness left. I didn't know what the border crossing was like physically—if it was a fence or a high berm, if it was heavily defended or not defended at all. And even if I did get into Syria during daylight hours, what sort of reception could I expect?

I was about a half mile south of the Euphrates and a half mile north of a town. The area was irrigated by diesel pumps at intervals along the river. The field crops were about eighteen inches high. I had kept off the tracks and moved through the center of the fields, putting my feet down on the root mounds of the plants. Even so, I knew I couldn't avoid leaving sign. My hope was that no one would be out in the fields the next day, tending what, apart from the frost, seemed to be a healthy young crop.

I was feeling very positive. I'd survived the contacts, and that was all that seemed to matter. The last contact was like a big barrier that I'd got over and got away from, and now I was a free spirit.

In many ways this was the most dangerous time. Probably since caveman times, people have been cautious when they plan an operation, aggressive when they execute it, and most open to error when it's finished and they're on the home straight. That's when people start to get slack and the major dramas occur. It's not over yet, I kept saying to myself—it's so near but also it's so bloody far.

Adrenaline during the contacts and the constant roller coaster of the night's events had blocked the pain signals from reaching my brain. A soldier of the Black Watch during the First World War was shot four times and still kept charging forwards. When he finally took the position and had time to assess his injuries, he keeled over. You don't realize what's been happening to your body because your mind blanks it out. Now I'd calmed down a bit and the future was looking rosy, I was starting to realize how physically impaired I was. All the aches and pains of the last couple of days suddenly started coming through. I was covered with cuts and bruises. In contacts you're jumping and leaping around, and your body's taking knocks all the time. You don't notice them at the time. There were deep pressure-cuts on my hands, knees, and elbows, and painful bruising on the sides of both my legs. I had scratches and scrapes from thorn bushes and gashes from wire; the sting of them added to the ambient pain level. We'd tabbed close to 125 miles over hard bedrock and shale, and the leather was starting to fall off my boots. My feet were in a bad way. They were soaking wet and felt like blocks of ice. I just about had some sensation left in my toes. My clothing was ripped and torn, and my hands were covered with thick grease and grime, as if I'd been working on an engine for the last couple of days. My body was covered in mud, and as I walked along it was slowly drying out. Trickles of sweat fell down my back, and big clammy patches formed between my legs and under my armpits. My extremities were frozen, but at least my trunk was warm because I was moving.

It was still very cold. The mud had a film of ice over the top. The first foot or so of any large pool of water was frozen solid. It was a beautiful crystal night. The stars were glittering, and had it been anywhere else in the world, you'd have gone out and marveled at it. But the clearness of the sky meant there were no clouds to obscure the full moon in the west, and no wind to disperse the noise.

Scattered here and there were little outhouses, some with a light on, some with a generator going. I could see lights from the town to the south. Dogs barked; I skirted around buildings, hoping that nobody would pay attention to them.

Car lights in the distance made me flap. Were they part of the follow-up? Were they going to start searching the fields now? It wasn't a very good place for me to be. There was only half an hour of darkness left— not enough for me to get around the town or even go straight through it and get into the cuds on the other side.

As the lights gradually faded I made a quick appreciation. Like the old Clash song, should I go or should I stay? Did I hide up or did I go for the border and try to get over before first light? What were the chances of the Iraqis following up during the day? There certainly hadn't been any follow-up so far. Perhaps they thought I'd already crossed the border and was away.

The houses looked so inviting. Should I get into one of these small buildings where you've just got the old boy and his fire and stay there with him for the day? I'd have shelter, and the possibility of food and water —and in theory a better chance of being concealed. But you never use isolated or obvious cover. It's a natural draw point for any hunter force. In films you see all these characters living in hay barns. It's pure and utter fantasy. If you're there they'll find you. None of this hiding under a straw bale business, just narrowly being missed by a probing bayonet.

My best chance was in the open but concealed, preferably from the ground and air. I had to assume the worst scenario, which was that the Iraqis would have spotter aircraft up. I found a drainage ditch that was about 3 feet wide and 18 inches deep, with water coursing through under gravity. I got in and moved along, pleased not to be leaving sign in the muddy water. The water was moving from east to west, my direction of travel.

I looked at my watch, checking off the minutes till daybreak. I stopped every few feet and looked around, listening, planning the next movement, planning my actions on: What if the enemy moved in from the front? What if I had a contact from the left? I remembered the ground I'd been over and planned the best escape route in each contingency.

After 900 or 1,200 feet I saw a dark shape ahead. It was either a small dam or a natural culvert. When I got closer, I saw that a track running north–south from the Euphrates to the built-up area had a steel plate over it as a makeshift bridge, the sort of thing you see at roadworks in the UK. It was just coming up to first light. I had to make a decision. I could go further along the ditch and hope to find something better, or I could just stay put. On balance, I thought I was better off where I was.

The only problem with the culvert was that when you look at things in the dark and under pressure, they can look pretty good, but in the daytime the picture can be totally different. You have to be so careful choosing an LUP at night in an area that is virgin to you. When I was in the battalion at Tidworth we had mirror image barracks, the Green Jackets in one, the Light Infantry in the other. One night, I came back from town with a bag of chips and curry sauce, pissed as a fart. I stumbled into my room, dropped my trousers, and got into bed. Sitting up eating my chips with my head spinning and the bedside light on, I couldn't understand it when a bloke called out, "Turn the light off, Geordie." I looked up and saw a Debbie Harry poster, and I didn't like Debbie Harry. "Who the fuck's that over there then?" the voice demanded, but by then I had realized what I'd done. I abandoned my chips, grabbed my trousers, and ran for my life from the Light Infantry barracks.

I belly crawled under the steel span. The culvert wasn't as deep as the drainage ditch itself because it hadn't been cleared, but the prospect of resting my limbs far outweighed the discomfort of lying in the cold mud.

I retrieved the map cover from the pocket on my leg and tried to use it as some sort of insulation, but to no avail. My mind strayed to food. I might be needing it later on, but then again I might be captured. It was better to get it down my neck than to have it taken away. I pulled my last sachet—steak and onions—from the pouch on my belt kit and ripped it open. I ate with my fingers and stuck my tongue into the recesses for the last of the cold, slimy gunge. For pudding, I put my lips to the level of the water and sucked up a few mouthfuls. I got the map on top of me, ready to look at when there was enough light, and just lay back and waited.

As dark turned to light, I heard trucks in the distance and isolated bits of hollering and shouting, but nothing near enough to cause alarm. It was almost peaceful. I started to shiver, and the trembling became uncontrollable. My teeth chattered. I took a deep breath and tensed all my muscles as tightly as I could. I stayed like that for two hours.

I had my fighting knife in my hand and my watch out on my chest so I didn't have to keep moving my hands. I studied the map to make an appreciation of where I was. If I had to leg it the last thing I wanted to do was map-read. I wanted to know that, as I came out, to my left would be the built-up area, to my right would be the Euphrates, and that I had however many miles to run to the border. I wanted to store as much information in my head as I could.

I went through different scenarios, fantasies really. What if I was already in Syria? I knew I hadn't crossed the border: the two countries were at war; there had to be some physical barrier between them, but that didn't stop me daydreaming.

It must have been about eight o'clock when I heard the scuffle of goats' hooves coming from the direction of the town. I tensed. We hadn't had the world's best luck with goats on this trip.

I didn't hear the goatherder until he was right on top of the metal plate. I took a deep breath, a really deep breath. Straining my neck, I saw the ends of two sandals and a set of big, splayed toes. One foot came down into the mud. I gripped my fighting knife. I wouldn't do anything until he put his head down and actually saw me, and even then I didn't know what I was going to do. Did I just bring the left hand up and stick him one in the face? If he started running, what then? I could tell by the big choggie, splayed feet that he wasn't military, so hopefully he wasn't armed.

He stooped to pick up a small cardboard box I hadn't noticed in the ditch. It was a discarded ammunition box for 7.62 short, the round that AKs fire. He disappeared from view. The box landed back in the water. He must have looked at it and decided it was of no use.

A couple of goats came and stood on the bank. I didn't want to breathe, I didn't want to blink. The goatherder made his way back on to the bridge and stood with his toes dangling over the edge of the steel. He coughed up a massive grolly out of the back of his neck and flobbed it into the water. It drifted down to me like a slimy green jellyfish and lodged itself in my hair. I was in such a mess anyway that it shouldn't have bothered me, but it did.

I was sure that one of the goats would get into the water and make the old boy come and rescue him, but nothing happened. The goats all trundled over, and the goatherder followed. I started to scrape the slime out of my hair.

I lay listening to noises. Looking out from my tomb, I could see that it was a crisp winter's morning with not a cloud in the sky. It was a view of the countryside, not at all a desert scene. All it needed was cows, and it could have been the fields around Hereford. There's a small footpath which follows the banks of the River Wye, and from a certain point you can look over to the other side at a dairy which has its own cows. Kate used to love being taken there. It looked nothing at all like the scene I was looking at now, but I imagined cows mooing and the sound of Kate giggling. The sun was out, but I was out of range of its warming rays. I felt like a lizard stuck where I was. It would be so nice to be out in the open, warming the bones.

I could hear vehicles in the distance—the springy, old metally, jangly sounds of them trundling along. Kids and older people hollered and shrieked. I was desperate to know what was going on out there. Were they looking for me? Or were they just going about their normal business? In one way it concerned me greatly that people were in the vicinity, but in another it just sounded nice and comforting to hear human voices because it meant I wasn't alone. I was cold and exhausted. It was good to have some kind of reassurance that I was on earth, not Zanussi.

Sometimes a vehicle would come nearer and nearer and nearer, and my heart would start skipping beats.

Are they going to stop?

Don't be so stupid—no drama, they're going to the river.

They must be looking.

But not intensively—it's too near the border.

The noises were scary. By the time they got to me my mind had magnified them a hundred times. I flapped about the kids being curious. Kids must play. Did they play in the water? Did they play with the goats? What did they do? A kid is shorter than an adult and would get a better perspective when looking at the culvert. Instead of seeing daylight a kid was going to see my head or my feet, and he wouldn't need to have passed his eleven plus to know that he should raise the alarm.

I wanted so much not to get caught. Not now. Not after so much.

I kept looking at the watch lying on my chest. I looked once and it was one o'clock. Half an hour later I checked again. It was five past. Time was dragging, but I started to feel better about my predicament. There had been vehicles, goats, and goatherds, and I'd got away with it. I was still trying to memorize the map, going through the routes in my mind. I was gagging for last light.

There was a deafening rattle of steel as a group of vehicles thundered across. This time they stopped.

You're compromised: what did they stop for? You're in the shit.

No worries, they're picking somebody up. Just keep remarkably still, control your breathing.

I tried hard to think positively, as if that would stop them coming and finding me.

7.62 is a big-caliber round. The sound of over a hundred of them reverberating on the steel plate just a fraction of an inch from my nose was the worst thing I'd ever heard. I curled up and silently screamed.

Fuck! fuck! fuck! fuck! fuck!

Men bellowed at the tops of their voices. They fired all around the drainage ditch. The mud erupted. I felt the tremors. I curled up even tighter and hoped nothing was going to hit. The cracks, thuds, and shouts seemed never-ending.

The firing stopped but the shouting continued. What were they going to do now—just stick a weapon underneath and blow me away, or what?

I was shitting myself. I didn't know what they wanted me to do. I couldn't understand what they were screaming. Did they want to capture me? Did they want to kill me? Were they going to throw a grenade in? Fuck it, I thought, if they want me out, they'll have to drag me out.

I was going to die in a drainage ditch two and a half miles from the border, of that I had no doubt. My nose was more or less touching the underside of the steel plate. I was stretching my neck, but I couldn't see much because of the perspective.

The muzzle of a rifle came down. Then a bloke's face. When he saw me there was a look of total and utter surprise. He did a little jump back and shouted.

The next thing I saw was a mass of boots jumping down all around the drainage ditch itself. Three blokes at either end, yelling their heads off. They motioned for me to get out.

No fucking way!

They wanted to see my hands. I was lying on my back with my feet and hands out straight. Two blokes grabbed a boot each and heaved.

I came out on my back and had my first view of Syria in the daylight. It looked the most beautiful country on earth. I could see the mast on the higher ground, tantalizingly close. I could almost have reached out and touched it. I felt burgled or mugged— the feeling of disbelief that this was happening to me at all, mixed with outrage that I was being robbed of something that was rightfully mine.

Why me? All my life I've been lucky. I've been in dramas that I've had no control of, and I've been in problems that I've created myself. But I've always been lucky enough to get out of them reasonably unscathed.

They gave a couple of kicks and motioned for me to get to my feet. I stood up straight, my hands up in the air, staring straight ahead. Nice blue sky it was, absolutely splendid. I turned my back on Syria and looked at the ploughed fields and green vegetation, and all the huts and tracks that I'd avoided during the night.

So much effort wasted. So few hours of daylight left.

They held their weapons nervously and jumped up and down, making weird warbling noises like Red Indians. They were as frightened as I was. They fired into the air on automatic, and I thought, Here we go, all I need is for one of these rounds to come down and slot me through the head.

Two Land Cruisers were parked to the right-hand side of the bridge. Three characters were pacing around on the steel plate; eight or nine others were charging around on the banks of the ditch.

The countryside looked even more European than I had imagined. I was pissed off with myself. To be picked up in featureless desert would have been bad luck, but to be captured like this on ground that could have been in northwest Europe was bloody bad management.

The squaddies were all over the place, gibbering and gabbering, still very wary. Now that they'd got me they were not too sure what to do with me. It seemed there were more chiefs than Indians; everybody wanted to give orders. There must have been some sort of reward coming their way. I stood motionless in the mud, a pathetic mess. I stared straight ahead, no smile of appeasement, no grim scowl of defiance, no hint of eye contact. My training had taken over. Already I was trying to be the gray man.

They started firing into the ground. They were in an unbelievable frenzy. It seemed wrong to me that I was going to get shot by accident rather than doing a job or in a contact with me firing back. Nothing death or glory about it: I just didn't want to die because some trigger-happy dickhead was going hyper. Or worse, get severely injured. But there's no way you show them that you're scared in a situation like that; you just stand there, take a deep breath, close your eyes, and let them get on with it.

The firing stopped after about fifteen seconds. One of the soldiers jumped down into the culvert and started rooting around for my kit. He came back with the map, which was unmarked, the belt kit, and the fighting knife. He brandished the blade in front of me and did the old throat-cutting motion. I thought, it's going to be one of them days.

One of the other soldiers was poking me with his weapon and gesturing for me to get down on my knees.

Is he going to kill me? Is it time to die now?

I couldn't think of any other reason why I'd get put

on my knees. If they were taking me away, they'd drag me away or motion me somewhere.

So do I get down and wait for the possibility of getting shot, or do I make a run for it?

I wouldn't get far. I'd be killed within five steps. I knelt down in the water and thick mud.

The bottom of the drainage ditch was about 18 inches lower than the level of the fields, so when I finally got down I was more or less at face level with the steel plate. I looked up.

The penalty kick that one of the lads aimed at my jaw knocked me backwards into the ditch. Water sluiced into my ears, and white blotches of intense light filled my vision. I opened my eyes. Through the starbursts, I saw the world closing in with people and a clear blue sky that was about to rain rifle butts.

Even when you're winded your body's self-protection mechanism makes it spin itself over. Face down in the mud, I curled up into a tight ball. There's an old saying in parachuting, if it's a bit windy and you know the landing is going to be fearsome: "Feet and knees together and accept the landing." I had to accept this one; there was nothing I could do to stop it. Compared with being shot, it was almost a pleasant surprise.

They were like little animals, putting in a bit of a kick, moving off, coming in again, starting to gain confidence. They grabbed hold of my hair and wrenched my head back. As they kicked and thumped my body in a frenzy of pent-up frustration, they screamed: "Tel Aviv! Tel Aviv!"

They jumped from the bridge onto my back and legs. You feel each impact but not its pain. Your system's pumping too much adrenaline. You tighten your stomach, clench your teeth, tense your body as much as you can, and hope and hope they're not going to start to give you a really serious filling-in.

"Tel Aviv! Tel Aviv!" they shouted over and over. It

dawned on me what they were getting at. This was not a good day out.

It can't have lasted for more than five minutes, but it was quite long enough. When they finally backed off, I turned over and looked up at them. I wanted them to see how confused and pitiful I looked, a poor fellow soldier who was terrified and meek and deserving of their pity.

It didn't work.

I knew it was going to start all over again, and I rolled into a ball, trying this time to get my arms underneath me. My mind was numb, but I was more or less conscious throughout. The thudding instep kicks to my head and sides were punctuated by telling, well-aimed toecap blows to the kidneys, mouth, and ears.

They stopped after a few minutes and hauled me to my feet. I could hardly stand. I was in a semicrouched position, trying to keep my head down, staggering about, holding my stomach, coughing up blood.

I swayed and lost my footing. Two boys came either side. They did a rough search—no more than a perfunctory frisk to make sure I didn't have a gun—then they knocked me to my knees and pushed my face down into the mud. They pulled my hands behind my back and tied them. I tried to get my head up so I could breathe, but they were standing on it to force me down. I gasped and inhaled mud and blood. I thought I was going to suffocate. All I could hear was hollering and shouting, and then the noise of more firing in the air. Every sound was magnified. My head raged with pain.

The next thing I knew, I was being frog-marched towards the vehicles. My legs wouldn't carry me, so they had to support me under the armpits. They were moving fast, and I was still coughing and snotting and trying to get some air into my lungs. My face was swelling up. My lips were split in several places. I just let them get on with it. I was a rag doll, a bag of shit.

* * *

I was thrown into the rear of a Land Cruiser, in the footwell behind the front seats. As soon as they put me down, I tried to get myself nice and comfy and sort myself out. It felt strangely secure to be in such an enclosed space. At least they'd stopped kicking me and I could breathe again. I felt the warm heater and smelled cigarette smoke and cheap aftershave.

I got a rifle butt to the head. It hurt severely and took me down. I wasn't going to come up from that one even if I'd wanted to. I was a bag of bollocks. There was massive pain in the back of my head, and everything was spinning. I took short, sharp breaths and told myself that it could be worse. For a second or two it looked as though I was going to be right. I wasn't being filled in any more, which I thought was rather nice. Then two lads jumped in the back and thumped their boots hard up and down all over my body. As the vehicle lurched across the field, they kept up the tempo.

I couldn't see where we were going because I had to keep my head down to protect myself from the flurry of boots. It would have been a pointless exercise anyway. As far as I was concerned, they were just going to shoot me. I had no control over it; I just wanted to get it over and done with. I'd had the initial shock of being captured, then the demoralizing glimpse of the Syrian border. It suddenly hit home. I was right on top of Syria and I'd got caught. It was as if I'd run a marathon in Olympic time and been disqualified a stride from the tape. I wondered again when they'd shoot me.

The vehicle swerved and lurched to avoid the crowds. When they slowed down, I could hear people hollering and shouting. Everybody was in a frenzy; they were really happy boys.

The jundies fired their weapons from inside the Land Cruiser. The AK47 is a large-caliber weapon, and when you fire it in a confined space, you can feel the increase in air pressure. It was deafening, but the familiar tang of cordite was oddly comforting. I started to taste the blood and mud in my mouth. My nose was blocked with clots.

I was bouncing up and down, the vehicle moving fast over the ploughed ground. The suspension groaned and screeched. All I wanted to do was snuggle up in a corner somewhere and be out of the way. One half of my brain was telling me to close my eyes and take a deep breath, and maybe it would all go away. But at the back of your mind is that tiny little bit of survival instinct: let's wait and see, maybe they won't, there's always a chance . . .

The crowds were making the fearsome Red Indian warbling noise. They were jubilant that they'd caught somebody, but I couldn't tell if the warble was a victory salute or a sign of even worse things to come. As we lurched over the field, I tried to concentrate on identifying the troops from their uniforms. They wore British-pattern DPM *(disrupted-pattern material)*, with chest webbing that held five magazines, and high-laced boots. They had Para wings, too, and red lanyards, which marked them out as élite commandos. It was only much later that I learned that the lanyards were to commemorate a victory from the Second World War, when they fought under Montgomery's command, of which they seemed quite proud.

We hit a metaled road and the bouncing stopped. I wasn't much concerned with where we were going at this stage—I just wanted to get there and to stop being filled in by these boys' boots. The soldiers jabbered at me fast and aggressively.

The vehicle stopped. We seemed to be in the town. Noise surged around us. I heard voices, many voices, and I knew from their tone that it was an angry mob. The sound of hatred is ugly and universal. I looked up. I saw a sea of faces, military and civilian, angry, chanting, shouting abuse. I felt like a child in a pram with a gang of adults peering in. It scared me. These people hated me.

An old man dug deep into his TB-riddled lungs and fired a green wad into my face. Other salvoes followed, thick and fast. Then came the physical stuff. It started with a poke in my ribs, a testing prod at the new commodity in town. The poke became a shove, then a slap, then a punch, and the crowd started pulling my hair. I thought it was going to be a case of mob rule. I felt I was going to get lynched, or worse.

They started to climb aboard. There was uncontrolled frenzy. Perhaps it was the first time they'd seen a white-eyed soldier. Perhaps they held me personally responsible for their dead and wounded friends and family members. They closed in and slapped and punched, pulled my mustache and hair. There was a gagging stench of unwashed bodies. It was like a horror film with zombies. All daylight was blocked out, and I thought I was going to suffocate.

More and more shots were fired into the air, and I began to worry that it wouldn't be long before they got bored with using clouds as targets. The useless thought came to me that they must be taking casualties from firing in built-up areas. Rounds have spent their explosive force when they come down, but they still come down with a deadly momentum. No doubt they'd blame me for those deaths as well.

What were the soldiers going to do, I wondered— just let the civvies have me? Kill me now, I thought. I'd rather have the squaddies do it than the crowd. The soldiers started pushing the people away. It was a wonderful feeling. Just a minute ago they were beating me up; now these boys were my saviors. Better the devil you know . . .

I was lying on my stomach at the back of the Land Cruiser, my hands still tied, and they started to drag me out feet first. The hollering of obscenities got louder. I concentrated on looking dejected and badly injured and on working out how I was going to protect my face as I fell two feet or so onto the tarmac. The solution was to spin around on to my back because then I could keep my head up. I managed to do it just in time. I lifted my head, and the base of my spine took the force of the drop, detonating an explosion of pain inside my skull. All the breath was knocked out of me. The soldiers were really playing the macho man, waving at everybody, shaking their AKs in the air Che Guevara style. They looked so butch, I thought, doing this in front of the girls. They were the real local teddies; they'd obviously be scoring tonight.

The vehicle had stopped about 50 feet from a big pair of gates set in a wall 10 feet high. I got the impression we were at the local military camp. They dragged me on my back towards the gates. I had to arch to save my hands from scraping along the road. Still there was mass hysteria. I was scared: the fear of the unknown. These people looked and sounded so very out of control.

At last I was dragged inside and the gates slammed behind us. I took in a large courtyard and a selection of buildings. The macho act ended at once, and the squaddies hoiked me to my feet and pulled me on by my arms. You've got to take time to have a look around, to tune in. If you do the hard man routine, stick your chest out and say fuck you, they'll fill you in again, and that's counterproductive. If you appear to be subdued and sapped, they've got the effect they want. It's now that you've got to start going to town with your injuries. You've got to look feeble, as if everything's on top of you and you're totally and utterly clueless. Quite apart from anything else, it preserves what energy you've got left so that you're ready for your escape, which is of primary concern.

I felt I'd passed a major test. I was in another world; another drama had ended. In a weird way I almost felt safe, now that the local population couldn't get their hands on me. The prospect of that seemed so much worse than anything fellow soldiers might do to me. I exaggerated the limp, shivering and coughing, and moaned every time someone got hold of me. It must have seemed a wonder I was alive, the way I was going on. I *was* in a bad way, but my mental state was good, and that's the one you've got to worry about and conceal from the enemy.

For a few minutes I stood there with a ring of guards around me. As I looked straight ahead, there was a metaled road going to a block about 300 feet ahead. Looking around from left to right, I saw barrack blocks to the right, following the line of the wall, and a small clump of trees.

Then I saw some poor bastard lying on the grass, trussed up on his stomach like a chicken, his ankles and wrists tied together. He was trying to lift his legs to take the pressure off his head. He'd obviously been given a good hammering. His head had swollen up to the size of a football, and his kit was torn and covered in blood. I couldn't even see the color of his hair or whether his clothes were camouflage-pattern. For a moment, as he lifted his head, we had eye-to-eye, and I realized it was Dinger.

The eyes give so much away. They can tell you when a person is drunk, when he's bluffing, when he's alert, when he's happy. They are the window to the mind. Dinger's eyes said: It's going to be all right. I even got a small smile out of him. I grinned back. I had a fearsome dread for him because he was in such a bad state, but it was wonderful to see him, to have somebody there to share my predicament. Selfishly, I was chuffed I wasn't the only one to be caught. The slagging if I got back to Hereford would have been unbearable.

The downside of seeing him was the realization that

it was my turn next. He was really in a bad way, yet he was much harder than me. It occurred to me that I could be dead by the end of the afternoon. If so, I just wanted to get it over and done with.

A couple of boys with weapons were lounging against a tree near Dinger, smoking cigarettes. They didn't stop when two officers and their little entourage came out of their office and walked halfway up the road to meet us. I just stood there, playing on the injuries, working on the principle that you don't know anything until you try. Mentally I prepared myself for another filling in. As the officers approached, I clenched my teeth and pressed my knees together to protect my balls.

The local military had incurred a lot of casualties, and it was clear that these well-dressed officers, a mixture of commando officers in DPM and ordinary types in olive green with stars on their shoulders, were not impressed. My head was pushed up, and one of them took a swing. I closed my eyes and braced myself for the next punch. It didn't come.

Another officer was jabbering away, and I opened one eye just enough to see what the conversation was about. The rupert who had hit me had a knife in his hand now and was walking towards me. Here we go, I thought, he's going to show the jundies how hard he is. He jabbed it under the bottom of my smock and ripped it upwards. The smock fell open.

The jundies were told to search me, but they didn't have a clue what they were doing. They must have heard weird stories about exploding suicide devices or something because they were paranoid. In my pockets they found two pencils and inspected them as if they contained arsenic or rocket fuel. One soldier cut off my ID tags and took them away. I felt suddenly naked without them. Worse than that, I was sterile, a man with no name. Removing my tags was as good as removing my identity.

The author with bergen, belt kit, and 203. *Robin Mathews*

The 209 lbs of equipment that each man carried.

Part of an SAS patrol armed with the 203.

RAF ground crew preparing the Chinook.

Left: Weather conditions at the FOB *(forward operating base).*

Below: Another patrol in their 110s on the billiard-table terrain of northwest Iraq.

My souvenir escape map, signed by members of the
squadron and General Schwarzkopf.

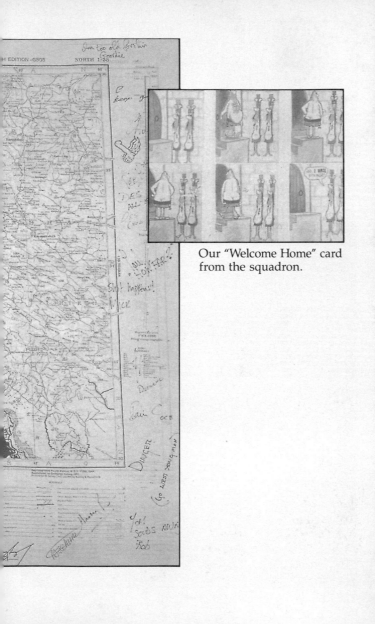

Our "Welcome Home" card
from the squadron.

Vince Phillips.

Bob Consiglio.

"Legs" Lane.

The Regiment's cemetery at Hereford.

M16 rifle fitted with the M203 40mm grenade launcher. *The Military Picture Library*

Minimi light machine gun. *The Research House*

The 66 shoulder-launched rocket. *The Military Picture Library*

Claymore antipersonnel mine, showing the firing wire and clacker and *(below, opened)* the ball bearings embedded in a curved layer of plastic explosive. *The Military Picture Library*

The Elsie antipersonnel mine, unarmed and armed. *The Military Picture Library*

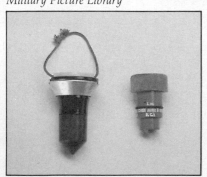

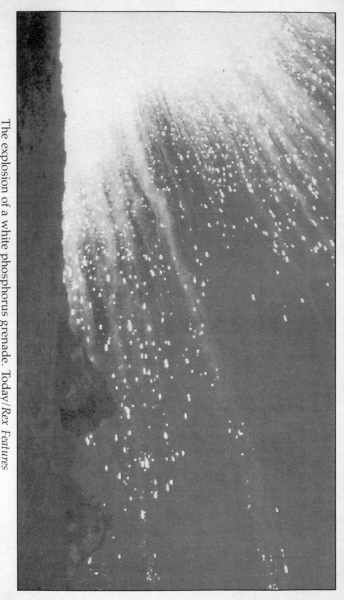

The explosion of a white phosphorus grenade. Today/Rex Features

The patrol radio—a PRC319 communications set, capable of sending encrypted short-burst transmissions. *The Military Picture Library*

Top left and above: The handheld Magellan GPS *(global positioning system)* navigation aid. *The Military Picture Library*

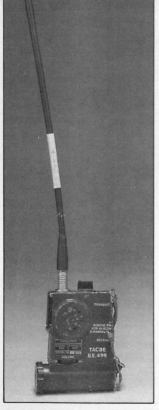

TACBE beacon/radio. *The Military Picture Library*

A Scud on its TEL *(transporter erector launcher)*. Crown Copyright (MOD). *London/MARS*

Launch.
The Research House

Preparation.
The Military Picture Library

S60 57mm antiaircraft gun. *The Military Picture Library*

Iraqi Commando AK with folding butt. *Jane's Information Group*

Two others took the Syrettes of morphine that were hanging round my neck and went through the motions of sticking them into their arms. They were cock-a-hoop and would obviously be shooting it up later on. I had a toothbrush in a pen pocket in the sleeves of my DPM shirt, but they refused to touch it. Maybe they didn't understand what it was doing there. Maybe, if the smell of the mob outside had been anything to go by, they didn't even know what a toothbrush was. Whatever, they weren't taking chances. They made me take it out myself.

The body search was from the top down, but it was badly done and they didn't even make me take off my clothes. They removed my boots and looted every item of kit. They behaved like old ladies at a jumble sale. We always use pencils rather than pens because pencils always work, even in the rain. I had a couple of three-inch stubs, sharpened at both ends so that if I was writing and one end snapped, I'd just have to turn it around and on I'd go. They went as souvenirs. So did the Swiss Army knife and a Silva compass I had in

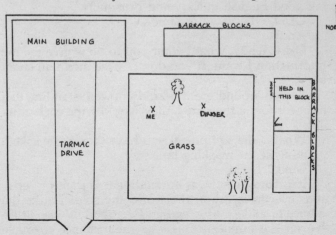

Commando camp

my pocket, both on lengths of paracord. Every bit of kit is attached to you securely. There was a notebook, but it had nothing in it. I'd destroyed its contents at the first LUP. There was my white plastic racing spoon from an American ration set, and that, too, was tied on a length of paracord in my pocket. My watch was around my neck on cord so that I couldn't be compromised by the luminous glow and it wouldn't catch on anything as I patrolled. Even the spare plastic bag I had in case I'd needed a shit while on patrol was snaffled.

Around my waist, however, on a one-inch webbing belt, was today's star prize: about £1700 in sterling, in the form of twenty gold sovereigns we had each been given as escape money. I had fixed my coins to the belt with masking tape, and this created a major drama. They jumped back, shouting what I assumed was the Iraqi for "Let him go! He's going to explode!"

A captain arrived. He couldn't have been more than about 5'2" tall but must have weighed over 13 stone. He looked like a boiled egg. He was aggressive, speaking good English quickly and brusquely.

"Okay, what is your name?"

"Andy."

"Okay, Andy, what I want you to do is give me the information I want. If you don't, these men will shoot you."

I looked around me. The soldiers were standing in a tight cordon; if they fired, they would wipe each other out.

"What is the equipment you have there?" he asked, pointing at the masking tape.

"Gold," I said.

That word must be as international as jeans or Pepsi, and in every army in the world the soldiers like the chance to make a little earner. Everybody's eyes lit up —even the jundies.' This was their chance to make more money in one hit than they probably earned in a year. I could see them planning their holidays and buying their new cars. I suddenly remembered a story I'd heard about one of the US soldiers who was among the troops who invaded Panama. In an office belonging to President Noriega he found three million US dollars in cash—and the knobber actually got on the radio and reported it. It was taken off to regimental HQ, and that was probably the last anybody ever saw of it. The bloke who told me the story said he couldn't sleep at night just thinking about the opportunity that had been thrown away.

The ruperts were taking no chances. They dragged me away to another office and told me to put the belt on the table.

"Why do you have gold?" the fat man barked.

"To pay people if we run out of food," I said. "It's bad to steal."

"Open it up."

The ruperts stationed two of the jundies in the room with me and then left, presumably in case I was lying and was about to explode a string of incendiary devices. I pulled out the first gold sovereign, and the ruperts were summoned. They dismissed the two squaddies and divided the sovereigns between themselves. They tried to look so official and solemn as they did it, but it was blatantly obvious what they were up to.

It was probably thanks to the ruperts' greed that my silk escape map and miniature compass weren't found. They were both hidden in my uniform, and a thorough search would have unearthed them. I was chuffed to have them still. It was a wonderful feeling: you don't know this, big nose, but I've still got an escape map and compass, so up yours. The best time to escape is as soon as possible after capture. The further you go down the chain, the harder it is to escape, because the system caters more and more efficiently for a prisoner. Frontline troops have other problems on their minds, but further down the line the security is better and you've most likely been stripped of your uniform. From the moment I was captured I had been trying to orientate myself so that I knew which way was west. If the chance came my way, I'd need these vital items.

Blindfolded now, I was taken to another room. I sensed it was large and airy. There were bodies in there talking; the atmosphere was more subdued. I could tell by the more regulated voices that this was the Head Shed's room. It felt strangely secure. I felt I was out of danger somehow, far from the madding crowd, even though I suspected what was going to happen. Then I realized that though the people sounded more in control, if they filled me in they'd do it more professionally.

There was a strong smell of coffee, Gitanes, and cheap aftershave. I was pushed down onto a chair with a cushioned seat and high back. Part of me felt I wasn't there. My mind was going into some sort of fantasy to block it out, as if it was all a dream. I had never once considered that anything like this could happen to me. The feeling was the same as if I'd been driving a car and knocked down a child: complete and total disbelief. My mind was hearing things, but I was enclosed in my own little world. I snapped out of it and thought about trying to get their pity, or a cup of coffee or something to eat. But I wasn't going to ask for jack shit. If they gave me something all well and good, but I wasn't going to beg.

I clenched my muscles, put my head down, gripped my legs together. I guessed that before they got down to some proper tactical questioning, they would take their frustrations out on me. They were murmuring to each other.

So what's it to be, I thought. A fearsome torture?

Or am I going to get fucked?

Men milled around, whispering. The tiniest sound is

magnified when you're trying so hard to hear. A chair scraped. Somebody got to his feet and came towards me.

I braced myself. *Here it comes.* I pretended to shiver. I wanted so much for these people to feel sorry for me.

Two seconds felt like two minutes. It was unbelievably frustrating not to be able to see what was going on. I shivered again, the injured, pathetic creature, the man who knew nothing, the man not worth doing anything to. But I knew I was grasping at straws. Head down, I tried to show no reaction as he approached.

There was a strong waft of coffee, and I longed to be in Ross's café in Peckham with a big frothy coffee in front of me. On Saturdays as young lads we'd go down and get two sausage and chips, pile on the salt and vinegar, and get a frothy coffee. Ross the Greek would let us spend all morning there. We can't have been more than eight or nine. My mum always gave me the money to go and get my dinner at Ross's; she knew it was the big thing. In wintertime there would be condensation running down the windows and that strong, strong coffee smell. It was such a snug and cozy place to sit. It came back to me so vividly that for a brief moment I felt like a child who has fallen over and is crying for his mum.

There was no way Dinger would have gone into his cover story yet. Name, number, rank, date of birth, the Big Four—that's all he would have given. I thought: I'm going to get severely filled in here because they're going to want a lot more than that. I sort of hoped maybe they won't be asking me now; maybe they'll be asking me later. Maybe they'll just be taking their frustrations out now. Maybe no one can speak English! My mind was racing at incredible speed as this character got nearer and nearer, and finally stopped just inches away.

He pulled my head up and punched me hard in the

face. The blow knocked me backwards and to one side, but they were surrounding me, and I was pushed back upright. Even when you're expecting a punch like that, you're shocked when it comes. I wanted to stay down because it would give me time to rest before the next one, time to think.

Everybody piled in. There was laughter as they tried to outdo each other's efforts. I felt drunk. You know what's happening, you know what's going on, but there's nothing you can do to control it. You begin to feel detached. It's happening to you, but your mind takes over and says Fuck this, I'm not having much more of this, and you start drifting into unconsciousness. You can feel it happening, but your mind goes off into a wander. I was being punched into a semistupor.

I let myself drop to the floor because at least then I could protect my face. I drew my knees up and kept them together, kept my head down, kept myself clenched up. As the blows rained down I screamed and moaned. Some of it was put on. A lot of it wasn't.

Then, as if on a signal, the beating stopped.

"Poor Andy, poor Andy," I heard, and a mock clucking of concern.

I got to my knees and put my head against the man and shook it. I leant against him, my breathing heavy and rasping because my nose was so clogged with blood and mud. I started sinking to the floor again. I needed his help to get me up. This gives time, I thought, this stalls the operation. Hopefully they'll come to their senses and see that I'm just a pathetic, useless cretin, not worth the effort, and leave me alone.

I was helped back into the chair and somebody deadlegged me. I screamed. Even as a schoolboy I used to hate deadlegs—and they were just the variety that were delivered with the knee. This was a full-blooded kick. Boots flew in from all directions again. I went straight down.

You know the sensible thing to do is to appear weak and plead with them for mercy, but something takes over. I was so angry that I made a conscious decision once more not to beg. There was no way I was going to demean myself. They were going to do it anyway. I knew it was counterproductive to resist, but you can't fight your pride and self-respect. If I moaned, that would only give them more pleasure. The only way I could beat them was by my mental attitude, and beat them I would. By keeping as quiet as I could, I was winning a small battle. Even the slightest imagined victory is magnified a thousand times. I'm winning this, I thought. Ridiculously, I felt my morale soar. Fuck 'em, I said to myself—don't give them the satisfaction of going home for their tea and saying to their mates, "Yeah, he was begging us to stop."

They didn't stop. Boots swung into my ribs and head, steel toecaps connected with soft shins. There was no point to what they were doing; everybody was just being macho. My only hope was that they'd get bored with it soon.

A couple of them started sounding off in English, denouncing Bush, Thatcher, everybody they could think of. My body was starting to throw its hand in. I felt limp and drained. It was difficult to breathe. I had already been deprived of my sense of sight; now everything was swollen and throbbing, and I felt my other senses numbing, too. My heart pounded so strongly it was creating its own chest pain.

I could hear screams and anguished groans. They must have come from me.

Somebody shouted into my face from inches away and then laughed manically "Ha! Ha! Ha! Ha!" and backed off.

I should have had the sense to become a quivering wreck and let them laugh about it and say, "Ah, bless his cotton socks, leave him alone, what a dickhead."

But I just lay there and took it.

"You are the tool of Bush, Andy," one of them said, "but you will not be for long because we are going to kill you."

I took the threat seriously. He had just confirmed my worst fears. They would give us both a good kicking, then take us off and slot us.

Good, I thought, let's get on with it then.

They dragged me to my feet again. Blood was pouring down my face from gashes in my scalp. It trickled into my eyes and mouth. My lips were numb, as if I'd been to the dentist. I couldn't control them to blow the blood away. I bent my head forward to redirect the flow and to avoid any eye-to-eye contact. I didn't want these bastards to see what I was thinking.

For another fifteen minutes people continued to take turns at punching and slapping, often not even bothering to put me back on the chair. I stayed crunched up as tightly as I could. A pair of hands grabbed my feet and started to drag me across the room so that the others could get an improved angle on their kicking. This is way out of control, I thought. Any more of this and I'm going to be well out of the game.

The blindfold had come off by now with the hustle and tussle of events. I didn't bother looking that much. All I saw was my knees hard against my face, and the light-cream lino floor, once beautifully polished but now smeared with mud and blood. I was finding it more and more difficult to draw breath. I was really getting concerned about the long-term effects. I felt my body disintegrating. I could die here—and the only good thing about it would be that I'd mucked up their floor.

The back of my throat was rattling. I coughed blood. Another twenty minutes, I thought, and we'd be into serious damage. That would really slow down my chances of escape.

At last they must have tired of the game. I was a bag

of shit, they'd got me where they wanted me, there was little point going on.

I lay there on the floor, drenched with my own blood. There was filth and gore everywhere. Even my feet were bleeding. My khaki socks were wet and dark red.

I opened my eyes for a moment and caught a glimpse of a pair of brown Chelsea boots with zippers on the side, and a pair of bell-bottomed jeans. The boots had cheap and nasty plastic heels, the stuff that Saturday markets are made of. The jeans were dirty and faded, and well and truly flared. Whoever was wearing them probably had on a David Cassidy T-shirt as well under his uniform shirt. Glancing up quickly, I saw that they were all ruperts, very clean-cut and smooth-faced, not a hair out of place. Everybody had a mustache and hair that was sleeked back. The Saddam look was in.

I lay in a corner against the wall, trying to protect myself. There were people on three sides of me. Their faces loomed down at me. One bloke flicked his fag ash at me. I looked up at him pitifully. His response was to do it again.

More people came into the room. I was lifted up and put back onto a chair and reblindfolded. I hoped it wasn't just a fresh crew coming in to take over from where the others had left off.

"What is your name?" I heard from a new voice in excellent English.

"Andy."

I didn't give my full name. I was determined to drag this out as long as I could. My surname was a whole new question. The trick is to use up time, but at the same time to appear to be wanting to help.

"How old are you, Andy? What is your date of birth?"

His diction was very precise, his grammar better

than mine. The slight Middle Eastern accent was barely detectable.

I gave him the answer.

"What is your religion?"

Under the terms of the Geneva Convention he wasn't allowed to ask that one. The correct response should have been: "I cannot answer that question."

"Church of England," I said.

It was inscribed on my ID tags and they had them, so why should I risk another filling in over information that they already had? I hoped the information would help confirm that I was from England, not Tel Aviv as the crowd had seemed to believe.

Church of England meant nothing to them.

"You are Jewish?"

"No, I'm a Protestant."

"What is a Protestant?"

"A Christian. I'm a Christian."

To them, everybody's a Christian who's not a Muslim or a Jew. Christianity embraces everybody from Trappist monks to Moonies.

"No, Andy, you are Jewish. We will soon find that out. Do you like my English, by the way?"

"Yes, it's good."

I wasn't about to argue. As far as I was concerned, he spoke better English than Kate Adie.

I had my head down, swinging it from side to side, looking and sounding confused. There were long pauses while I appeared to be trying to think of things. I slurred my words, played on the injuries, played for time, dragged everything out.

"Of course my English is good," he snapped, coming right up to my face. "I worked in London. What do you take me for—an idiot? We are not idiots."

He had been asking questions from maybe 10 feet away, as if from behind a desk. But now he was up and walking around as he launched into a torrent of rhetoric about how intelligent and wonderful the Iraqi nation was and what tremendously civilized people they were. He was beginning to shout. Flecks of spit landed on my face. They smelled of tobacco and cheap cologne. The speed and harshness of his verbal assault made me wince a little; I clenched my teeth. I had to fight to control my reactions; I didn't want him to know I was in a better state than he thought. You've got to take it for granted that these people are switched on.

"We are an advanced nation," he spat. "As your country shall soon find out."

I had been feeling a bit like a child on the receiving end of a scolding, who puts his face down while he's being yelled at and his whole body starts to shudder.

He mentioned London and I thought, This is all getting on rather well here, we're going to talk about London.

"I love London," I said. "I wish I was back there now. I don't want to be here. I don't know what I'm doing here. I'm just a soldier."

We went through the Big Four again. In my mind's eye I tried to race ahead and compare what I was going to say with what I'd already said. I could hear lots of writing going on. All the pens seemed very close to me. I heard paper being folded and the shuffling of feet.

My interrogator moved away and sat down. His tone switched to something soothing and approachable.

"I know you're just a soldier," he said. "I am a soldier myself. Let us just get this done in a civilized manner. We are a civilized nation. There are certain things we want to know, Andy. Just tell us. You're just a tool. They are using you."

It was pretty obvious what was going on. My job now was to make them think that their methods were working.

"Yes, sir," I said, "I'm so confused, I really want to

help you. I don't know what's happening. I'm so worried about my friend outside."

"Well, tell me what unit you're from. Just tell us and you won't have to go through this pain. Why are you doing this to yourself?"

"I'm sorry, I cannot answer that question."

It all started again.

When the new characters had come in, one of them must have slipped in behind me. When I gave the dud response, he must have got the nod because he threw a massive hook with a rifle butt into the side of my head. It took me straight onto the lino.

If you're in a fight as a schoolkid, you're all revved up for it, and you're expecting the blows. They don't hurt so much when they come. If you're not expecting it, the pain is intense. The shock from the rifle butt was horrendous. I passed out. I went to another world, and although it hurt intensely, it was actually quite a pleasant place to be.

As I lay on the floor, I noticed that my breathing was very shallow now and my heart was pumping more slowly. Everything was slowing down. I could feel myself gradually declining. I couldn't swallow. Everything was a haze.

I took another blow from the rifle butt. Bubbles of vivid light exploded before my eyes. Then there was darkness.

I was semiconscious when they lifted me back onto the chair.

"Look, Andy, we just need to know some things. Let me do my job. We don't have to do this. We are all soldiers. This is an honorable profession." All of this in a low, soft, comforting voice. A sort of "Let's get it over with, let's be mates' sort of tone.

"We could just leave you out in the desert to be eaten by the animals, Andy. Nobody would care, except your family. You're letting them down, you're not being brave, you're just playing into the hands of the people who sent you here. They're having a good time while people like you and me are fighting each other. You and me, Andy—we don't want to fight this war."

I was nodding and agreeing with everything he said, and all the time I was doing it the wonderful feeling was growing inside me that I had actually beaten him: he saw me nodding, but he didn't know that inside my head my attitude was totally different. I started to feel better about my capture. Everything had felt so negative up till then. I was thinking: He must be believing this crap. He's chatting away and I'm agreeing with him. I couldn't believe I was getting away with it. I was on top of this discussion, and he wasn't even aware of it. I'd got something over him. This could be the start of a wonderful relationship.

I was winning.

"Just tell us, Andy, and we shall send you back to England. What unit are you from?" He made it sound as if he had the power to summon a private jet there and then to whisk me back to Brize Norton.

"I'm sorry, I cannot answer that question."

This time, as the kicks connected with my skull, there was a hissing, popping sound in my ears, and as I clenched my jaw, I heard the bones creak together. I felt blood trickle out of my ears and down my face. I was worried. Blood coming out of your ears is not a good sign. I thought, I'm going to be left deaf. Shit, I was only in my early thirties.

"What unit are you with?"

I was hoping desperately that he'd get on to something else, but he wasn't going to let go.

I said nothing.

"Andy, we are not making much progress."

Bizarrely, the voice was still soft and chummy.

"You must understand, Andy, I have a job to do. We're not getting very far, are we? There is no big problem, just tell us."

Silence.

More kicks. More punches. More screams.

"We already have this information from your friend, you know. We just want to hear it from you."

That was a lie. He'd have got jack shit out of Dinger. Dinger was harder than me; he wouldn't have said a word. The reason he had got himself so badly filled in was probably because he'd treated them like anybody else he didn't like the look of and told them to fuck off.

"You must understand, I'm a soldier," I said. "You're a soldier, too—you must understand I can't tell you this."

I was trying to get some affiliation, I was trying to put it over in a sobbing, pathetic way. I hoped to appeal to their own traditional fear of loss of face.

"My family would walk around in shame for the rest of their days," I cried. "They would be disgraced, I'd be discredited for ever. I just can't tell you these things, I can't."

"Then Andy we have a big problem. You're not telling us what we need to know. You're not helping the situation, you're not helping yourself. You could be dead very soon, for something that means nothing to you. I want to help you, but there are people above me who don't want to do that. Admit it," he said, in the tone of my best mate giving me advice. "You are an Israeli, aren't you? Come on, admit it."

"I'm not an Israeli," I sobbed. "Look—I'm not dressed like an Israeli. This is British uniform, and you've seen my identification tags. I'm English, this is British uniform. I don't know what you want from me. Please, please. I want to help. You're confusing me. I'm scared."

"This is stupid."

"You've got my identification tags, you've seen that I'm English. I'm scared of what you're saying."

His tone suddenly changed. "Yes, *we* have your identification tags, you haven't," he exploded angrily.

"You're who we say you are, and as far as we're concerned you're an Israeli. If not, why were you so near Syria? What were you doing? Tell me, tell me, what were you doing?"

Even if I'd wanted to answer, he wasn't giving me time. He hit me with a nonstop torrent of questions and raging rhetoric. "You mean nothing to us! You're nothing, nothing!"

It must have been fun in his house. The kids wouldn't have known if he was coming or going.

What do I do now? I asked myself.

Let's get back to the Israeli thing.

A dread was creeping into my mind concerning Bob. Bob had tight, curly black hair and a large nose. If he was captured or they found his body, he could be taken as Jewish.

"I'm British."

"No, no, you're Israeli. You are dressed like commandos."

"Everybody in the British army wears this uniform."

"You'll die soon, Andy, for being so stupid, for not answering simple questions."

"I'm not Israeli."

It had got to the stage where I was having to remember what I'd been saying and what I had not been saying, because I knew that if these things were being written down—and I could hear the scribbling—I was going to get myself into severe shit.

Let's keep on the Israeli thing. Maybe if this character keeps on talking to me, we can get a relationship going. Him and me. He's mine. He's my interrogator. He just might take pity on me.

"I'm a Christian, I'm English," I set off again. "I don't even know whereabouts in Iraq I am, let alone if I'm near Syria. I don't want to be here. Look at me, I'm scared."

"We know you're an Israeli, Andy. We just want to hear it from you. Your friend has already told us."

I thought, Dinger looks like he could be a bit Jewish also, with his tight, wiry blond hair.

"You're commandos."

In their army only commandos wear DPM.

"We're not! We're just ordinary soldiers."

"You'll die for being so stupid. All we want is simple answers from you. I'm trying to help you. These people want to kill you. I'm trying to save you. How do you expect me to do that if you're not helping me? We want you to answer these questions. We need to hear it from you. You want to help us, don't you?"

"Yes, I want to help." I was sobbing again. "But I can't help you if I don't know anything."

"You're so stupid." The voice was aggressive, but he mixed some compassion with it. "Why aren't you helping us? Come on, I'm trying to help you. I don't want you to be in this situation any more than you do."

"I want to help you, but I'm not an Israeli."

"Just tell us and we'll stop. Come on, you're so stupid, aren't you? What's the matter? We're civilized people. But I need you to tell me that you're an Israeli. If you can't tell me that, then tell me why you're so near Syria?"

"I don't know where I am."

"You're near Syria, aren't you, so just tell me. These people will kill you. Your friend's okay, your friend has told us. He will live, but you're going to die, for something stupid. Why die? You're stupid."

I heard his chair scrape on the floor. I was trying to take in what was going on without showing that I could focus. I was physically wrecked. I was hoping for just the slightest hint of humanity in this man. Shit, I could always turn the waterworks on so easily as a kid, win my aunties round, and get a packet of crisps. What was wrong with these people?

I was going for an Oscar without a doubt—but a good percentage of what I was doing was for real. I was in real pain. It was a good catalyst for the reaction I wanted to portray. It was good to have this Israeli thing. Let's keep on that and hopefully they'll keep away from the other questions.

"I can't help you, I just can't help you."

I heard a big sigh, as if he was my best mate in the world and there was nothing left he could do to help me. The sigh said: I am your contact; it's only me that's keeping everybody at bay.

"Then *I* cannot help *you*, Andy."

As if on cue I heard another chair scrape and feet moving towards me. When I smelt the waft of after-shave, I just knew that the lad who was a dab hand with the rifle butt was on his way over to give me the good news.

He was, too. He really read me my horoscope.

I must have been getting used to being blindfolded because my senses of hearing and smell seemed to be more acute. I was starting to tell these people apart by their smell. The boy who was handy with the rifle butt wore freshly laundered clothes. Another one liked pistachio nuts. He'd put them in his mouth and chew, then gob the mashed shell into my face. The one who spoke good English smoked incessantly and had breath that smelled of coffee and stale cigarettes. When he launched into rhetoric, I got his spit all over my face. He also stank like a color supplement aftershave ad.

His chair would scrape, and I'd sense him moving around. He'd speak like a Gatling gun, then he'd do the Nice Guy bit and give me lots of "Everything's quite okay, it's going to be all right."

As he was chatting very gently, I could hear him getting closer and closer until we were nose to nose. Then he'd yell in my ear.

"This is no good, Andy," he said. "We shall have to get this out of you another way."

What worse way could there possibly be of doing it? We'd had intelligence reports of interrogation centers and mass killings, and I thought, Here we go, we're going to get severely dealt with now. I had visions of concentration camps and electrodes clamped to my bollocks.

Two of the boys set to with rifle butts.

One particularly heavy blow caught me on the jaw, directly over my teeth. Only the skin of my cheek lay between the edge of the butt and two of my back molars. I felt the teeth crack and splinter, and then the pain of it hit me. I was down and screaming my head off. I tried to spit out the fragments, but my mouth was too swollen and numb. I couldn't swallow. The moment my tongue touched the sharp, tender stumps I passed out.

I came to on the floor. The blindfold had fallen off, and I watched as blood poured from my mouth into a pool on the cream lino. I felt stupid and useless. I wanted nothing more than for the handcuffs to fall off so I could get up and deal with these guys.

They carried on, giving me some good stuff around the back with the butts, twatting my head, legs, and kidneys.

I couldn't breathe through my nose. When I screamed, I had to draw breath through my mouth, and the air hit the exposed nerve pulp of my broken teeth. I screamed again, and went on screaming.

It was getting outrageous.

They picked me up and put me back on the seat. They didn't bother putting the blindfold back on, but I kept my head down anyway. I didn't want eye contact, or to risk another filling in for looking up. I was in enough pain. I was a big, incoherent mess, honking away, sniveling to myself as I slumped on the chair.

My coordination was well and truly gone. I couldn't even keep my legs together any more. I must have looked like Dinger's double.

There was a long silence.

Everybody was shuffling around, leaving me to ponder over my fate. How long could I go like this? Was I going to get kicked to death here or what?

There was a lot more sighing and clucking.

"What are you doing this for, Andy? For your country? Your country doesn't want to know you. Your country doesn't care. The only ones who will really worry will be your parents, your family. We don't want a war. It's Bush, Mitterrand, Thatcher, Major. They're sitting back there doing nothing. You're here. It's you that will suffer, not them. They're not worried about you.

"We've had war for many years. All our families have suffered. We're not barbarians, it's you who are bringing in war. This is just an unfortunate situation for you. Why don't you help us? Why are you letting yourself go through all this pain? Why do we have to do this sort of thing?"

I didn't answer, I just kept my head down. My game plan was not to go into the cover story straightaway, because then they've got you. I was trying to make it look as if I was prepared to give them the Big Four and that was all. Queen and country and all that. I would go through a certain amount of tactical questioning and then break into my cover story.

They were talking between themselves in low tones, in what I took to be quite educated Arabic. Somebody was scribbling notes.

The writing was a good sign. It intimated that there wasn't just a big frenzy going on, with them getting what they could and then topping me. It made it seem there was a reason for not shooting me. Was there some sort of preservation order on us? It gave me a sense of security, a feeling that some officialdom somewhere was directing operations. Yes, said the other side of my brain, but you're getting further and further down this chain, and the longer this goes on the less chance you have of escaping. Escaping must always be foremost in your mind. You don't know when the opportunity is going to arise, and you've got to be ready. *Carpe diem!* You've got to seize that moment, but the longer you are in captivity the more difficult it becomes.

I thought about Dinger. I knew he wouldn't have substantiated any of this stuff about Tel Aviv. He would have done as much as he could, and when he decided that he'd physically had too much and was going to be kicked to death, he'd have started to break into the search and rescue story.

It occurred to me I might feel better if I could see my environment, absorb my surroundings. I looked up and opened my eyes. The venetian blinds were down, but one or two thin shafts of light shone through. Everything was twilighty and in semishadow.

The room was quite large, maybe 40 feet by 20. I was sitting at one end of the rectangle. I couldn't see a door, so it had to be behind me. The officers were at the other end, facing me. There must have been eight or nine of them, all smoking. Smoke haze hung from the ceiling, pierced here and there by the sun coming through the blinds.

Halfway down the room, on the righthand side as I looked at it, was a large desk. On it were a couple of telephones and piles of normal office paper, books, and clutter. A big leather executive-style chair was empty. Behind it was the world's biggest picture of Saddam in his beret, all the medals on, smiling away. I guessed it was the local commander's office.

General admin notices hung on the wall. In the center of the lino floor and continuing under the desk was a large Persian carpet. On the left, facing the desk, was a large domestic-type settee. The rest of the walls were lined with stackable plastic chairs. Mine, the guest chair, appeared to be a plastic cushioned dining chair.

More tut-tut-tuts and sighs. People were talking to themselves as if I wasn't there and this was just a normal day at the office. I rolled my head, and blood and snot dribbled down my chin. I didn't know how much longer I could bear the agony in my mouth.

I worked out the options. If they started to fill me in again, I'd be dead by the end of the afternoon. The time had come to start spilling the cover story. I would wait for them to initiate it, and I'd go ahead.

When I had refused to answer their questions, I wasn't being all patriotic and brave—that's just propaganda that you see in war films. This was real life. I couldn't come straight out with my cover story. I had to make it look as if they'd prized it out of me. It was a matter of self-preservation, not bravado. People sometimes do heroic things because the situation demands it, but there's no such thing as a hero. The gung ho brigade are either idiots or they don't even understand what's happening. What I had to do now was give them the least amount of information to keep myself alive.

"Andy, you're just sitting there. We're trying to be friendly, but we have to get the information. Andy, this could go on and on. Your friend's outside, he's helped us and he's Okay, he's out there on the grass, he's still alive, he's in the sun. You're in here in the dark. This is no good for you and it's no good for us. It just takes up our time.

"Just tell us what we need to know and that's it, everything's ended. You'll be Okay, we'll look after you until the end of the war. Maybe we might be able to organize it for you to go home to your family straightaway. There's no problems, if you help us. You look bad. Are you aching? You need a doctor—we'll help you."

I wanted to appear utterly done in.

"Okay," I said in a hoarse whisper, "I can't take any more. I'll help you."

Everybody in the room looked up.

"I am a member of a search and rescue team who were sent to lift downed pilots."

The interrogator turned around and looked at the others. They all came forward and sat on tables and desks. Everything I said had to be translated for them.

"Andy, tell me more. Tell me all you know about the search and rescue."

His voice was very nice and calm. He obviously thought he'd cracked it, which was fine—that was exactly what I wanted him to think.

"We're all from different units in the British army," I said, "and we're all drawn together because of our medical experience. I don't know anybody, we were just brought together. I'm medically trained, I'm not a soldier. I'm stuck in this war and I don't want to be a part of it. I was happy working back in the UK on sick parades, and all of a sudden they've put me on one of these search and rescue teams. I haven't got a clue about any of this, I'm a medic, that's all I am."

It seemed to go down rather well. They chatted about it amongst themselves. It obviously squared with what Dinger had told them.

The trouble is, once you start there's that chink in the armor, and you've got to carry on with the story. If there's too much detail, you'll start cocking things up for the other prisoners. You have to try to keep your story nice and simple—then it's easy for you to remember as well. The best way to achieve that is to be the total bag of shit. You can't remember because you're in such a bad physical state. Your mind just can't recollect anything; you're just a thick, bone squaddy, one of the minions, and you haven't got a clue, you don't even know what kind of helicopter it was. My mind was racing to think of the story and what I was going to say next.

They knew I was a sergeant, so I threw that one in again. In their army, sergeant is a buckshee rank. It's their officers that do everything, including the thinking.

"How many of you were there?"

"I don't know. There was lots of noise and the helicopter came down. We were told there was danger of an explosion and to run, and they just took off and left us." I played the confused bonehead, the scared, abandoned squaddy. "I just do first aid, I don't want any of this. I'm not used to all this. All I do is put plasters on wounded pilots."

"How many were on the aircraft?" he tried again.

"I'm not entirely sure. It was nighttime."

"Andy, what's going on? We gave you a chance. Do you take us for idiots? Over the last few days many people have been killed, and we want to know what's happened."

This was the first time they had mentioned casualties. I had been expecting it, but I didn't want to hear it.

"I don't know what you mean."

"We want to know who's done it. Was it you?"

"It wasn't me. I don't know what's going on."

"You *must* give us a chance. Look, just to show you how much we want to help you: You tell me your mother's and father's names, and we will write to them and let them know you're all right. You write them a letter and put the address on, and we'll post it."

It was something straight out of training. You are taught never to sign anything. This goes back to Vietnam days where people signed pieces of paper in all innocence, and the next thing they knew there was a statement in the international press saying that they'd slain a village full of children.

I knew it was bollocks. There was no way they'd actually send a letter to Peckham. It was fantasy land, but I couldn't just come out with Fuck you, big nose. I had to get round this somehow.

"My father died years ago," I said. "My mother went away with an American who was working in London. She's somewhere in America now. I haven't got any parents; it's one of the reasons I'm in the army. I've got no other immediate family."

"Where did he work in London, this American?"

"Wimbledon."

Another classic. They were trying to get me to open up my heart, and everything would come rolling out. I'd been put through all this before in E&E and capture exercises.

"What did he do?"

"I don't know, I didn't live at home then. I had big family problems."

"Do you have any brothers or sisters?"

"No."

I wanted to base my lies on the truth. If it's something that you know and it's the truth, you stand a better chance of remembering it. And they might run a check and be able to confirm that what you're saying is true and not go any further into it. I had in my mind a friend who had been in that sort of family situation. His father died when he was 13. His mother met an American, wanted nothing more to do with the son, and buggered off to the States. As far as I was concerned, it sounded quite convincing.

I took my time. My speech was slurred, I was still dribbling, I couldn't talk properly.

"Are you in pain, Andy? Help us and everything will be fine. We'll get you medical attention. Carry on, tell us more."

"I don't know any more."

Then another classic. He must have been working his way through the manual.

"Sign this piece of paper, Andy. All we want to do is prove to your family that you're still alive. We will make attempts to find your mother in America. We have contacts there. All we need is your signature so she knows you're Okay. And we can actually prove to the Red Cross that you're still alive, you're not dead in the desert, and the animals aren't eating you. Think of it, Andy. If we get you to sign your name and go to the Red Cross, we're not going to kill you."

I couldn't believe anybody would actually come out with such a comical ploy. I tried to be noncommittal. "I don't know any addresses, I haven't got any family life."

You could give a fictitious address, or you could give a real address in case they checked up. But Mrs. Mills of 8 Acacia Avenue might open her door one morning and get blown away. You never know how far this sort of thing will go.

"Andy, why do you keep on obstructing us? Why are you doing this to yourself? These people, my superiors, they won't let me help you unless you tell them what they need to know. I'm afraid I can't help you any more, Andy. If you don't help me, I can't help you."

He just walked away. I didn't know what to expect now.

I had my head down, and I could hear them coming up. I clenched my jaw and waited for it. This time there were no rifles, just several quite severe smacks around the face. Every time they hit near the broken teeth I screamed.

I shouldn't have done that.

They pulled my head up by the hair to get a better aim. Then they slapped several more times over the site.

The slaps became punches that knocked me off the chair, but it wasn't very exciting compared with the last beating. Probably they thought they'd now cracked it and I just needed a bit more encouragement. It lasted less than a minute.

Back on the chair, I was breathing heavily, blood trickling down my front.

"Look, Andy, we're trying to help you. Do you want to help us?"

"Yes, I do, but I don't know anything, I'm helping you as much as I can."

"Where are your mother and father?"

I went through the same story.

"But why don't you know where your mother is in America?"

"I don't know because I have nothing to do with her. She didn't want me. So she went to America and I joined the army."

"When did you join the army?"

"When I was sixteen."

"Why did you join?"

"I've always wanted to help people, that's why I'm a medic. I don't want to fight. I've always been against fighting."

This business about family was a red herring. I didn't know if it was just a matter of pride that he wanted to crack it.

"Andy, look, obviously this way is not working."

The filling in started again.

Your body adapts and it passes out quicker. Your mind is working in two ways. One half is telling you you're out of it, and the other half really is out of it. It's like lying on your bed when you're pissed—your mind is spinning and a little voice is saying: Never again. This time I was totally out of the game. It was a good kicking. I wasn't exaggerating anything after this one. I was incoherent. I flaked out, and when I came to I was still incoherent.

What woke me up was a boy stubbing his cigarette out on my neck.

I was in blackness, blindfolded and handcuffed, lying face down on grass. I had an excruciating headache. My ears tingled and burned.

I felt sunlight on bits of my face. I sensed the brightness of it. My mind was a blur, but I worked out that at some stage I must have been dragged from the room and trussed up outside. I wanted to rest my head, but I couldn't lie on one side because of the swelling, and I couldn't rest on the other because of the cuts.

I heard Dinger's voice just behind me. They were stubbing cigarettes out on him as well. It was good to hear him, even though he was moaning and groaning. I couldn't see him or touch him because I was facing the other way, but I knew he was there. I felt a bit safer.

There must have been three or four guards using us as ashtrays. They'd had a bad time with us over the last few days, and they were obviously enjoying getting their own back.

Other squaddies came around to see the sideshow and get in a poke and a kick. They gobbed on us and laughed. One put a lit cigarette behind my ear and left it there to burn down. His mates loved that one.

Even though I was blindfolded, I kept looking down, trying to look scared. I wanted to see Dinger. I needed the physical contact with him, I needed to feel near him. I wanted some form of attachment.

I was writhing face down as the cigarette burned behind my ear and managed to wiggle the blindfold down my nose. I could see daylight at last. You have a horrible sense of insecurity when you're blindfolded because you're so vulnerable.

If this is my last hour, I said to myself, let's see as much as we can. It was a lovely clear sky. We were under a small fruit tree with a little bird in it. It started singing. The odd vehicle would start up about 60 feet away, there was talking, it was all rather sedate and nice. On the other side of the wall there was the hustle and bustle of the town, the hooting and revving of vehicles and general shouting. I heard the main gate open and close about 150 feet away, vehicles drive out and fade away. It felt as cozy and safe as being in a walled garden in a different century.

I thought: I've seen and I've done as much as I can. If it's going to happen, let's do it now. I didn't have much thought about Jilly or Kate. I'd gone through all that in the culvert, thinking there wasn't much I could do about it, this was not the time to worry about them. I'd done the best I could to look after them financially. I'd got the letters sorted out, and at the end of the day they knew that I loved them, and I knew that they loved me. There were no big problems; they'd be told I was dead and that would be that.

There were other things I wanted to concentrate on now. In *Breaker Morant*, the film about the Boer War, as the characters walked to the spot where they were going to get executed, they reached out and held hands. I didn't know whether I wanted to physically grab hold of Dinger or whether I wanted to say something. I just wanted some sort of connection with him for my last moment.

More squaddies came round, kicking and poking. They looked down at these two pathetic messes on the ground, and they gobbed and took the piss, giggling like a bunch of kids, which some of them probably were. But none of it seemed as bad as before. Either the novelty was wearing off for them or I was just getting used to it. I just kept my head down and clenched my teeth. Both of us moaned and groaned with each kick because it hurt—but it was not so much the power of the kick as the effect it had on the aches and pains from before. They denounced Mitterrand and Bush, and when they saw my blindfold was down, they did cutthroat signs and waved their pistols and mimed *bang-bang*. I could have taken it if it was

part of a master plan, but these wankers were just doing it for their own enjoyment.

Vehicles started up, and the drivers revved the engines. There was a lot of shouting and barking of orders from the buildings behind us, and that got me
flapping. It was a horrible sinking feeling: Here we go
again, I thought, why not another hour here? It's all
rather nice in the sun; we've had such a good period of
sedation.

I hoped the noise came from officers and it didn't
just mean that the jundies were getting all sparked up
again. You felt there was some purpose with the officers; you could converse with them quite well. With
the squaddies it was just boots and fists.

Vehicle doors were slamming. There was a general
hum of activity. Something was definitely about to
happen. I braced myself, because it was going to happen whether I liked it or not.

I didn't know what I was going to shout to Dinger.
"God Save the Queen!" maybe. But then again, probably not.

Somebody untied my feet, but the blindfold and
handcuffs stayed in place. Hands on either side
grabbed me roughly and hauled me upright. My body
had started to seize up after the long rest. Bruises
throbbed. Cuts which had clotted were reopened as I
was pushed and shoved. My feet wouldn't carry me
and I had to be dragged.

I was thrown onto the back of an open pickup and
man handled to the front. They bent me over the cab, a
jundie either side of me; I assumed I was being taken
away to be shot. Was this the last time I was ever going to see or hear anything? My great game plan to say
something to Dinger had gone to rat shit, and I was
annoyed with myself.

They took my blindfold off, and I blinked in the
harsh sunlight. There was nothing in front of us. They

wouldn't let me turn around, so I couldn't tell if Dinger was behind. The jundies were banging on the roof; the driver and passenger had their arms out, and they were slapping the metal as well. There were happy noises everywhere.

One of the ruperts came up and said, "We are now going to show our people."

I was still trying to adjust my eyes, totally bemused by the noise and the sun. We seemed to be part of a convoy of five or six brand-new Toyota pickups and Land Cruisers. Some still had the plastic over the seats. They were covered with desert dust, however, and they'd had to scrape it off the rear windscreen of the cab beneath me so the driver could see out.

They opened up the large double gates for the vehicles to come out of the camp, and we were greeted by the surging roar of a crowd, as if two Cup Final sides were emerging from the tunnel at Wembley. There was a solid mass of people ahead of us—women with sticks, men with guns or stones, all dressed in their dish-dashes and waving pictures of Saddam Hussein in their hands. Some were jumping up and down with joy; others were ranting rhetoric, pointing and throwing stones. The jundies tried to stop them because they were getting hit as well.

And this was just as we drove out of the gate. I thought: That's it, we're off to be shot without a doubt. We'll have a quick drive around town, they'll make a video, and then they'll do the business.

We turned right onto the main boulevard, and the crowd surged around us. We had to stop almost immediately, as the jundies tried to push people off and the driver jammed his hand hard on the horn. We inched forward, trying to pave a way through the mob. They chanted "Down with Boosh! Down with Boosh!" and I just stood there like the president at the head of a cavalcade.

The squaddies were chuffed as hell. Everybody was

firing into the air. Even kids of ten were letting rip with AKs. All I could think was: One of these rounds is going to hit me. It was such a lovely hot day as well.

I got twatted now and again by a stick or stone. The jundies either side of me were jumping up and down with excitement. I only had socks on my feet, and they landed on them with their boots. I felt weak and wanted to lean against the cab, but they pulled my head back to make sure everybody could see me.

Dinger came up on the right-hand side. He, too, was riding a Toyota pickup. As he drew level, we got some eye-to-eye and managed to swap a smile. It was the best thing that had happened all day. Dinger was looking how I felt. He was the bog monster at the best of times, but I looked at him and thought: Fucking hell, I didn't know he could get even uglier than he was. It was the happiest time since the capture, without a doubt. The wink and the small smile, that was all I needed. I drew immense strength from that one small gesture. It was a matter of personal credibility. If he could get through this and grin about it, I thought, fuck it, so can I. I felt incredible affection for him, and I hoped that he did for me. This, as far as I knew, was my last look at a mate.

We trundled along on our carnival floats, driving down the main boulevard of the town. The crowd chanted and shook their fists. The noise was incredible. They didn't even know who or what we were. We could have been spacemen for all they knew, but whatever, we were the bad guys.

Some of the squaddies were chanting with them. Others were running around trying to control the crowd. All of them were trying to avoid the stones and sticks that were meant for us. There were bursts of fire going off all over the place, the jundies with us firing in the air as well.

"Down with Boosh! Boosh!"

People were diving in and out of the little Arab

shopfronts with their concertina railings. "Thou shalt not steal," the Koran proclaims, but everywhere you go in the Middle East the shops have these railings as security against thieving fellow Muslims. Everybody had pictures of Saddam and was pointing at his face and kissing it and shouting up to Allah.

We would move at walking pace, then stop for a bit to move the crowd. My legs couldn't hold me up. I looked over at Dinger, and he was grinning from ear to ear. I wondered what on earth he was laughing at; I thought he'd gone demented. Then I realized: He was taking the piss out of them! I thought, Blow this, we're on our way to die here, so who gives a monkey's? I started myself. Fuck 'em! Suddenly all that mattered to me was not looking a bag of shit. You've got to make sure you look good. I got some eye-to-eye going with the crowd and smiled away. One of the guards spotted me and got the chance to look a right hard man, landing a slap and a punch. I looked at Dinger, and we grinned at them like Leslie Grantham opening a supermarket. If our hands hadn't been tied, we'd have been doing the royal wave.

It really sparked them up, the grinning. Some took it well, most of them didn't. They were going crazy. It was the wrong thing to do and totally counterproductive, but it had to be done. The guards gave us a slap to get us all subdued again because it made them look good. But what the hell, I felt better. A large white American sedan came through on the left-hand side. Two ruperts in it looked up, pointed, and laughed. They were in a good mood about it anyway. I gave them my big presidential smile in return. They loved it, but that gave the jundies the hump and they had another go at us.

We paid the price for all the piss-taking when we got to the other end of the town. Crowds of people were waiting for us, trying to break through the cordon, arguing with the squaddies because they wanted to have a go at us. They were jumping up and down, and it was obvious it was only a matter of time before the cordon was either broken or deliberately removed. My only worry was the thought of me getting shot and not Dinger.

I was dragged off the vehicle. I searched desperately for Dinger. I needed him. He was my only link with reality.

Then I saw that the same was happening to him and I thought: It's going to happen round here somewhere.

I was not too worried about the actual dying bit. Never had been; just as long as it was as quick and clean as Mark's.

Would Jilly ever know? Did she even know I was missing? Everything materialistic was squared away; there was nothing else I could have done for her. But it was the emotional thing: it would have been lovely to have the chance to say my farewells.

What a way to go.

Fuck it! Fuck it! Fuck it!

The stench of the town was overpowering. They were primitive, caveman smells of cooking, old embers, and stale piss, mixed with rotting garbage and diesel exhaust.

The town was an odd mixture of the medieval and the modern. The main boulevard was freshly tarmacked; the rest was dust and sand. There were Land Cruisers straight from the showroom and jundies with shiny boots and clean, western-type uniforms, and the crowd in their stinking dish-dashes and flip-flops or plain bare feet. I was knocked to the ground at one point, and right next to my eye was a big toe splayed out like a split sausage, grimed with a lifetime of dirt. There were immaculately groomed officers and healthy-looking young soldiers, and the locals with just three teeth between them and even those were black and decayed, and Negro Arabs with scarred faces and white, scabby knees and elbows from lack of washing and moisturizing, and dusty, matted rasta hair.

The buildings were of mud and stone, square with flat roofs. They must have been a couple of hundred years old, and on their sides were the latest posters for Pepsi Cola. Old, skinny, mangy dogs skulked in the shadows, scavenging and pissing. Rusty tin cans lay in piles everywhere.

Running down the middle of the boulevard was a central reservation, and in the middle of it, just opposite us, was a children's playground, full of tubular steel frames and swings in old faded blues and yellows. It was the sort of thing you'd find on a normal housing estate in Britain, but it looked so out of place and weird in this kind of world. They'd been fighting a war for years, and there was poverty, shit, and grind all around us. Fuck knows what the Arabic for "Tidworth" is but this was it—an old shit-arse tip of a place.

We were standing at the roadside awaiting death. The jundies grabbed us, but my legs had given up and I stumbled. They had to drag me towards my public. They showed us off like hunting trophies, pushing our heads up, making sure everybody got a good look.

I wasn't smiling this time. I was looking out for Dinger; I was scared of losing him in the crowd. I just wanted to keep by him. I could hear him yelling and shouting as much as I was, and from time to time I caught glimpses of him. It was a bad time.

The mob ruled. I had been right cocky when we got dragged off the vehicle, but now I was plain scared. They were all warbling the Red Indian war cry. Were we going to be left to the crowd? Were they going to rip us apart? Old women came up and pulled my hair and mustache and hit me with sticks or punched. The men would start by poking, then end up punching and thumping. I fell to the ground, and all the bodies closed in. They thrust pictures of Saddam in front of my face and made me kiss him.

I doubted whether some of these people even knew there was a war on. As for the women, repressed by centuries of culture and religion, this was probably the one and only chance they'd ever have to strike a grown man.

As time wore on, I started to think that perhaps they were not going to shoot us after all. Surely they would have done it by now? Maybe there was some system for dealing with prisoners. Certainly the jundies were controlling the crowds as much as they could. They obviously didn't want the local population to kill us, because I noticed that they were fending off any men they saw with rifles and pistols. Perhaps the parade was just a PR exercise, a morale booster for the locals and a chance for them to vent their frustrations.

Women were scratching and tearing at my skin. I had grease and old bits of food shoved in my face and pisspots emptied over the gashes in my head. Old newsreels of Vietnam flashed through my mind. I remembered images of pilots who looked beaten and pissed off getting dragged through towns they'd just bombed. It was exactly how I felt.

All I wanted was contact with Dinger—preferably verbal. I could hear him shouting as he was being filled in, but I hated not being able to see him. He was my only link to the world. I didn't want to lose him.

I couldn't move any more. I fell onto one of the squaddies and put my arms around him. The other lad came and helped him lift me. As they dragged me along the ground, the tops of my toes were scraped away. We had to stop now and again for a 60-year-old to come and punch me in the stomach. I was well and truly gone. I didn't really care about anything any more.

I didn't know how long it lasted, but it seemed like a lifetime. There was gunfire in the distance, and officers came running to try and control the soldiers, who in turn were trying to control the crowd. It was so ironic to be protected by the same jundies who an hour ago had been stubbing out their cigarettes on our necks. Then they were the bastards; now they were the saviors.

I heard Dinger retaliating. I knew we should be trying to play the useless being that's not even worth worrying about. But we were tuned in to this drama now; we had got used to it, and it was getting on our tits. The time had come to do something about it.

I gave the old girls the evil eye, and they waded in. I went down on the floor under a flurry of slaps and scratching, and two soldiers moved in to pick me up. Still on my knees, I looked up at one of them and said, "Fuck you, you ugly bitch!" They understood what I meant; the translation was in my eyes. It was not a good move. The jundies picked me up. I shoved them off and said "Fuck you!" again. I didn't give a shit now what they did; I was demolished anyway. But they'd suffered loss of face, so they had to give me the good news to restore their credibility.

I remembered a lecture we'd had from an American POW just before we left Hereford. He had been an aviator at the time of the Vietnam War, after transferring from the Marine Corps. His Marine training had been that the harder you are and the more aggressive you are if you're captured, the sooner your captors will leave you alone. He stood there in front of us hardened cynics at Hereford, crying his eyes out as he told us about the five years he had been a prisoner of the Viet Cong.

"What a load of shit," he said. "The unbelievable nightmares and pain I went through because I really believed what I'd been taught."

And I was doing exactly what he'd told us not to do. But you can't just do nothing. Pride and credibility are at stake. I was suffering a massive loss of dignity and self-respect, and I couldn't take any more. I knew it was totally counterproductive, I knew it wouldn't pay off, but God it felt good. For one split second I was back on top, and that was all that mattered. I was not a commodity, I was not a bag of shit, I was Andy Mc-Nab.

The squaddies were giggling as we drove back to camp. They'd had a wonderful day out and were happy to leave me to my own devices on my hands and knees in a corner of the pickup, bleeding and gasping for breath as they smoked and laughed and relived the battle. I was rather pleased that it was over and done with and I hadn't been shot.

It was more or less last light when we got back inside the gates, and they didn't bother replacing the blindfold as they dragged me towards the single-story barrack block.

There were five beds around the edge of the room. The blokes didn't seem to have lockers or any personal kit. All they had were the beds, with blankets on top—commercial, fluffy blankets with pictures of tigers and weird and wonderful patterns. On top of the blankets was their belt kit. Everything pointed to this being a transit camp rather than a permanent barracks.

The only light was from a paraffin heater in the center of the room. As it flickered, shadows flew around the room. It was beautifully warm—the sort of warmth that immediately makes you tired and sleepy. It was a warmth that I recognized. Even the shadows were familiar. A nice, comfortable, secure feeling washed over me. I was back at my Aunty Nell's in Catford. I loved going there as a kid. She had a big three-bedroomed semi that she ran as a B&B. Compared with my family's flat, to me it was a hotel. At night Aunty Nell would put the paraffin heater in my room to warm it through. I'd lie there in bed, nine years old and blissfully happy, watching the shadows dance on the wallpaper, looking forward to the next day's meals. Aunty Nell used milk with the cereals instead of the hot water and a dash of Carnation I was used to, and she cooked packets of Vesta curry for her B&B guests. If my uncle reported that I had been a good boy, I used to be fed one as well.

The old boy, George, was a keen gardener. He had a massive garden with a shed at the bottom where I'd play. He was a crafty old bugger. He'd say to me: "Start digging around here, Andy lad, and you can count how many worms there are. We need to know how many worms there are so we can work out how good the mud is."

I'd be digging away, a boy with a mission, and he'd be sitting there drinking tea in his deckchair, laughing his head off. I never saw through it. I used to think it was great, counting the worms for my Uncle George.

I was left alone with my thoughts for twenty minutes or so, one hand cuffed to a metal fixture on the wall. I tried to get comfortable, but the cuffs worked on a ratchet—if you moved the wrong way they would tighten up even more. I got into a semilying position, the hand defying gravity at an angle of 45 degrees.

I carried out a damage assessment. My whole body was aching, and I was worried I might have broken bones. My legs were the main concern. They were hurting badly, and I knew they couldn't carry me any more. I checked the bones one by one, starting off with my feet, looking for deformities, making sure there was movement. Everything seemed Okay. There was a good chance nothing was broken.

I was breathing through crusted blood and dust and snot, and every time I blew to clear it the bleeding started again. I was badly cut. My face was swollen, my lips split, and every exposed area of skin was lacerated. Now that I actually had time to draw breath and think about it, my whole body was starting to

sting. The scrapes were far more painful than the cuts.
The framework, however, was still intact. The injuries
were just muscular with cuts and bruises. I was weak
and exhausted, but I'd still get up and run for it if the
chance came.

I had been trying to gather as much information as I
could to keep myself orientated. I went over what I'd
seen and exactly where I was. I was annoyed that I
hadn't done a better job of it. I had been looking down
too much when I should have been taking it all in. If I
escaped and got past the gate, which way would I go?
Would I turn left or right, or go straight? Which way
was west? If I got out the back way, what then? How
far inside the town was the camp? I'd need to get out
of the built-up area as soon as possible. It was something I should have been checking as we drove out,
but like a dickhead I'd let myself be distracted by the
crowd. I was quite pissed off with myself for my lack
of professionalism.

I went through the scenarios. The process was part
fact and part fantasy. Fact because I was doing what
you're supposed to do—appreciations on how you're
going to get out. Fantasy because I was imagining me

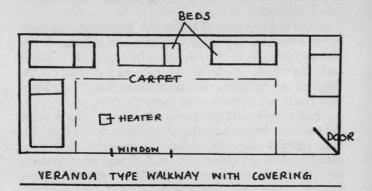

Barrack room at Commando center

actually getting out and turning right, imagining what I would see and what would be behind me. I wanted to escape.

I looked around the room. Above me was a window. Only one of the sections was clear; the rest were boarded up where they had been smashed, or perhaps to stop the sun coming in. I could hear the soldiers mooching around outside, and in the middle distance there was shouting. The voices just outside the window were low and quiet, a mumble from no more than 20 or 30 feet away, and underneath the veranda, as if they'd been told to stand there and talk to make me flap.

I hoped Dinger was getting the same treatment as me because it was all rather nice sitting there on the carpet. It felt wonderful to be on my own. I felt quite happy and content in the dark, watching the warm glow of the paraffin heater and inhaling the familiar fumes. There were no hassles, just me on my lonesome with my hand pinned to the wall. It was real prime time.

I started to think about the patrol. Had the others been caught? Were they dead? Did Dinger know anything about them? Was I going to get the chance to speak to him?

I tried to keep as still as I could. My heart was pulsing slowly, and my body was stiff and aching. It was painful to move, and I wanted to find a comfy position and stay there. Some of the cuts had clotted to the fabric of my uniform; as I moved they reopened. Blood had glued my socks to my feet.

I must have looked like a vagrant. It was a week now since I had washed and my skin was black. My hair, matted from the drama of the E&E, was now caked with dried blood and mud. It was hard to make out the camouflage on my DPM because of blood, grease, and grime. My trousers looked like a biker's jeans.

Why had we been taken back to the camp? I didn't have a clue. This was obviously still the tactical questioning phase. I was waiting for something or someone. I took a deep breath, breathed out, and started to think about methods of escape. I suddenly remembered that I still had my escape map and compass. I could actually feel them in the drawcord of my trousers. I felt really good about that: at least I'd got something, I had the mental edge over them.

I thought about all the good stuff I'd done with Jilly, all the stupid holidays we'd had together, all the ice creams I had squashed in her face. Things came into my mind that had made me giggle with her, all the silly immature little things. I tried to visualize what she'd be doing right now. I had a pleasant picture in my mind of a Saturday two weeks before I left for the Gulf. Kate was staying with us as usual that weekend, and she was lying on the floor with me watching *Robin Hood* on video. Little John was doing his dance, and I got up and did it with her. We danced and danced around the room, trying to do high kicks, until we collapsed on the carpet, dizzy and laughing.

I thought back to the time of her very first Christmas. I hadn't seen much of her because I was away when she was born in February and didn't get back until she was six weeks old. Then I saw only the next three months of her, on and off. That Christmas I was free, and we were staying at a friend's house on the south coast. Kate wasn't sleeping very well, which I thought was great because it was the first time we'd had together alone. I got the pram out at midnight, wrapped her up well, and we went walking along the coastal path until six in the morning. She fell asleep after the first half an hour, and as I walked I just looked at her beautiful little face and clucked like a hen. When we got back, she woke up again so I put her in the car and we went for a drive. I kept checking over my shoulder to see that she was all right. She had fearsome big blue eyes that stared at me from inside all the wrappings of woolens and a bobble hat. It was a very special time. Soon afterwards I had to go away again, and in the next two years I only saw her for a total of twelve weeks.

There were noises outside. My little dreamworld was about to be invaded. I was flapping. Were they coming to give me another beasting? After the calm, it was a horrible, apprehensive feeling, a fierce dread of a world about to collapse. I put my head down and clenched the stiff, sore muscles. Shit, I thought, they've had their tuppence worth, why can't they just leave me alone?

There was a draft as the door opened. I glanced up and saw a character in the middle of the room. He was in his mid-50s and only about 5'3" tall, with a big middle-age paunch beneath his woollen dish-dash. His mustache was well trimmed, and his jet-black hair was swept back. He had manicured hands, and his teeth flashed when they caught the light. He was ranting and raving at me in Arabic. The two guards who had come in with him went and sat on one of the beds, smoking and chatting, but keeping a watchful eye.

There was a pistol in the character's belt, which I didn't take much notice of to start with because every man and his dog was armed. He stood over the paraffin heater, hollering and gesticulating. With the glow of the heater beneath him his face looked like a Hallowe'en monster with treble chins.

He came over to me and got hold of my face. He squeezed my jaw in his hand. The smashed teeth were agony. I groaned and closed my eyes. I didn't want to know what was going on. He stayed close to me. I smelt spicy food on his breath. He prized my eyes open with his thumb and forefinger. What the fuck was he going to do?

He had an exchange with the guards, very fast and

aggressive, then slapped my face a few times. I had no idea what he was on about. Then he walked backwards away from me and pulled out a Makharov pistol. This is all rather nice, I thought, what's the story here then? He pointed it at me but he didn't cock it.

Was this bluff kit or what?

The hammer of the Russian-made pistol stays to the rear when you cock it—i.e., put a round into the chamber. If you pull the trigger, it will fire and reload itself again with the hammer still to the rear. If you don't want to fire, you put the safety catch to safe. The hammer will still go forward but is stopped just short of the firing pin by the sears that come out because you have moved the safety catch. This is unlike some semiautomatic pistols. They still have a safety catch, but the hammer will stay to the rear when it's applied.

I was looking in earnest to see if the hammer was back. If it was, I knew that he wasn't bluffing, and that if he was nervous, he might have a negligent discharge and shoot me anyway. I looked at his face. His expression was very serious, and the eyes were welling up. I could see the shine of the tears. Our eyes met. He started to cry, and the pistol wobbled in his hand.

Surely the guards wouldn't let him do it in their nice clean barrack room? But his eyes gave it away. He intended to pull the trigger, without a doubt. It didn't look official. This was off the cuff. But the bloke had got the hump, so even if it was unofficial, so what? He'd do it anyway. I might get slotted here through emotion rather than a decision made, and I found that scary. The character really looked as if he might squeeze the trigger, and there wasn't a thing I could do about it.

Come on then, arsehole, let's get it over and done with.

The guards seemed to wake up to what was happening. They jumped to their feet, shouting angrily, and grabbed his arm. They took away the pistol.

That single act gave me the biggest piece of information I had received since my capture: either these characters simply didn't want to get their barrack block messed up, or, more likely, they were under orders to keep us alive.

One of the guards came over and squeezed my cheeks. "Son, son," he said. "Boom boom boom."

One of us had killed the man's son. Fair one. In his shoes I'd be doing the same. Unfortunately it was me that he was doing it to.

I was sitting cross-legged on the floor with one of my arms up in the air, handcuffed to the wall. He came over and started to try and fill me in. I put my head down and brought my knees up, crouching forward to protect my bollocks. I got as close to the wall as I could. Only my arm was vulnerable now. It was funny, he had been willing to kill me with the weapon, but he found it quite hard to lay hands on me. He was kicking, but it wasn't much good because he had leather sandals on. He'd throw a punch, but it had no weight behind it. He was clearly upset, but really he didn't have it in him to do anything severe. He lacked aggression and strength, and I was delighted.

I was exaggerating, moaning and groaning as he kneed me in the back and slapped and spat. If it was my son who had been killed, and I was in the same room as the perpetrator, he'd have been honking good style by now. In a way I felt quite sorry for him, because his son was dead and he was too nice and gentle a man to do anything about it. Maybe, after all, he couldn't have pulled the trigger.

The squaddies started to get bored—and perhaps a bit worried that they might have to clean blood off the floor and walls. They calmed him down and led him away. When they returned, they sat on the beds again and smoked more cigarettes.

"Boosh, bad, bad," one of them said.

"Yeah, Bush, bad," I nodded and agreed.

"Major," he said, and did an oinking noise.

"Yep, Major's a pig," I said, and oinked.

They thought this was great stuff.

"You," he pointed at me and brayed loudly.

"Me, donkey. *Ee-aw!*"

They held their sides and fell over on the beds. They rolled up.

They came over and poked me. I didn't really know what they wanted from me, so I just did another loud bray. They loved it. I didn't give a shit if they wanted to have fun at my expense. It didn't mean a thing to me. I thought it was just as funny. I wasn't getting filled in, that was all that mattered. It was absolutely splendid.

This went on for about a quarter of an hour. There'd be a couple of minutes' silence, then somebody would get up and poke me again, I'd give them a good *ee-aw*, and they'd crack up. What a bunch of tossers.

I thought I'd try to have my handcuffs sorted out while they were in such a good mood. I was at a 45-degree angle, and my hand was elevated. Gravity was pulling my hand onto the handcuff, and it was swelling up badly. It was agony. I wondered if they'd strap me onto something lower down, like a pipe.

I pointed at my hand and said, "Hurts. Please. Pain. Aaah."

They looked at me and poked, and got another donkey bray. They had another roll-up, and I tried to indicate that my hand was agony. It didn't work. They just laughed. Then they suddenly got all serious. They must have thought that it was time to assert some authority. So they started to carry out their own questioning, as if I was supposed to think they weren't just guards, they were big-time interrogators.

"Who? Who?"

It was hard to make out what they were saying.

"What? I don't understand."

I kept pointing at my wrist, but to no avail. They

asked more questions, their Hallowe'en faces lit from below by the heater, but I couldn't understand them.

One of them went and fetched another guard. He could speak fair English. They'd obviously told him that I couldn't understand what they were on about.

"What's your name?"

"Andy."

"Commando, Andy? Tel Aviv?"

"British."

"British. Gascoigne? Rush? Football?" He beamed big smiles and scored an imaginary goal with his right foot.

Everybody's face lit up, mine included—even though football did nothing for me. When I was a kid, Millwall was the local team, but I only went to see them three or four times. I stood there like a dickhead on the terraces and wondered what all the fuss was about. I couldn't see a thing because I was too small, and all I knew was that it had cost loads of money to get in. I went on a Wednesday night once and left halfway through because it was so cold. That was the extent of my football knowledge, and that was all football did for me—it reminded me of wet, cold, windy terraces. I had no interest in it whatsoever, yet here I was, a prisoner of soccer-mad Iraqis, and it might be my lifeline.

"Liverpool!" he said.

"Chelsea!" I said.

"Manchester United!"

"Nottingham Forest!"

They laughed and I joined in, trying to form some sort of bond. This was good, textbook stuff, but I couldn't sustain it for much longer. My knowledge was just about exhausted.

"How long am I here?" I tried. "Do you know how long I'll be here? Can you give me any food?"

"No problems. Bobby Moore!"

I thought I'd try another ploy.

"Mai? Mai?" I asked for water. I coughed dryly and gave it the old puppy dog look.

A bloke went out and came back with a glass of water. I gulped it down and asked for more. That cheesed them off so I just thanked them again and decided to keep quiet for a while.

They were all in their late teens, growing their first wispy mustaches. They behaved like young squaddies in any army, but what surprised me about them was the standard of maintenance of their uniforms and weapons. I had imagined the ragheads to be a bit of an undisciplined rabble, their kit dirty and shabby. But their uniforms were well laundered and pressed, and their boots were highly polished. Their weapons were in excellent order and well maintained. The buildings, too, were in a good state of repair, and spotlessly tidy. This was good; I felt that in their discipline lay some sort of protection for me. They were unlikely to do anything unless they were told to do it. It made me feel a bit happier that they weren't just a bunch of headbangers, rushing around wanting to kill and maim. Somebody, somewhere, made them clean their weapons; somebody, somewhere, made them clean their boots and their rooms.

What was more, there were obviously ways of striking up a relationship with these people, a fact which might help me at a later date. It was not just black and white in their eyes, as I was expecting it to be, with me the bad guy, them the good guys. There was this gray area of shared interest that we had already started to explore. So far, we had something in common in football. We were all talking and replying; it wasn't just me on the receiving end of rhetoric, abuse, and tactical questions. Relationships, however tenuous, can almost always be formed, and in the situation I was in this could only be good. I had engineered getting the water, and in that exchange I was doing the controlling. Well, there was no harm being optimistic.

It went through my mind that maybe they were being friendly because it was all over now and the questioning was finished with. I was trying to think of all the optimistic things, but really you should be thinking of the pessimistic things, the worst-case scenarios, because then anything else is a bonus. At the end of the day they were just young lads. Dinger and I were the new kids in town, the commodities they wanted to have a look at, the new toys, the white-eyed prisoners. They'd probably looked on Dinger and me with a bit of awe, something to tell the grandchildren about. And now they'd seen us, spoken to us, taken the piss out of us, they were bored. They started to look tired, probably from the warmth of the heater and the excitement of the day. They tucked their weapons under their beds and got their heads down.

My mind turned again to thoughts of escape. I couldn't get out of the handcuffs, and even if I could what was I going to do? Was I going to garofe them all and run away? Things like that just do not happen. It's a fantasy that comes out of films. Are you going to kill number one without number five hearing?

My hand was fixed to the wall. I wasn't going anywhere. There was nothing I could reach from where I was. I would have to wait for the next stage of transit or some other opportunity.

I was feeling a lot more at ease with my situation. I'd been caught, I'd gone through the initial drama, and now I was sitting in a warm room with people who weren't kicking the shit out of me. I wasn't going to be there for ever, but apart from the pain in my wrist, it was nice and relaxed. The people here didn't want to fill me in; they just wanted to talk about Gazza and Bobby Charlton. I had the hopeful thought—and even as I thought it I knew it was fruitless—that maybe this was the way ahead: that they were fed up with me and maybe I'd just be chucked in as one of Saddam's human shields.

* * *

As the night wore on, my arm and hand started to hurt quite badly. I tried to keep my mind off the pain by going through the escape scenarios again, doing my appreciations.

Out of the top of the window I could catch a little bit of the stars. It was a beautiful, clear night. I looked back at the sleeping jundies.

If I managed to get away, could I get to Dinger? Where was he? I was assuming that he was on the camp somewhere, but was he next door? I couldn't hear anything. Was he along the veranda? I came to the conclusion that I'd have to grab the opportunity if it came, but I couldn't leave without making the effort to get hold of him. I knew that he'd be thinking exactly the same, as any member of the patrol would. Was it worth waiting until we were together? No, I'd grab any opportunity that came along. So—what was the first thing I was going to do? How was I going to find out where he was? Was I going to look through the windows for him or was I going to shout? Would his guards be awake?

You've got to have a game plan and contingency plans. Hesitation is fatal. I would avoid being overt if possible—that's just another bit of madness from Hollywood. In the films they come at you one at a time so you can slot them neatly like ducks at a funfair. In real life everybody jumps in together and they kick you to pieces. It would have to be as covert as I could make it: just get out, get some firepower, get Dinger, get a vehicle. Easy! All that in an enclosed camp with troops, and me with maybe a 30-round magazine.

Once we were out we would just have to move west. On foot or in a vehicle? Crosscountry or through the town? The drive from the culvert to the camp had been very short: we were still close to Syria. Our next transit was bound to take us into more secure areas, further from the border.

I dozed off and woke in pain. My head was hurting, my body ached. I had to sort out the blood and snot in my nose.

I heard hooting in the distance and the sound of vehicles. The big corrugated iron gates were being kicked open. It was still dark. People were walking along the veranda outside, guided by Tilly lamps. They were talking. I felt a stab of apprehension. What was happening now? I took a deep breath and tried to calm myself down. One of the guards woke up and gave the other two a kick. They got to their feet.

The five or six blokes who came into the room were strangers. I felt helpless, that little kid feeling you get when you know you're cornered by the rival gang. They towered above me in the shadows and flickers.

When my hand was released from the wall it was well past the pins and needles stage. It was swollen and completely numb. Two blokes held me either side and lifted me up. Somebody handed me my boots, but my feet were too swollen to put them on. I carried them the way an old granny carries her handbag, clenched to my chest. I wanted to keep them; I didn't want to spend the rest of my days without any footwear.

As they frog-marched me outside I played on the pain, moaning and groaning. I must have looked a right dickhead. The blokes did lots of mock "tut-tut-tuts." One pulled a face of feigned concern and said, "We're really worried about you."

The cold air hit me. It was a refreshing, bracing feeling, but I would have preferred to be back in Aunty's nice warm room. I started to shiver. It was a beautifully clear night. If we managed to get away, we'd be able to navigate westwards very easily.

Nobody said where we were going. They dragged me along, and I had to take silly little steps because my feet weren't carrying me properly. We stopped by

a Land Cruiser, and they shoved me into the back with
my boots on my lap. They squeezed the ratchets of my
handcuffs and tied a blindfold painfully tight.

I tried to lean forward to rest my head on the seat in
front to relieve the pressure on my hands, but a hand
on my face pushed me back upright. The interior light
shone through the blindfold. I could tell there were
two in the front. The door slammed noisily and made
me jump. I clenched my teeth, ready for a twat around
the head.

I was sitting on the right. There was the sound of
shuffling to my left, then I heard: "All right, mate, all
right, mate."

Dinger was honking as he hit his head on the way
in. This was really excellent news. I instantly felt
happy, that wonderful feeling again of being in it together.

He was positioned with his knees pressing against
mine.

"Can you help my hands?" I asked into the darkness.

I got hit around the back of the head, but it was
worth it. I'd let Dinger know that I was there, and I'd
learn that there was a guard in the back with us and
that these people meant business.

The driver sounded like an officer. "You, no talking.
Talking—boom boom!"

Fair one.

Every movement brought a retaliatory prod from
the guard, but I couldn't avoid taking deep, sighing
breaths because my hands were so painful.

The vehicle stank of the usual cigarettes and cheap
cologne. I ran through an appreciation. This transit
probably signified the end of the tactical phase. We
were getting moved further down the chain. I had no
idea whether it was going to get better or worse. The
optimistic side was saying: Right, I'll just go to prison

now. The professional side was saying: Let's wait and see. You don't know what's going on.

I tried to concentrate on keeping my orientation. We came out of the gate and turned left. That meant we were heading east, not west, so we weren't going in the direction of Syria. As if we would. He was driving like an idiot. Normally you'd consider it very handy to have a crash, but at the speed he was going we would all die in the wreckage.

I once saw a film of Houdini clasping his hands behind his back and stepping through them to bring them round to his front. I wondered if I would be able to do it with the injuries. Then I thought: You dickhead, you've never done it in your life anyway, what are you on about? But I would have turned myself into an elastic band if it had meant getting away. All I needed was an opportunity.

I felt incredibly tired because of the heater and the heavy cigarette smoke, but the pain in my hands kept me awake. As if to make sure we stayed awake, they put on a cassette of Arabic music. It was so loud that at first I didn't hear the bombs falling.

9

They must have been thousand-pounders. We heard several explosions; the area was getting severely hammered. The pressure waves hit us and the car rattled. The guards cursed.

The vehicle stopped. I heard all the typical noises of disaster—the screeching of brakes, screams of pain and loss, shouts of panic and anger, a distressed woman crying, a child whimpering, metal scraping on stone. The driver and guards jumped out and cold air rushed over us. This could be our moment. The blokes had gone, the doors were open, but I could hear talking. I couldn't see what was going on. It was unbelievably frustrating. I had to piece things together purely by sound. Was the road bombed? Was it an obstruction? Had he stopped to help somebody? And more to the point, were they now going to come around and fill us in, purely because we were white eyes and they'd just been bombed? The thoughts raced through my mind, but before I even had time to speak to Dinger, the Iraqis got back in and we started moving again.

We drove for about an hour and a half. My sense of direction had gone to rat shit as soon as we'd come out of the camp and turned left, and I didn't have a clue where we might be. I was pissed off with myself again.

When we finally stopped, we could have been in Timbuktu for all I knew.

They dragged us out of the vehicle, and I was put back into what I sensed was the same room as before. I had the feeling the guards were still in bed. Somebody pushed me to the floor and handcuffed me to what I assumed was part of a bed. It was actually quite comfortable. I wasn't crunched up in the back of a vehicle, my knees weren't up around my ears, and my arm wasn't chained high up in the air. I sat cross-legged on the floor, trying to sort myself out, trying to tune in. I sensed that I was facing the wall. I tried putting my head right back so I could see past the bridge of my nose. I couldn't see anything except a bit of the glow from the paraffin heater.

I sat there for an hour, the scenarios rushing around my head. We had definitely been going through a built-up center of population when the bombs fell. Was it Baghdad? Why take us to Baghdad? So that people could see us? To be part of a human shield? Would the Allies bomb a position where prisoners were? Damned right they would. Schwarzkopf would hardly stop the war effort because Dinger and Andy were held in a radar center. Who were we going to get handed over to? Would we make a video? I wouldn't mind. I wanted people to know that I was still alive.

I could hear two sources of slow, regular breathing. To test if they were asleep I leaned forward and rested my head on the bed. Nothing happened. I slid over onto my right side and got my head down on the carpet. Still nothing. I put pressure on the blindfold against the carpet and managed to slide it down a little. I was indeed back in the same room.

I tried to work out what had happened to the others. Were we the only two survivors? Would they say if people had got across the border? I didn't come up with any answers, but it was good mental exercise. I might have to be doing a lot of that. I was already pacing myself for a long capture. It would obviously be nice to get released as soon as the war was over, but I couldn't really see it at this stage. There would most likely be a hostage period to come after this, lasting perhaps a couple of years.

I thought back to the American POW. He had endured years in solitary, and everybody back home assumed he was dead. It was only because an exchange took place that the truth came out. There was a US sailor that the Viet Cong had taken for a bit of a bonehead and used for menial tasks like mopping up. He was released because he was just an able seaman of no consequence who had fallen overboard—the classic gray man. In fact this character had taken it upon himself to remember the names, ranks, and numbers of over 200 prisoners. When he came back he reeled them all off. Our POW was among the names. It was a traumatic discovery for his family. I was trying to relate my experience to his, and there was no comparison. A year or so was bugger all. I'd only start worrying after two.

My hands were agony. I tried to work them out of the cuffs, but it was futile. They were far too swollen. I considered waking the guards up and asking to be released for a while, but they wouldn't have the keys —and they certainly wouldn't bother going and getting them.

My thoughts turned to Jilly. I wondered what she was doing.

Two hours later the boys came back with their Tilly lamps. Just as before, they undid my handcuffs and picked me up and dragged me back into the cold. It was a nice feeling on the body; I kidded myself I was about to start a long country walk or ski a good mountain.

Nobody talked. I hoped and prayed that Dinger was coming too, but I couldn't hear him. I was put in the

same position at the back on the right-hand side, behind the seats, legs up around my head. This time I
took the precaution of arching my back to make space
for my sore hands, so that I wouldn't have to make the
movement later on and earn myself a whack on the
head.

"No talk or shoot," the driver said.

"Okay."

"Yeah, okay mate," said Dinger from beside me.

I could tell by the tone of his voice that he was as
relieved to hear me as I was to hear him. But the relief
was short-lived. Just as we were setting off, somebody
leaned into the vehicle and said: "I hope that Allah is
with you."

I didn't know if it was said to spark me up, but if it
was, it succeeded.

We got the same bad driver as before and were soon
being flung around all over the place. There was no
music this time, just small talk between the blokes in
the front. Occasionally a window would go down as
one of them snotted up a grolly and gobbed it, or
shouted a greeting at somebody in the darkness.

We stopped on one occasion while the driver had a
long conversation with somebody in the street. I got
the impression he was showing us off. I heard giggles
from two or three people outside the car, then hands
came in and tugged our mustaches and slapped our
faces. I clenched up. It pissed me off more than the
kickings. That had been tactical questioning, and I
could understand the reasons behind it. But these
dickheads were having fun at my expense, pure and
simple.

We drove on in silence. We were going further and
further from the border, but I was just about past caring. I was too worried about my hands. They were
swollen to nearly twice their normal size, and I had no
sensation left in the fingers. I could feel nothing be-

yond the wrists, where the handcuffs had dug in so deeply that I was bleeding. The pain was becoming unbearable. I feared that at this rate I was going to lose the use of my hands for ever.

I tried to think of the positives. At least I wasn't dead. It was now about twelve hours since my capture, and I was still alive.

I started to think about the patrol as a whole. What would the Iraqis know about us? I had to assume that they'd link us with the contact at the MSR. They would know how many of us there were, because they would have found eight bergens. They would have found the LUP as well, with the cache of water and food.

What would give us away in the bergens? Because of SOPs, I knew there wouldn't be any written details of codes or our tasking. What about the equipment? How would we get around the explosives, timing devices, and detonators? I'd say they were area protection devices—they would have found the claymores, which would add weight to my story. Perhaps they wouldn't even know what the timing devices were. And maybe the jundies would have been so busy looting the bergens that all that kit would have disappeared anyway. I almost giggled when I imagined them rifling through the bergens in darkness and sticking a finger straight through one of the plastic bags of shit.

One thing I could be sure of was that nothing remained that was compromising to the task. We always refold our maps so that they aren't on the part we've been using, and we never put markings on them. Everything was in our heads.

I was feeling confident at this stage about the lack of knowledge they'd have on our equipment. If they knew more than I expected, we'd just have to waffle our way through and make excuses. The only problem really was that we didn't exactly look like your average search and rescue team. But by this stage we didn't exactly look like anything anyway, apart from total and utter bags of shit.

The vehicle stopped, and by the sound of things there was a reception committee waiting. I'd started to feel secure in the car: I'd got adapted to it, and now we were starting all over again.

They were talking in a low mumble, perhaps because it was the early hours of the morning. As the back doors opened there was a rush of cold air. We were pulled out and marched across a courtyard at quick pace. The cobblestones were agony. The cuts reopened, and my feet were soon slippery with blood. I stumbled and started to fall, but they grabbed me and kept on going. We went up a step, turned right along a veranda, and came to a door. I stubbed my foot on the doorframe and cried out. There was no reaction from them at all. They were very professional. It was all well rehearsed.

We went straight in. There was the usual smell of paraffin and the hissing sound of Tilly lamps, and I almost felt at home. They shoved me onto the floor and arranged me so that I was sitting cross-legged with my head down and my hands behind my back. I let them do whatever they wanted. It was pointless resisting. I clenched up, fully expecting something to happen. They ripped my blindfold off. The cloth had scabbed to some pressure sores on my cheekbones and the bridge of my nose. I flinched with pain and felt warm blood dribble down my face.

The pain was forgotten the instant I saw Dinger. I hadn't heard him get out of the car, and I'd had the horrible feeling I was on my own again. They yanked his blindfold off as well, and we got some eye-to-eye. Dinger gave me a little wink. I'd been avoiding eye contact with my interrogators since I'd been captured.

It was fantastic to have human contact again. Just a little wink was enough.

We were in a semidark room that had a medieval feel to it. The walls were bare stone and glistened with damp. It was cold and smelt musty. The windows were bricked up. The concrete floor was pitted and uneven.

I raised my head a little, trying to stretch my neck, and a guard I hadn't noticed behind me pushed me back down. I saw that his uniform was olive drab, not the commando DPM we'd become accustomed to.

I had managed to see that facing us was a six-foot folding table and a couple of foldaway chairs. Everything looked temporary. The Iraqis drink their coffee and sweet, black tea out of small, fruit juice-size glasses. There were two or three of them on the table, half-full of drinks that must have been old because they weren't steaming. Two ashtrays were heaped with stubs. Bits of paper were littered around. They'd put their weapons on the table as well.

There was activity by the door, and I lifted my eyes. Two characters came in. One was dressed in a green flying suit with a civilian leather jacket over the top and Chelsea boots with big heels and elasticated sides. He looked like the oldest swinger in town. I looked at the shape of him and had to try hard not to laugh. He was tall, but with a massive pot belly that was straining against the flying suit. He obviously thought he still had a 30-inch waist, the dickhead. He had all this Gucci kit on, and it was obvious he saw himself as a really smart, tasty geezer, but in fact he looked like a bag of bollocks.

The other character was much shorter and smaller-framed. He was a skinny, sunken-cheek type, wearing a terrible suit that he must have been issued with and hoped one day he might grow in to.

Guards brought in our belt kit and weapons and dumped them on the table. What did I have in my belt kit that would give me away? Were they going to bring in the bergens as well?

Mister Tasty handed a large brown envelope to the skinny runt. The back was covered with rubber stamps of nine-pointed stars, and there was Arabic writing on the front. This was a definite handover—either commandos to military intelligence, or military intelligence to civilian police. Whichever, we were going further down the chain, and it was going to be more difficult than ever to escape.

Nobody spoke to us. All this was going on as if we weren't in the room. There seemed to be no reference to us, no looks or nods in our direction. We stretched our legs out with cramp, and they came and pushed them back up. I looked at their wrists when they bent down to see if I could find out the time. It was irrelevant, but I wanted some sort of grip on reality. But nobody was wearing a watch, which was ominously professional. And yet they let us witness the handover, which seemed strange.

The *Top Gun* geezer in the flying suit left the room, and soon afterwards I heard transport moving off.

So this was it—we were with our new hosts.

I started to worry. Soldiers don't wear suits. Who was this guy? With soldiers you know where you stand, and you can understand what's going on. Now we were getting handed over to somebody in civvies. I'd heard all the horror stories from the Iran–Iraq war. I knew all about electrodes and meat hooks in the ceiling. These boys had been doing this professionally for years; they'd got it well squared away. We were not a novelty: we were ten years down the line; we were just another couple of punters. I was filled with dread. But there was nothing I could do about it; I had to accept the landing. The only hope was that they wouldn't want to damage us too much; they'd want to keep us looking nice for a video. Perhaps they would be less physical than the last bunch—but I doubted it.

The skinny runt's shirt was dirty and the collar a good four sizes too big for him. He wore a big kipper tie and trousers that were turned up at the bottoms. He looked as if he'd borrowed his wardrobe from Stan. He gobbed off some orders in a dull monotone to the guards. They picked up Dinger before we could get any eye-to-eye.

They left and I was on my own in the semidarkness with three or four guards. Some were in olive drab uniforms. Iraqi NCOs wear their insignia on their collars, very much like the Americans, and I could see that one of these guys was a warrant officer, class 1 equivalent, with two stars. He spoke fairly good English.

"You—look up," he growled.

This was great. Now I could have a proper look around. I looked up with an obedient expression on my face, trying hard to appear pitiful.

He was in front of me with two cronies in uniform and one who was dressed in traditional Arab dishdash, nothing on his head, and a pair of canvas pumps.

"What is your name?"

"My name is Andy, sir."

"American?"

"No, I am British."

"You're American?"

"No, I'm British."

"You're lying! You're lying!"

He hit me hard across the face. I rolled with it and went down.

"Sit up. You're British?"

"Yeah. I'm British."

"You're lying. You're Israeli."

This wasn't interrogation as such; he was just having his fun.

"Tonight, many people died because your country is bombing our children. Our children are dying in their schools. Your country is killing thousands of people every night, and it is time for you to die."

I was sure he was right and I was going to be topped. But they were not the ones who would do it. These weren't the teddies in charge; these were dickhead administrators doing a bit of freelance.

"What do you think about that?"

"Well, I don't want to die."

"But you're killing thousands of people. You're killing them, not us. We don't want this war."

"I don't know anything about that; I'm just a soldier. I don't know why we're at war. I didn't want to go to war; I was just working in England, and they made us join the army."

I spouted off any old bollocks, just to show I was confused and didn't really know what was going on or why I was there. I was hoping they might take a bit of pity and understand, but obviously not.

"Mitterrand is a pig. Bush is a pig. Thatcher is a pig. She is making the children die of starvation."

"I don't know anything about that; I'm only a soldier."

I got another slap around the head and went down.

The other two came up and had their fun. One was walking up and down. He'd come and put his face up close and shout, then pace up and down and come up again and twat me around the head.

The warrant officer said: "This man wants to kill you. I think I'll let him kill you now."

I could tell they were just getting rid of their frustrations. With luck they'd eventually get bored. It was no big problem.

I saw that our belt kit had gone. It must have been taken when they took Dinger away. I was concerned. Had we been split up for good? Was I never going to see him again? It was a disheartening thought. It would have been so nice to have seen him one last time before I died.

They were starting to get more confident. They'd had their little slaps and everything, and now they were recycling all the propaganda that they had been fed—all the wonderful things that were going to happen when they finally kicked the imperialist Western powers out of the Middle East.

"The Americans and the Europeans are taking all our oil. It is our country. The Europeans divided our country. The Middle East is for the Arabs: it is our land, it is our oil. You bring your culture in, you spoil everything."

I said I knew nothing about it: I was just a soldier, sent here against my will.

They started punching me in the head. One came up behind me and kicked me in the back and around the sides of the trunk. I went down and crawled into a ball, my knees right up to my chin. I closed my eyes, clenched my teeth, just waiting for it, but they lifted me up and straightened me out.

"Why are you here, killing our children?" they asked again, and it was sincere stuff. Obviously kids were getting killed in the bombing, and it had got to them. This wasn't the "You bastards!" and good kicking that I was used to; these guys really had the hump. The kicks were from the heart.

"Why are you killing our children?"

"I was sent here to save life," I said, glossing over the fact that this statement did not entirely reflect our activities of the past few days. "I'm not here to kill."

I started to bleed as the old wounds reopened. My nose was pouring blood, and my mouth started to swell up all over again. And yet I got the feeling there was a bit of control here. One of the boys must have said, "That's enough for now," because they stopped. They'd obviously had some instruction not to go overboard. They obviously wanted us to be able to talk. And that could only mean that things were going to get a whole lot worse.

"We've been fighting wars for many years, do you know that?"

"No, I don't. I don't know anything about that sort of thing. I'm all confused."

"Yes, my friend, we have been fighting wars for many years, and we know how to get information. We know how to get people to talk. And, Andy, you will talk soon . . ."

He coughed with a long, loud bronchial rumbling of the chest, and the next thing I knew—*whoomph, splat*—I got a big green grolly straight in the face. I was really pissed off at that, more than I was at getting filled in. I couldn't wipe it off, and it was all over my face. I had visions of contracting TB or some other outrageous disease. The way my luck was going, I'd get through all the interrogation and imprisonment shit, get back to the UK and find out I'd got some incurable form of Iraqi syphilis.

The rest of the blokes thought this was a good one, and they started gobbing as well, lifting my face right up so they had a bigger target.

"Pig!" they shouted, pushing me down onto the floor and spitting more.

The kickings you accept, because you can't do anything about it. But this—this really got to me: the fact that it had been snotted up out of their guts or their nose and was now on my face and trickling into my mouth. It was just so disgusting. They kept it up for about ten minutes, probably the time it took to exhaust their supplies.

They moved me into the corner of the room and made me face the wall, looking down. I was cross-legged, my hands still handcuffed behind my back. They blindfolded me again.

I stayed in that position for maybe forty-five minutes with not another word said to me. I could hear low voices and the sounds of people moving around. A Tilly lamp hissed on the other side of the room. It was very cold and I started to shiver. I felt the blood on my wounds begin to clot, and it was a very strange sensation. When you're bleeding it actually feels nice and warm. Then it starts to go cold and clots, and it's viscous and unpleasant, especially if your hair and beard are matted with it.

My nose was blocked with solid blood, and I had to start breathing through my mouth. It was total agony as the cold air got in amongst the stumps of enamel and pulp that had once been my back molars. I began to hope for an interrogation, just anything to get lifted out and taken somewhere warm.

I didn't have too much of a clue about what was going on. All that I knew was that we'd been handed over to a man in a Burton suit that was five times too big for him and he seemed to be in charge. I said as little as I could get away with, just waiting to see what was going to happen. I worried about Dinger. Where had they taken him? And why? The runty bloke had left with him. Were they going to have a go at him first? When he came back, was I going to have to look at Dinger battered and bleeding, and then get dragged away myself? I don't want that: I'd rather get taken away without seeing Dinger come back kicked to shit.

The door opened and the guards came in again. There was a brief exchange with the lads in the room, and they had a good giggle about the gob all over my face. They picked me up and dragged me outside. We turned right as we came out of the door, then followed a pathway and turned 90 degrees left at the end. I couldn't walk properly, and they had to prop me up under the armpits and half carry me. It was very cold. We went over more cobblestones, and I was in real trouble. The tops of my toes had been scraped away in the town, and I was frantically trying to get on the balls of my feet and sort of pigeon-toe along so I didn't scrape the lacerations.

It was only another 20 or 30 feet to where we were going. The heat hit me straight away. It was beautifully warm, and the room was full of aromas—burning paraffin, cigarette smoke, and fresh coffee. I was pushed down to the floor and made to sit with my legs folded. Still blindfolded and handcuffed, I put my head down to protect myself and instinctively clenched my teeth and muscles.

People were shuffling around, and through chinks in the blindfold I could see that the room was brightly lit. It seemed a furnished, used room, not a derelict holding area like the one I had just come from. The carpet was comfortable to sit on, and I could feel the fire really near me. It was all rather pleasant.

I heard papers being shuffled, a glass being put on a hard surface, a chair being moved across the floor. There were no verbal instructions to the guards. I sat there waiting.

After about fifteen seconds the blindfold was pulled off. I was still looking at the floor. A pleasant voice said, "Look up, Andy: it is all right, you can look up."

I brought my head up slowly and saw that I was indeed in a plush, well-decorated, quite homely room, rectangular and no more than 20 feet long.

I was at one end, near the door. I found myself looking directly ahead at a very large, wooden executive-type desk at the other end. This had to be the colonel's office, without a doubt. The man behind the desk looked quite distinguished, the typical high-ranking officer. He was quite a large-framed person, about 6-footish, with graying hair and mustache. His desk was littered with lots of odds and bods, an in and out tray, all the normal stuff that you would associate with an office desk, and a glass of what I took to be coffee.

He studied my face. Behind him was the ubiquitous picture of old Uncle Saddam, in full military regalia and looking good. Either side of the desk and coming down the room towards me against the walls was a collection of lounge chairs without arms, the sort that can be put together to make a long settee. They were crazy colors—oranges, yellows, purples. There were three or four of them each side with a coffee table between.

The colonel was in olive drab uniform. On the left-hand side from my view, and about halfway up the row, was a major, also in olive drab and immaculately turned out—not boots but shoes, and a crisply pressed shirt. You can tell staff soldiers no matter what army they come from.

The major was paying no attention to me at all, just flicking through what appeared to be papers from the handover, making the odd note in the margin with a fountain pen. He started talking in beautifully modulated, newscaster English.

"How are you Andy? Are you all right?"

He didn't look at me, just carried on with his paperwork. He was mid-thirties, and he wore half-moon glasses that made him tilt his head back so that he could read. He had the Saddam mustache and immaculately manicured hands.

"I think I need medical attention."

"Just tell us again, will you, why are you in Iraq?"

"As I said before, we're members of a search and rescue team. The helicopter came down, we were all told to get off, and it took off and left us; we were abandoned."

"How many of you were there on the helicopter, can you remember? No problems if you can't at the moment. Time is one commodity your sanctions have not affected."

"I don't know. Alarms were ringing inside the helicopter. We were told to get off, and then everything got very confused. I'm not too sure how many were left on and how many were off."

"I see. How many of you were there on the helicopter?"

It was the schoolteacher talking down to a kid he knows full well is lying—but he wants the kid to squirm before he confesses.

"I don't know, because when we got on it was dark. Sometimes there's only four, sometimes there's twenty. We're just told when to get on and when to get off. It always happens so quickly. I didn't know where we were going or what we were doing. To be honest, I'm not really interested. I never take that much notice. They treat us like shit; we're just the soldiers who do the work."

"All right. So what was your mission, Andy? You must know your mission because it's always repeated twice in your orders."

It's standard British army practice to repeat the mission statement twice in orders. It astounded me that he knew. If he understood British military doctrine, he must have had some training in the UK.

"I don't really know about my mission," I said. "It's just a case of: go here, go there, do this, do that. I know we're supposed to know the mission, but we are not told half the time what's going on; it's total and utter confusion."

My mind was racing, good style, trying to do several things at once. I was listening to this character and I was trying to remember what I'd already said and what I was going to say in the future. The problem was, I was knackered, I was hungry, I was thirsty. This boy was sitting up there all rather comfy and contented, just having a bit of a waffle. He was far more switched on at this stage than I was because I was such a physical wreck.

"Well, what were you going to do once you were on the helicopter?"

"We're all drawn together from different regiments

to form these rescue teams. We haven't been together long because we're all from different places. We haven't formed into teams yet. Look, we're here to save life, not to take life away. We're not that sort of people."

"Hmmm."

The colonel hadn't stopped staring at me since the blindfold was removed. Now he sparked up in passable English.

"Where is your officer who commands you?"

I was happy about this question. In the Iraqi system there's an officer in command even at the lowest level; it was good that they found it incomprehensible for a long-range patrol to be in the field without an officer. I'd been portraying myself as thick and confused, and maybe they'd been taken in. Now they wanted the officer: he was the man in the know. I decided to play on the deserted soldiery bit.

"I don't know, it was dark. He was there one minute and gone the next. He must have stayed on the helicopter. He wouldn't bother coming out with us if he knew the helicopter was taking off again. He deserted us."

"Do you think there could have been eight of you?"

That meant they were aware of the problem at the MSR and were trying to make the connection—if they hadn't already done so. In my heart I knew it was only a matter of time.

"I don't know, there were people running around everywhere. We're not trained for this sort of thing, we're trained to render first aid—and all of a sudden we're stuck in the middle of Iraq. There might have been eight, I haven't got a clue. I was confused and I just ran for it."

"Where did the helicopter land?"

"I really don't know. They just put us down. I don't know where it was. I wasn't map-reading on the aircraft; it's the pilots that do everything."

Could they believe this shit? I felt I was flogging a dead horse, but I had no choice now—I'd gone down that path, and I had to keep going, right or wrong. I didn't know if they were just fishing or not. I'd just have to play the game out. Anybody else who'd been caught would be doing the same. No need to panic; the conversation was still all very nice.

"Tell me about some of the equipment that you have, Andy. We are somewhat confused about it."

I didn't know if he was trying to get me to talk about the bergens which had been dropped or our belt kit. He was talking as if we were the eight-man patrol that had got bumped, and I was talking as if we were the search and rescue team.

"It's just standard sort of issue—water, ammunition, and a bit of extra first aid kit and our own personal stuff."

"No. Tell me about the explosives that you had in your packs."

Hang about, I thought—it hasn't been confirmed yet that I was in this patrol.

"I don't know what you mean."

"Come on, Andy, let's sort this out. There is no big problem. Just sit there, take your time, and it will all be done tonight. You were carrying explosives, Andy. We've followed you all the way since you were first found. We know it was you and your friends. We've been following your exploits."

"I'm sorry, I don't know what you mean."

"Well, you do really, don't you, Andy? Such a large quantity of plastic explosive. Did you intend to blow something up?"

His tone was still very pleasant and gentle, the GP enquiring about my general well-being. I knew it wouldn't last. In training, you are taught to try and take advantage of whatever you can whenever you can, because you don't know if it's ever going to come your way again. A golden rule is that if you can get something to eat, take it every time. They were trying to be the nice guys and help me as much as they could, so I felt it was time to try and take advantage of the situation.

"Would it be possible to have anything to eat, please, because I haven't eaten for days and days," I said. "I've got stomach pains from hunger. It would be nice to have something to eat."

"Of course you can have something to eat, Andy. It might be difficult to find, of course, because the sanctions mean that we have children starving in the streets. However, we will try to find you something. We are a good and generous people. We will look after you. If you help us, who knows what else you can get? You might be home soon. Think about that, Andy—home."

The rice was hot and so was the bowl of delicious stewed tomatoes and two chapatis. The water was refreshingly cool and served in a clean glass.

At first one of the guards picked up the spoon and started to feed me.

I said, "Would it be possible to undo one of my hands so I can feed myself?"

The major said No, but the colonel Okayed it with a wave of his hand. One of my handcuffs was undone, and the release of pressure was absolutely splendid. The only problem was that I couldn't hold the spoon properly because of the numbness in my hand. I balanced it between my little finger and the finger next to it and then rested it above the web of the thumb as a sort of lever.

The colonel pointed at the picture of Saddam.

"Do you know who this is?"

I hesitated, as if trying to put a name to a face at a party, and said, "Yes, that's Saddam Hussein. President Hussein."

"Yes it is. What have you heard about him?"

What was I supposed to say? "I've heard about him all right. I've heard he's pretty good at gassing kids in Iran?"

"I know that he's a man of power, a strong leader."

"This is correct. Under his leadership we shall soon be rid of all you Westerners. We have no time for you. We don't need you."

It wasn't rhetoric; his tone was still conversational.

I finished the rice and got stuck into the tomatoes. I had great trouble eating them because my mouth was so swollen and numb. It was like coming back from the dentist after an injection and thinking you'll have a cup of tea, but it dribbles down your chin because you have no control. I was noisy and uncouth as I slobbered away, tomato juice trickling down my chin. The tomatoes tasted lovely, and I was just sorry that the sores in my mouth stopped me from chewing them properly and extracting all the flavor. The bread was a problem, too. I just gulped down big hunks without chewing. No matter: I wanted to get it all down my neck as fast as I could in case they started playing games and took it away from me halfway through.

The colonel peeled an orange as he watched me. In contrast with the chimpanzee's tea party down on the carpet, he did it with studied elegance. With the aid of a small knife he made four careful cuts down the skin, then peeled off each quarter in turn. He opened out the orange segment by segment.

The fruit had been presented to him on an ornate china plate on a tray, with a silver knife and fork. There was a definite class system in operation, the jundies running around with a teapot pouring tea for these two lads, while they just sat there.

Now and again the colonel would pick up a piece of orange and put it in his mouth. Down on the carpet his prisoner slobbered and slurped. Talk about Beauty and the Beast.

My stomach was feeling really good, but it wasn't just the food that was making me happy: while I was eating they weren't asking me questions. It gave me time to think.

Sure enough, as soon as I'd finished I was handcuffed again, and we carried on the conversation from where we'd left off. He was still talking as if we'd already agreed that the equipment found after the initial contact on the MSR was ours.

"So, Andy, explain to me some more about the equipment. What else did you have? Come on, we need your help. After all, we have helped you."

"I'm sorry, I'm getting all mixed up. I don't understand."

"What were you doing with explosives?"

The tone still wasn't aggressive.

"We didn't have any explosives. I don't really know what you're on about."

"Andy, you were obviously going to destroy something because you were carrying PE4, which is a high explosive that is designed to destroy things. You appreciate why I cannot really believe the story you are telling me?"

His mention of PE4 was another indication that he was UK-trained, but I ignored it. "I really don't know what you're on about."

"We have some of your men in hospital, you know."

That one got me. I tried not to show any shock or surprise; I wasn't supposed to be connected with any villains from the MSR.

"Who are they?" I asked. "What condition are they in?"

My mind was racing. Who could it be? What might they have said? Was he just bluffing?

"They're Okay, they're Okay."

"Thank you very much for looking after them. Our army would be doing the same for your injured."

If they had anybody in hospital, it must mean they were interested in keeping them alive.

"Yes," he said casually, "we know everything. A few members of your group are in hospital. But they are fine. We are not savages; we look after our prisoners."

Yes, I know, I thought—I've seen the footage of the Iran–Iraq war; I've seen how you look after your prisoners.

There was nothing I could do about it, but I had to respond the way I thought they wanted me to. It's all a big game, one that you start training for as a kid. You learn how to lie to your mother or teacher, and turn on the tears whenever you want.

"Thank you for helping them," I said, "but I don't know anything that I can tell you."

"Well, we agree that you were with the group that abandoned its packs, and that we followed you all the way along."

"No—you're confusing me. I don't understand what you mean about abandoned packs. We don't use packs. We were deserted; we were stuck in the middle of your country. I'm just a soldier; I go where I'm told and I do what I'm told to do."

"But, Andy, you have not explained to me what you were told to do. You must have had a mission."

"Look, I'm on the lower echelon of the military system. As you know yourself, we work on a need-to-know basis. We are only told what we need to know, and because I'm so low down on the chain I get told nothing."

Bingo—this seemed to strike a chord. At the top of the card which gives the sequence for an orders group it says: *Remember Need To Know.* He had obviously had some sort of teaching from the Brits, probably at Sandhurst or Staff College: the Iraqis had been in the Western powers' Good Lads Club for a number of years.

The colonel looked puzzled and asked the major something in Arabic. The junior officer gave a lengthy explanation. I felt good about this. I'd actually come back at him with something that they seemed to accept. Maybe they thought I really did know jack shit. Maybe they could equate my situation with their own. We were all soldiers. Obviously he was a major and the other one was a colonel, but they would still receive orders from brigadiers and generals. The long shot was that they'd take a certain amount of pity on us, or think that we were really not worth the trouble of trying to get any more information out of because we were just a bunch of bonehead squaddies who'd screwed up.

"That is fine, Andy. We will see you later on. It is time for you to go now."

He sounded like a therapist winding up a session.

"Thanks very much for the food. I am trying to help, really I am, but I just don't know what's required of me."

They put the blindfold back on and, rather surprisingly, took the handcuffs off. I felt the blood rush back into my hands. They lifted me and took me outside. The cold hit me. It had been so warm in the office, scoffing tomatoes, bread, and rice.

I was quite happy that this was another major hurdle over with, and that I'd got some food out of them. Chances were they'd been going to give me some anyway as part of the good-guy routine, but it just made me feel better to have asked for and received it. I was fairly confident at this time that my story was holding up, even though I wasn't entirely happy with the performance I'd given. At the end of the day, whether they believed it or not, as long as they had me down as thick and ignorant, it didn't really matter to me. Hopefully I'd just be pigeonholed as totally irrelevant and too thick to get any creditable information out of.

* * *

I still hadn't got my boots, and I couldn't walk properly on my raw feet. But I was mentally fit, and that was all that mattered. They can break any bone in your body that they choose, but it's up to you whether or not they break your mind.

I hobbled down a long, cold, damp corridor with lino floors, and they sat me down at the end. It was completely dark—not a flicker of light came through my blindfold. From time to time I could hear the echo of footsteps moving along other corridors and crossing this one. Perhaps it was an office complex.

After an hour or so there was again the sound of footsteps, but they were more irregular and shuffling than usual. Shortly I heard the sound of labored breathing. A guard took my blindfold off, and I watched him walk away. The corridor was about 8 foot wide, with tiled walls and doors every 15 feet or so. Down to the right there were two other intersections with corridors coming off, and that went down maybe 100 or 125 feet. It was dark. There was a Tilly lamp right at the other end of the building, glowing at the junction.

I looked to my left and saw Dinger. He had a huge grin on his face.

"Come here often, wanker?" he said.

The guard came back with our boots and went out and joined his mates who were sitting a few feet away, keeping an eye on us.

"Muslim or Christian or Jew?" one of them said.

"Christians," I said. "English. Christians."

"Not Jew?"

"No. Christians. Christians."

"Not Tel Aviv?"

"No, not Tel Aviv. English. Great Britain."

He nodded, and gobbed off to his mates.

"My friend here," he said, "he's a Christian. Muslims and Christians are Okay in Iraq. We live together. No Jews. Jews are bad. You are a Jew."

"No, I'm a Christian."

"No, you are a Jew. Tel Aviv. Tel Aviv no good. We don't want Jews. We kill Jews. Why you come in our country? We don't want war. War is your problem."

He was just talking, rather matter-of-factly, and seemed quite sensible. Iraq has a large Christian population, especially around the port of Basra.

"We are not Jews, we are Christian," I said again.

"Aircrew?"

"Not aircrew. Rescue."

If he'd wanted us to be Muslims or members of the Church of the Third Moon on the Right, that's what we would have been. I was just nodding and agreeing with everything, apart from the Jew bit. It was the early hours of the morning and we could sense the guards' attitude: "We're bollocksed, you're bollocksed,

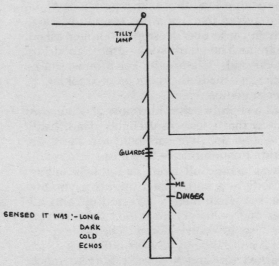

Hallway of handover location from Commando to Secret Police?/Intelligence?

we have to look after you, let's just do it without any problems."

Dinger was rubbing his feet.

"Is it all right if I help him?" I said.

They gave a wave that said: Yeah, do what you want.

Dinger and I leant forwards to examine his feet.

"Bob?" I whispered in his ear.

"Don't know."

"Legs?"

"Probably dead. What about Mark?"

"Dead. When did you get caught?"

"Mid-morning. I heard you being brought in in the afternoon."

"Are you all right?" I said. I couldn't believe I'd asked such a bone question. What a dickhead statement.

He eyed me with a look that said: You knobber!

The guards sussed that we were communicating, and one of them came over to stop it. Dinger asked him for a cigarette. The guard spoke pretty good English, but Dinger said, "Cig-ar-ette?" as if he was talking to a lunatic, and made the motions of smoking. It didn't get him anywhere.

We both had a slightly better idea now of what was going on. I knew that Legs was probably dead. I still didn't know about Bob. We sat there for about an hour, but couldn't communicate any more.

My body was aching all over, and I was falling asleep. Your body gets so psyched up when you are being filled in, but when there is a period of calm, all the little aches and pains get magnified because you have nothing else to worry about. The feeling reminded me of school. When you have a fight as a kid, you're all sparked up, and it doesn't hurt so much initially. It's a couple of hours later that the pain comes out. My lips were still bleeding. My mouth had been split in several places during the beatings, and the wounds kept trying to congeal. But even the slightest movement made them reopen. My arse and lower back were sore from sitting all day on the hard concrete. The injuries made me feel even more exhausted, and I wanted to get my head down. I nodded off, my head lolling on my chest, then jerked awake a minute or two later. This went on for about half an hour. Then Dinger and I leant against each other and dozed.

We were woken by the slamming of doors and the sound of talking. The glow of a Tilly lamp appeared at the bottom of the corridor and got bigger and bigger. Finally the lamp appeared, with lots of bodies behind it. We knew we were off again.

We were handcuffed and blindfolded—not aggressively, rather nonchalantly. We stood up and shuffled together along the corridor and out into the open air. A Land Cruiser was waiting with its engine running.

Our blindfolds were taken off again as we got in, though I had no idea why—perhaps there was just a breakdown in communications. Off we went, two guards in the front and one in the back.

"Baghdad? Baghdad?" Dinger sparked up, nice and friendly.

"Yes, Baghdad," the driver replied, as if he was stating the obvious.

The driver knew all the back doubles. We drove for ten minutes through busy back streets. The vehicle had its headlights blazing. The guards didn't seem particularly bothered when I strained to see road signs and street names. I didn't see a single written word. There were no large magnificent buildings to be remembered and identified later. All the houses had flat roofs. By the look of it this was the slum area of the city. It must have been a residential area because there were no signs of bombing. It didn't even look as if there was a war on. The roads were tarmacked but full of potholes, and the sidewalk areas were just dust. Old cars were abandoned at the roadside, being pissed on by dogs.

We stopped outside a pair of large, slatted wooden gates. They opened inwards as soon as the vehicle arrived, and we drove into a small courtyard not much bigger than the Land Cruiser's turning circle. Squaddies were waiting for us, and I felt the familiar knot of apprehension tighten in the pit of my stomach. Dinger and I looked at each other blankly.

I wanted to look up as we were hustled out of the vehicle but made sure my head was down so I didn't antagonize anybody. It was pitch-black, and at every moment I expected the filling in to start. We were dragged into a block and along a corridor that was hardly wider than my shoulders. It was totally dark, and the jundie in front of me had to use his torch. We got to an area where there was a row of about a dozen doors, all very close together. The jundie opened one, pushed me inside, took off my handcuffs, and closed the door. I heard a bolt sliding and a padlock being applied.

There was no ambient light whatsoever. It was so dark in the room that I couldn't even see my hand in front of my face. There was a gagging stench of shit. I got down on my hands and knees and felt my way around. There wasn't much to feel. The room was tiny, and it didn't take me long to discover the two porcelain footpads either side of a hole about eight inches in diameter. No wonder my new bedroom stank. I was in a minging Arab shithouse.

You have to take advantage of every situation, and here was an opportunity to get the sleep I desperately needed. I wasn't going to waste time thinking about anything. There wasn't room to stretch out so I maneuvered my body so that I was bent around the pan.

There was no ventilation and the smell was overpowering, but there you go. It was just a relief not to have been beaten up.

I fell asleep immediately.

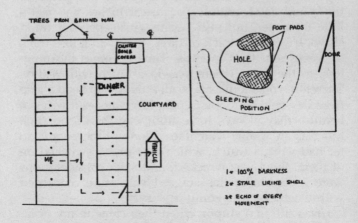

Toilet and courtyard

10

I woke up feeling as if I'd been drugged. Doors further down the corridor were opening noisily. There was some talking; I could hear it but I was not really conscious of it because I was in such a daze. I wondered what time it was. My body clock had completely packed in, and I didn't even know if it was night or day. It should be a priority to keep track of times and dates, mainly because it makes you feel a little bit better, but also because it keeps your mind sharp. If you lose track of days, then you'll lose track of weeks and then months. Time becomes meaningless, to the point where you lose touch with reality. Therefore you should make all attempts to keep a grip from day one. You look at people's watches if you can because they always have numbers; there's no such thing as an Arabic watchface. None of the guards so far had worn a watch, which was pretty switched on of them. But I was wrecked, and such considerations were irrelevant at this stage. I was more concerned with whether I was going to survive.

I was still in a stupor when they came to my door. "Andy! Andy! Andy!" a guard shouted through the door in a jovial, holiday camp kind of voice. "Is it Okay, Andy?"

"Yep, yep, I'm all right!" I tried to sound happy and polite.

My muscles had seized up; I was as stiff as a board. I tried my best to stand up. If they saw me just lying there, making no effort, they'd fill me in. But I couldn't move.

The door opened and I saw daylight. I stretched out my arms, palms upwards, in a gesture of helplessness.

"I can't move," I said. "Stiff."

He called to another guard. I clenched my sore muscles in readiness for the kicking I was about to receive.

They came into the toilet and bent over me.

"Up, up, aaah," one said, all nice and gentle. They put my arms around their necks and lifted me upright, almost with compassion. They were actually concerned. I couldn't believe it.

The crash of a door bolt and the friendly shout of "Good morning! Good morning!" echoed around the block as they helped me towards the door to the courtyard.

The light was dazzling, even though the toilet block was in shadow. I squinted at the sun. It was fairly low, and I guessed the time was about eight o'clock. The sky was a beautiful, cloudless blue, and the air was cool and crisp, with just enough nip to make your face tingle and let you see your breath as you exhaled. It could have been an early spring morning in England, and I could have been coming out of my house and setting off for work.

Directly in front of us was a vehicle, and beyond it a single-story building. The noises were subdued—vehicles in the distance, disembodied voices shouting further down the camp, city noises the other side of the walls. I heard a bird singing to my left. I turned my head and looked up; it was in a tree that grew on the other side of the courtyard wall. It sang its heart out and it was lovely to hear.

Below it, in the corner where the toilet block met the

wall, there was a pile of large metal segments. When aircraft drop cluster bombs, the ordnance breaks up at altitude and releases the payload of smaller bombs. The large outer casings fall to earth, and these were obviously being collected by somebody. They had English writing on them. It gave me a good feeling to see something from home. Somebody friendly was up there in the sky, not watching over me or even looking for me, but at least they were there, and they were hosing these people down.

The vehicle was facing outwards, ready to go, and as we approached the engine fired up. I got in and was left with a couple of guards. One of them, the first black Iraqi soldier that I'd seen, reminded me of my battalion days. In the early eighties, when the Afro was in, our black dudes used to buy pairs of tights and cut the legs off to use as sort of bank robber masks to squash their hair down at night. The effect of this was to make their Afros really tight in the morning, so that when they put their berets on, their hair didn't poke out and look ridiculous. As soon as we were off duty, they'd get out the Afro comb and frizz it all out again.

This lad had the mop on top, then the ring where the band of his beret had dug in, but all the rest was sticking out. Obviously he didn't put his head in a stocking bottom at night, and I wondered if I should pass on the beauty tip. It gave me a little giggle to remember the battalion. It seemed a lifetime ago.

Dinger was in a bad way, shuffling like an old man, moving along about a foot every pace, being supported either side by two lads. It was quite funny to watch because Dinger towered a foot or so above them. It looked like a pair of little Boy Scouts helping an old-age pensioner.

The bright light hit him, and he shuddered up like a vampire, putting his head down to protect his eyes. We'd been blindfolded and in darkness for so long, and all of a sudden we were getting full wattage, like bats caught in a searchlight.

I saw that the guards were commando again, in DPM and carrying AK47s. Dinger didn't have his boots either, and his feet were cut. Much the same as me, there were big red scabs on the outside of his socks where the blood had congealed. His hair wasn't its usual dirty frizzy blond; it was matted and a dark reddish brown. His face was covered with a week of growth, and that, too, was covered with mud and scabs.

As he was helped into the vehicle, he put his hand out and I grabbed hold of it and pulled him in.

"All right, mate?" I said.

"Yeah, I'm all right."

I got the grin. The house might be bomb-damaged, but the lights were still on in the attic.

It was another major victory. We'd made physical contact, we'd exchanged words. It was a big boost to my morale, and I hoped I'd had the same effect on him.

The guards put the blindfolds on again, breaking the scab on the bridge of my nose and squashing my eyeballs so hard that I got snowstorms in front of my eyes. One of Houdini's secrets was to tense all his muscles as tightly as he could when they were tying him up, so that when he relaxed he had some room to play with. As they tied the blindfold, I tensed my cheek muscles to give me some slack later on. It didn't work.

They put the handcuffs on again, good and tight. My hands were very tender, and the pain was unbearable. Perversely, I took a deep breath and clenched my teeth as the ratchets bit into the flesh because I didn't want them to see that they were hurting me. I'd been going through the process of playing on my injuries, and now I was being counterproductive again by trying not to show the pain.

We sat and waited. As I listened to the engine tick-ing over, I wondered where we were going to. Had we convinced them we were inconsequential nuggets, not worth any further waste of manpower? Were we now on our way to a prison where we would just sit out the rest of the war in relative comfort?

My thoughts were broken by what I assumed was one of the guards. Just as the driver put his foot on the clutch and engaged first gear, he poked his head through the open window and said quietly, "Whoever is your God, you will very soon be needing him." I didn't know if he was saying it out of compassion, or as a cruel and deliberate ploy to make us flap. But it had the effect of totally saddening me. My whole body dropped, as if I'd been told my dad was dead. It was a massive shock. Things had seemed to be on the up, and now this.

Whoever is your God, you will very soon be needing him.

The sincerity in his voice alarmed me. I thought: That's it then, it is going to get worse. The mention of God was horrifying because there was so much concern in the guard's voice when he said it, as if it really was only God who could save us now. Did it mean we were going to be executed? That was fine—I'd just have to hope it was publicized and the people back home got the news. What about torture? We'd heard the horror stories during the Iran–Iraq war, and the thought now crossed my mind that this was it: Here we go, it's time for the old chop your bollocks off routine, followed by ears, fingers, and toes, all nice and slow. But the optimist in me was fighting hard, saying: No, they wouldn't do that: they must realize they're going to lose the war; they don't want another Nuremberg.

If the desired effect was simply to piss me off, then it succeeded—severely. The same went for Dinger. As the Land Cruiser lurched across the courtyard, he muttered out of the corner of his mouth, "Well, at least they can't make us pregnant."

I giggled. "Yeah, fair one."

The boy in the passenger seat turned round and gobbed off angrily, "No speak! No talk!"

They might not be able to make us pregnant, but they might try and fuck us. It was a crazy assumption, but your mind does that sort of thing under duress. The thought worried me more than getting killed.

Alone with my thoughts, I brooded about the conversation I'd had with Chris back at the FOB.

"That's all you need on top of getting captured," Chris had joked. "To have six chutney ferrets roaring up your arse."

We drove for about fifteen minutes in brilliant sunshine. I could tell we weren't heading out of town because we were still turning corners at quite frequent intervals and the noise of human activity didn't drop. People in the streets were shouting at one another; drivers were leaning on their horns.

One of the blokes in the front farted. It was outrageous, a really putrid bastard. That's nice, I thought: on top of everything else I've now got to chew somebody else's shit.

They thought it was hilarious, and the guy on the passenger side turned around and said, "Good? Good?"

"Mmmm, yum yum," Dinger said, full of appreciation, inhaling deeply as if he was on the seafront at Yarmouth. "Lovely, good stuff."

Our noses were so clogged that not too much of the smell was getting through, but it was important to show them that we didn't care about anything they did. After a while the blokes up front couldn't hack it themselves and had to wind the window down.

It was lovely to feel the cool breeze hitting my skin. I turned my face into it until I tingled. It kept my mind off my hands. I had perfected a technique of leaning forward and keeping my back straight to take the pressure off the cuffs. The problem was that every time I moved, they thought I was doing something to try and get away, so I'd get shoved back. But what was fifteen minutes of this between friends?

The driver stopped laughing, and I sensed that we had arrived. Gates were being opened, and we drove over a different surface for another couple of hundred meters. The Land Cruiser was surrounded by angry voices. We had a reception committee.

The moment the vehicle stopped the doors were pulled open. Hands grabbed my hair and face and pulled me out on my side. It was straight out and onto the ground, no messing. It wasn't the worst beasting we'd had—slapping, hair pulling, punches to the side, all the normal harassment stuff—but it came as a big, big shock. People were laughing and gobbing, and I got my head down, clenching up, just letting them get on with it. It was their party.

After two or three minutes I was hauled to my feet, and they started dragging me away. My legs wouldn't function, and I tripped and stumbled. They just kept dragging, very quickly, very rehearsed, like porters at an abattoir processing carcasses. There was hollering all around me, but I was trying to listen out for another group so I could keep tabs on Dinger. I couldn't hear anything outside of my own little environment.

I kept trying to lift my feet so they wouldn't scuff on the floor and get damaged even more. We only went about a dozen meters. While they fiddled with the door, I tried to catch my breath. We went up a couple of steps that I didn't know were there, and I banged my toes and groaned. I went down, but they dragged me up again, shouting and slapping. We went along a corridor. The echoes were eerie and ugly. It had been hot, and now suddenly it was cold and damp and musty again. The building seemed derelict.

The cell door must have been already open. They threw me against a corner and pushed me down onto the floor. I was arranged so that I was cross-legged but with my knees right up, my shoulders back, and my hands behind my back, still handcuffed. I didn't say or do anything; I just went with the flow. After another couple of slaps and kicks and a burst of rhetoric for good measure, they slammed the door shut. It sounded as if it was made of sheet metal bolted to a frame, but the frame must have been warped because they had to slam it really hard, and it banged and rattled with an echo that frightened me shitless.

You're alone. You think you are alone. You can't see what's going on, you're disoriented, and you're worried. You're fucking worried. You're breathing heavily, and all you're thinking is: Let's just get it done. You can't be sure there's nobody in the room. Maybe they haven't all gone; maybe somebody's still looking at you, watching for a mistake, so you keep your head down, clench your teeth as best you can, keep your knees up, try to protect yourself against the punches and kicks that could start again at any instant.

I heard the crash of another door. Dinger getting locked away, I assumed. It gave me a bit of consolation to know that we were both still in the same boat.

There wasn't a lot I could do except just sit there and try to calm myself down. I took deep breaths and exhaled very slowly as I analyzed the events and came to the obvious conclusion that something unpleasant was definitely going to happen. We had been moved to a place that felt organized and geared up. There was a reception party to deliver a short, sharp shock; they knew the score, they knew exactly what they were going to do and when. But was this the prison we were going to stay in now, or were we still in transit and these boys just asserting their authority? Was I going to stay blindfolded and handcuffed for the rest of my days? If so, I was going to be in a desperate state. Would I come out with my eyes impaired? And Jesus —what about my hands?

I calmed myself with the thought that once I'd

tuned in to the new environment, I'd be all right. It was like going into a house that you haven't visited before. It feels strange, but after a couple of hours you feel a bit more affinity with it, you feel more at home. I knew that as long as my blindfold came off, that was what would happen eventually. I still had my escape map and compass safely tucked away, so at least I had something over them.

It was cold: a dank, dilapidated sort of cold. The floor was damp. I was sitting in wet mud and shit. I found that my hands could touch the wall. It was plaster that had chips and chunks out of it, and where it met the floor there were gaps. The concrete floor was very rough and uneven. Pressure sores on my arse made me try to adjust my position. I tried straightening my legs out but that didn't work, so I brought them back up and tried to lean on one side. But wherever I leaned my hands were painful; I just couldn't get comfortable.

I heard noisy talking and the sound of people walking up and down outside. There was obviously a gap in the door or a window, and I sensed them looking in at me, checking out the new commodity, just staring with blank, gormless eyes. It flashed through my mind that if I got out, I'd never visit a zoo again in my life.

The pain from the handcuffs and the stress position had become too much. Whether or not I was being watched, I had no choice but to try and lie down to relieve the pressure. There was nothing to lose in having a go. You don't know until you try. I shifted on to my side, and the relief was immediate—and so was the shouting. I knew they were coming for me. Every nerve in my body screamed: "Fuck! Fuck! Oh no, not again . . ."

I tried to pull myself up by putting my weight against the wall, but I ran out of time. The bolt flew undone, and the guards battled to get the warped door open. It shook and rattled like an up-and-over garage

door as they kicked at it in a fury, and when it did
finally swing open, it was still rattling like a panto-
mime thunderstorm. It was the most frightening noise
I'd ever heard, horrendous, absolutely horrendous.

They were straight in, grabbing me by my hair, kicking and punching. Their message was very clear. They
forced me back into the stress position and left the cell,
slamming the door behind them. The bolt crashed
home, and their footsteps echoed and faded.

*This feels like a proper prison; this is a purpose-built cell.
I'm under their total control. So this is where it's all going
to happen? There's no chance of escape, and if conditions
stay like this there never will be.*

These boys knew what they were doing all right.
Their reactions were well rehearsed and orchestrated.
This suddenly felt like it was going to be for ever. I
was without hope. I thought it would be impossible
ever to feel lower, or lonelier, or more abandoned and
lost.

My mind rambled. I wondered if Jilly had been told
I was missing in action or presumed dead. I hoped
she'd been told jack shit. I hoped that somebody had
got over the border or that the Iraqis had spoken to the
Red Cross. Some chance. Maybe I'd land up on the TV
soon, which would be all rather nice. But then again
would it? The next of kin would be pacing up and
down enough already, just because there was a war
on. Jilly had always been quite good about my work.
She took the view that what she didn't know wouldn't
hurt her. She was able somehow to just cut it out of
her mind. This time, however, it was obvious where I
was, and the same went for my parents.

My only fear of dying was if nobody knew I was
dead. I couldn't bear the thought of my family's anguish at not having a body to mourn, of going through
their lives not knowing for sure.

The Iraqi Head Shed obviously didn't want us dead
at this stage, because if people had been left to their

own devices we'd have been topped a long time ago. And if they wanted us alive, it must be for some purpose—whether for propaganda or just because they knew they were going to lose the war and it wouldn't look good if prisoners were getting slotted.

You have to accept the circumstances and do the best you can in them. There was nothing I could do to help the people back home, so I turned my mind elsewhere. Should I have gone for the border that night? It was obvious to me that I should have taken my chances. But then, with hindsight, I'd have got eight score draws on last week's coupon.

I was injured and disoriented. I couldn't even remember what day it was. I knew I had to get a grip. Disorienting the prisoner is a good start to breaking him, and I knew it. But there was nothing I could do but put it out of my mind until I got a chance to see a clock or a guard's watch.

Interrogators have two hurdles to get over: the straightforward one of cracking you physically, followed by the more difficult one of breaking you mentally. They don't know your psyche, your weaknesses, your inner strengths. Some people might break the first day, others will never give in—and spread along the spectrum in between lie all the rest of us. The interrogator cannot be sure that his objective has been achieved. The telltale signs are hard to detect; he'll know he can't judge by your physical condition because you're exaggerating your injuries. But he'll have been taught that the eyes don't lie. It's up to you to make sure he can't see through the window; you have to mask your alertness. You have to make people peering in believe that they're looking at empty premises, not the shop front of Harrods.

I forced my mind to focus on more productive thoughts. I ran through the story once more, trying to remember what I'd said, hoping that Dinger had said more or less the same thing. The aim had to be to hold out for as long as we could so that a damage assessment could be made back at the FOB. The question our Head Shed would be asking was: What do members of Bravo Two Zero know? They would come to the conclusion that we knew our own tasks, but nothing of other people's, present or future, so nothing could be compromised. Anything that we did know that could affect other operations would have been changed or canceled.

We had to keep to our story. There was no turning back.

I was still in the stress position in the corner an hour later, or maybe it was ten minutes.

People paced up and down, looked in, mumbled.

As far as my body was concerned, it was the lull in the battle. It hadn't been complaining of such things while I was getting filled in, but now that nothing physical was happening to me it screamed that it was hungry and thirsty. I wasn't too worried about food. My stomach had been kicked about a bit and probably couldn't have taken it anyway. The priority was water. I was so, so thirsty. I was gagging.

I heard them fiddling with the padlock and throwing back the bolt. They banged and kicked the door to get it open, and the steel juddered and jarred. They were coming for me. Thirst vanished. Fear was everything.

They came in without a word, just straight over and grabbed me and lifted. I couldn't see them, but I could smell them. I tried to look as though I was doing my best to help them, despite the injuries I was playing on. But I found I was kidding myself more than them. It was well and truly past the stage of playing. I couldn't stand up. My legs would not obey me.

They dragged me out of the cell and turned right, heading down the corridor. My feet trailed in their wake, the scabs on my toes scraping off on the floor. I could see a little through the bottom of the blindfold. I saw the cobblestones and a trail of blood. I saw a step coming but had to trip over it because I didn't want them to realize that I could see. I didn't want to get punished more than I was going to be anyway.

It was warm in the sun. I felt it on my face. We went along a pathway and brushed past a small hedgerow. Up onto another step, then back into darkness. A long, black corridor, cool, musty, and damp. I heard office-type noises and the sound of footsteps on lino or tiles. We turned right and entered a room. It was cold and damp, but as they carried me in we went past isolated centers of heat. It wasn't at all the nice, comfy, Aunty Nelly feeling of a room that had been flooded with heat for a long time.

They pushed me down onto a hard chair. There was the usual strong smell of paraffin and cigarettes, and this time some acrid body odor. Whether it came from the people in the room or a previous prisoner, I couldn't tell. I tried to lean forward, but hands grabbed me and pulled me back.

There were lots of people in there, shuffling their feet, coughing and muttering to one another, and they seemed to be arranged on either side of the room. I heard Tilly lamps. I didn't know if the room was windowless or if the curtains were drawn, but it was very dark apart from their glow.

I clenched my muscles and waited. There was silence for a minute or so. I was worried. We'd got to the serious place. This was the real world; the people here would not be idiots.

A voice spoke to me from the top of the room. It sounded like somebody's favorite grandad, a sort of old, gravelly voice, very pleasant in tone.

"How are you, Andy?"

"I'm not too bad."

"You look quite injured." The English was fluent

but with a marked accent. "Perhaps when we have finished our business and we have an understanding, we might be able to get you some medical attention."

"It would be very nice if I could have some. Thank you very much. And my friend also?"

We were in a new environment now, with a new gang. If this was going to be the good boy routine, maybe I'd get something to eat, maybe I'd get medical attention, maybe I'd be able to get medical attention for Dinger. I might even find out some information. Maybe they might be able to let me have my blindfold off or my handcuffs—maybe, maybe, maybe. Even if it was for ten minutes, it would be better than a kick in the tits. If they're promising you things, you must try and see if they'll deliver. Take what you can, while you can. Right, let's go along with this.

"All we need to know, Andy, is what you were doing in our country."

I went through my story again. I tried to look scared and humble.

"I was in a helicopter as a member of a search and rescue team. I'm a medic: I wasn't there to kill people. The helicopter came down, there was some form of emergency, we were all told to run off the helicopter quickly, and then it just took off. I don't know how many people got off the aircraft or are on the ground and still running around. You have to understand, there was total confusion. It was at night, nobody knew where the officer was; I think he might even have run back on the helicopter and deserted us. I had no idea where I was and no idea where I was going. I was just running around, scared and confused. And that's all there is."

There was a long pause.

"You understand, do you Andy, that you are a prisoner of war, and prisoners of war are required to do certain things?"

"I understand that, and I am helping you as much as I can."

"We need you to sign some things. We need to get some signatures from you so they can be sent to the Red Cross. It's part of the process of letting your family know that you're here."

"I'm sorry, but under the Geneva Convention I'm told that I must not sign anything. I don't really understand why I have to sign anything, because we're taught that we don't have to do that sort of thing."

"Andy," The Voice became even more grandfatherly. "We need to help each other, don't you agree, so that things will run smoothly?"

"Yes, of course. However, I don't know anything. I've told you all I know."

"We really must help each other; otherwise things will have to get painful. I think you understand what I mean by that, Andy?"

"I understand what you're saying, but I really don't know what you need. I've told you everything that I know. I don't know anything else."

There's a technique that high-pressure salesmen use to get you to tell them that you want to buy the product. It's called something like the Creative Pause. Victor Kiam explained it in one of his books: when he was going through his sales pitch, he would stop and pause, and if the person he was trying to sell to actually felt that they had to carry on the conversation during this gap, Kiam knew that he had a sale. The punter felt he had to do something, and that was to agree to buy.

I kept quiet and looked confused.

"You're really looking quite poorly, Andy. Do you require some medical assistance?"

"Yes, please."

"Well, Andy, you have to pay for things. What we require in return is a little assistance. You scratch my back and I'll scratch yours! I believe it's an old English saying, yes?"

He must have looked around the room for approval because the others laughed hard—a bit too hard. It was the sound of the chairman of the board making a bone joke and everybody chortling because they have to. Half the people in the room probably didn't even know what he was saying.

"I will be helpful," I said. "I'm trying to be as helpful as I can. Would it be possible to have some water or some food, I wonder, as my friend and I haven't eaten or had anything to drink for a long time. I'm very thirsty and feeling very weak."

"If you are helpful, we might be able to come to some sort of agreement—but you cannot expect me to do something for nothing. Do you understand that, Andy?"

"Yes, I understand, but I really don't know what you want from me. I've told you everything I know. We're just soldiers; we were just told to get on an aircraft and go. We don't know what's going on. The army treats us like dirt."

"I think you will find we treat people better here. I am willing to supply food, water, and medical assistance for you and your friend, Andy, but it must be a fair trade. We need to know the names of the other people, so we can inform the Red Cross that they are in Iraq."

It went without saying that this was a load of old bollocks, but I had to appear as compliant as I could without actually giving anything away. I wanted to keep this interview in the hands of Mr. Nice Guy. He was being polite, cordial, gentle, soft, concerned. I wasn't looking forward to the bad guy stuff, which I knew would happen sooner or later.

"The only name I know is my friend Dinger's," I said. He would have given his name, number, rank, and date of birth anyway as required by the Geneva

Convention. I said his full name. "Apart from him, I have no idea who is here and who isn't. It was very dark, everybody was running all over the place, it was chaos. The only reason I know about Dinger is because I have seen him."

Something told me the cover story was crumbling. It just didn't feel credible to me any more. It was starting to get holes picked in it, as any story will unless it's deep cover. It was just a matter of playing for time. I had no idea what they were thinking at this stage; it was just cat and mouse. He'd ask a question and I'd give one of my bone answers, and he'd just go on to the next one without even questioning what I had said.

The Voice must have realized I was giving him a load of old pony, and I, in turn, realized that what I was giving him wasn't what they wanted. Despite that, bad things weren't happening—but happen they certainly would.

Mentally I was fine. Your mental state can be altered by drugs. I just hoped they weren't that advanced and were still into caveman tactics. Physical abuse can only get the interrogator to a certain point; beyond that, it's not a viable inducer of the goods. They can assess your physical state from the beatings they've given you. What they can't gauge for sure is your mental state. For that, they need to know your level of alertness, and the only visible clue to that is your eyes. Some people would get totally wound up if an interrogator laughed at the size of their cock, or accused them of being a homosexual, or said their mother was a whore. They would spark up, and this would show that they were not as out of it as they wanted to appear. Everybody has a chink in their armor, and the interrogator's job is to find it. From that moment on, they can really go to town.

We were trained to expect it, and we were lucky that within the Regiment everybody is taking the piss all the time. Daily life revolves around personal insults. But it would still be a battle.

If you're physically and mentally exhausted you shouldn't have the energy even to comprehend what's being said, let alone react to it. Your bluff job won't last long if you as much as blink when he laughs at the size of your cock or asks about your wife's favorite position. The effect you're striving for is that you're exhausted, everything's really too much bother for you to understand, you've told them everything you know, and there's nothing more you want to do than go home. The advantage we were starting with was that, to them, even a senior NCO is a nobody. Their army is run by the officers for the officers. Other ranks are just ignorant cogs in the wheel. They didn't have my mind and they would never get it; it was just a case now of reminding them that I was just a cretinous bumpkin, not even worth the bother.

I asked if it was possible for the handcuffs and blindfold to come off. "I can't think straight," I said. "My hands are numb and my eyes are in trouble. I've got a headache."

"It is for your own security," The Voice replied.

"Of course, I understand, sir. I'm very sorry for asking."

It was for their security, not mine. They didn't want me to be able to identify them.

"I'm trying to help," I went on, "but I'm only the sergeant. I don't know anything, I don't do anything, and I don't particularly want to do anything. If I did know any more, I'd tell you. I don't want to be here. It's the government that sent me. I was just riding in the back of a helicopter, I didn't even know we'd landed in your country."

"I understand all that, Andy. However, you must realize that we need to clarify a few things. And for us to help you you need to help us, as we have discussed. You understand this?"

"Yes, I understand, but I'm sorry, this is all I know."

The game went on for about an hour. It was played very cordially, there was no mistreatment whatsoever. But the undertone was that they knew I was lying through my hind teeth. The only problems were of my own making, when I failed to keep two steps ahead of him and ended up contradicting myself.

I did it a couple of times.

"Andy, are you lying to us?"

"I'm confused. You're not giving me time to think. I'm worried about getting home alive. I don't want to be in this war, I'm just very, very scared."

"I shall give you time to think, Andy, but you must think clearly, because we cannot help you unless you help us."

He started then to talk about my family life and my education. "Have you got a degree?"

Degree? I didn't have so much as a CSE.

"No, I've got no qualifications. This is why I'm a soldier. In Mrs. Thatcher's England, unless you've got education you can't do anything. I'm just a working-class person at the bottom of the heap. I had to join the army because there's nothing else I can do. England is very expensive, there are many taxes. If I didn't do this I'd starve."

"Have you any brothers and sisters?"

"No, I haven't any brothers or sisters. I was an only child."

"We need to know your parents' address so that we can send them notification that you're still alive. They must be very worried about you now, Andy. You need to get a message to them; it would make you feel better. We can do this for you. We are willing to help you, as long as you help us. So if you would just give me your parents' address, we shall send them a letter."

I explained that my dad had died of heart trouble, and my mother had run away and was now living somewhere in America. I hadn't seen her for years. I hadn't got any family at all.

"You must have friends in England who would need to know where you are?"

"I'm just a loner. I drifted into the army. There's nobody."

I knew he didn't believe me, but it was better than a point-blank refusal. The end result was the same, but at least I didn't get a beasting in the process.

"Andy, why do you think the Western armies are here?"

"I'm not entirely sure. Bush says that he wants the oil of Kuwait, and Britain just goes along with it. Basically we're the servants of Bush, and I'm the servant of John Major, the new prime minister. I don't really understand this war. All I know is that I was sent out to do a medic's job. I have no interest in war; I don't want to go to war. I was just dragged in to do their dirty work for them. I know Thatcher and Major are sitting at home with their gin and tonics, and Bush is jogging around Camp David, and here I am, caught up in something I don't really understand. Please believe me —I don't want to be here, and I'm trying to help."

"Well, we will see you very soon, Andy," he said. "You can go now."

The blokes behind me picked me up and dragged me away at the double. I didn't manage to get my feet going at their speed, and they dragged me all the way down the corridor, along the path, down the step, across the cobbles, and back to the cell. They put me back in the corner, in the same agonizing position.

When the door slammed, I let all my breath out with relief. I started trying to sort myself out.

Two minutes later, the door banged and crashed, and a guard came in. He took off my blindfold, but I didn't look up. The last thing I wanted was another filling in. He walked out again, leaving me to see my surroundings for the first time.

The floor was concrete—really bad, decaying concrete, full of little dips and very damp. There was a window to the right of the door, a small, slim, long opening. As I looked up at it, my eyes fixed on a large hook in the middle of the ceiling. My heart started pumping hard. I had visions of me hanging up there very soon.

The walls had once been cream but now were covered with muck. The surfaces were chipped and etched with Arabic writing. There were also a couple of Nazi swastika signs, and on one wall a back view, about A4 size, of a dove flying up towards the sky. The bird had chains joining its legs together, and underneath, in English amongst the Arabic, were the words: "To my only desire, my little boy Josef, will I ever see him again?" It was a beautiful piece of artwork. I wondered who had done it and what had happened to him. Was this the last thing that anybody did around here?

Splashed over the walls were two enormous bloodstains, two or three pints of blood per stain, dried onto

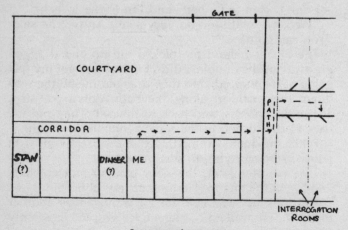

Interrogation area

the plaster. By one of them was a scrap of cardboard. I stared at it for a while, then shuffled across on my arse until I was close enough to read what was on it. It was from a box which had held sachets of fortifying drink. The packaging said how wonderful it was to drink: it gave you vitality and energy. I read more and got a shock that made my heart jump. The product came from Brentford in Middlesex. That was where Kate's mother came from. I knew the place well; I even knew where the factory was. Kate still lived there. It depressed me beyond belief to think of her. How long was I going to be here? Was this it for the war? Was this it until they'd finished with me? Would I just end up as one of the statistics of atrocity?

My defense was to get back to business and think about possible scenarios. Did we have any more survivors? Had the Iraqis made a connection between us and the compromise at the MSR? Had they already got people who had confirmed this, and were they just playing games? No, the only fact I knew for sure was that they had me and Dinger.

About a quarter of an hour later I heard muffled voices in the corridor. My heart pounded. They walked on, and I let go a big breath. I heard another door open. Probably Dinger, being taken for an interrogation.

An hour later I heard his door being slammed and locked down. It was starting to get last light. It must have been very dark out in the corridor because the shadows weren't coming under the door any more. I listened as all the voices walked away to the door at the end of the corridor, and then that was locked as well, for the first time since we'd got there. Did that mean we were there for the night? I hoped so. I needed to get my head down.

Darkness brought with it a strange sense of security because I couldn't see, mixed with dread because I was cold and had time to think. I tried sleeping on my front, with my head resting on the floor, but the best position turned out to be lying on my side with my cheek resting on the concrete. The only drawback was the pressure that was exerted on my hip bone; I had to move every few minutes to relieve it and ended up not sleeping.

The glow of Tilly lamps shimmered under the door, and I heard footsteps and the jangle of keys. The bolt thudded. They started to kick the door. It was even scarier than in the daytime. I could hear Dinger's being done at the same time. It was all so intimidating: they had the power and the lamp, and I was just the dickhead in the corner.

The door was kicked open. I got myself sitting up. I pulled my knees in and got my head down, ready for the inevitable kicking. They came over, picked me up, and guided me out into the corridor. My feet were agony, and I had to collapse to take the weight off them. They dragged me a few meters and stopped. They took me into another cell. I couldn't work out

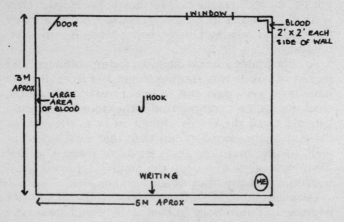

Interrogation cell

what was happening. Was it some sort of punishment cell? A toilet? Another interrogation room?

They pushed me down to the floor. The handcuffs were removed, but reapplied to the left wrist. My right hand was free. The other wrist was handcuffed to something.

One of them said, "You stay here now."

They left the cell, locked the door, and their footsteps receded down the corridor.

I felt with my free hand to find out what I was anchored to and came into contact with somebody else's arm.

"Dinger?"

"Wanker!"

I couldn't believe it.

We were chuffed to fuck to be reunited. For a few minutes we just sat there amazed, hugging each other and swapping greetings. Things were absolutely splendid. Then we heard footsteps in the corridor. The guards started kicking the door to come in. I looked at Dinger. His face looked as disappointed as I felt. I looked up as they came in, ready to say: Nice stitch, guys. But they'd come back with a blanket for us to share. Was it Saddam's birthday or what?

"How's your hands?" I whispered into Dinger's ear, unsure if we'd been put together because the cell was bugged.

"Shit state," he said.

That pleased me. I'd have been pissed off if mine were worse than his.

"I've still got my map and compass," I said.

"Yeah, same here. I can't believe."

"Gold?"

"Civvies took it. And yours?"

"The ruperts had it away."

"Wankers, the lot of them."

For the next half an hour we were like a couple of

kids comparing wounds. We took the piss out of the guards and generally let off steam. Then we got the blanket sorted out so that it was under our arses but also coming up our backs and over our shoulders. As we moved around to make ourselves comfortable, the handcuffs got tighter and tighter.

Sitting with him in the darkness, I learned what had happened to Dinger, Legs, and Bob after we got split up.

As they patrolled along the hedgeline, Dinger heard a noise and stopped. Behind him, Legs and Bob followed suit. They couldn't shout a warning forward. The patrol was split.

The noise subsided. They waited for ten minutes but no one returned. They carried on, moving on the bearing. They had only gone 600 feet when there was a challenge from about 50 feet away. Two incoming shots went very close. Then there was fire from many positions. There was a contact, during which Bob got separated from the other two.

Dinger and Legs fired and maneuvred back down to the river. They heard a clearing operation about 450 feet away, lots of firing and shouting. The Iraqis were coming down in extended line.

Dinger and Legs had thirty rounds of link for the Minimi and a mag between them. There was no way they could fight their way through. They had no choice but to cross the river. They got right down to the water's edge and found a small boat. They tried to unchain it. No luck. They didn't want to shoot the padlock, so there was only one escape route left.

The river only looked about 300 feet across and slow-flowing. The water was so cold it took Dinger's breath away. As they staggered ashore they found that all they'd done was swim a tributary. They were stuck on a spit of land in the middle of the river, there was firing and shouting on the bank they'd left, and torchlights flashed over the water. They looked for cover.

The spit was overlooked by a roadblock on a pontoon about 250 meters away. There was no cover; both men were freezing cold and shaking convulsively. Legs recce'd around to find how they could get off, and where. They could still hear all the other contacts going on, including one very long one with a Minimi. It must have been Bob. Then there was silence.

Legs found a polystyrene box, which they broke up and stuffed down their smocks for buoyancy. The only exit point from the spit was guarded by the bridge; there was so much enemy activity that their only chance was to swim the main river.

They lay on the ground for an hour, waiting for an opportunity. Their wet smocks and trousers were icing solid; they had to move. Dinger stalled. He'd had a tough enough struggle getting this far, and he doubted his ability to swim the main river. Legs urged him on. They waded in up to their waists and started to swim. The river was 1,600 feet across, the current was flowing fast, and Dinger was soon struggling.

"We can do it, mate," Legs said. "We can do it."

At last, Dinger's feet touched the ground. "That's bottom," he whispered as he staggered onto dry land, instinctively carrying on up the shoreline to check for enemy activity.

Looking back across the river, he saw that the current had carried them about a kilometer and a half downstream. He also saw that Legs was still in the water. Dinger ran down to the water's edge and hauled him out. Legs couldn't stand.

Dinger had seen a small pump-hut about 30 feet from the bank. He dragged Legs up to it and carried him inside. Dinger was so tired himself now that it took him two hours to get the wet clothes off him.

It was first light. Dinger carried Legs out into the sun, no longer caring about a compromise: the most important thing was to keep him alive. People were starting to work in the fields, forcing Dinger to drag the injured man in and out. He knew it wouldn't be long before they were discovered. There seemed to be hundreds of troops on the ground.

Legs was going to die. Dinger had to make a decision: did

he stay concealed and just watch him die, or did he compromise the position and give Legs the chance of medical attention? It didn't take much thinking about. Dinger left the hut and stood around until a farmer spotted him.

Dinger ran back inside and closed the door behind him. The farmer ran up, locked it, and took off into the fields ranting and raving. Dinger had already organized an avenue of escape from the back of the hut. Legs was by the generator, his breathing labored. Dinger told him what he was doing and left. He didn't know if Legs understood. He hoped he did.

He was running along the floor of a dry wadi when a local spotted him. Soon there were whole groups of them, twenty or thirty at a time, paralleling him on either bank. They started shooting. He knew he was going to get caught, but he kept running. He'd had his shamag around his head to try and pass himself off as a local; when they finally converged on him, they knocked him down and used it to bind his hands behind his back. As Dinger looked up, he saw one of them pull a knife. The man started to cut his ear off.

Dinger reckoned this was as good a time as any to indicate the gold on his belt. The locals thought it was Christmas. Off it came, and they started squabbling about it. When they had sorted themselves out, they frog-marched Dinger into their town.

The civvies were trying to pull him apart. Several shots were fired, and he thought the end was near. But the shooting had come from a squad of jundies; they waded into the mob and pulled him clear. There must have been some sort of order or reward to deliver prisoners alive.

He was put into a convoy of vehicles, and they crossed back over the river and drove to a camp. Everybody was excited; Dinger was the first white-eye they'd caught.

He was handcuffed to a chair in a room full of officers. They spoke good English and asked him the Big Four. Then they said, "What is your mission?" to which he replied: "I cannot answer that question."

They said that things would get very bad for him if he

didn't answer the questions: this was war. They asked him again, and he started to reply. He got as far as "I cannot . . ." and they launched him. He was kicked to the floor and filled in. It sounded as though there was a competition going on; there was a lot of high spirits and chat. Dinger was starting to get worried.

The beasting went on for about thirty minutes. No questions were actually being asked. Then one of the officers jumped up and left the room, and one of them said, "You will be sorry now."

The man returned with a wooden pole about 4 feet long and 3 inches in diameter. He waded straight into Dinger with it.

It only lasted for about ninety seconds, but Dinger was sure he was going to die. He started going into the cover story.

They asked how many people there were in the search and rescue package, and when Dinger said, "I cannot answer that question," they started again with the pole.

They brought in an empty 66 and a 203 and asked him how the weapons worked. Dinger refused to show them, which earned him another seeing to with the pole. Then Dinger thought: It's a weapon, for Christ's sake, not a state secret. They could find out how to work it from a copy of Jane's.

He told them the pilot rescue story, and it seemed to work well, but this was an early stage in the questioning. He knew things were going to get a whole lot worse.

We compared notes on the rest of the patrol. The last thing Dinger had seen of Legs was him lying on a stretcher, absolutely motionless. As far as he was concerned, Legs was dead. We had no idea about Bob. Dinger had thought he was with us, and we had thought he was with them. Dinger had seen some of Bob's equipment when we first got moved to Baghdad; it was part of his webbing and it was badly burnt. It didn't bode well. Whilst I had been getting interrogated just after capture, Dinger was in another room with all our captured equipment.

"They had some weapons there. The blokes were fucking about with a 203, and I started shouting to leave it alone because it still had a round in. All I got for my pains was a smack in the mouth. The nuggets fired it, and it went off."

Luckily for Dinger, a 40mm bomb needs to travel about 60 feet before the inertia device kicks in and it self-arms. The bomb hit the ceiling and bounced down again. Allah was smiling on him that day: if the bomb had popped it would have taken everybody in the room.

"There was a mega flap at that stage, and obviously I got filled in for it," he said.

We were rolling up about the 203 but trying hard not to giggle. It was such a relief to listen to Dinger's voice again. All my problems seemed to fade away.

"The sergeant major picked up a compass, and the knobber didn't have a clue what he was doing with it," Dinger went on. "He knew it was a compass, but he really didn't know how to use it. He daren't lose face in front of the jundies, so he acted as if he knew. It really kept me happy. He had the fucking thing upside down trying to open it, and there was me, keeping my head down, a bit of a smile on my face, trying not to laugh. They were dragging little bits and pieces like batteries out of the kit, and everything to them was an explosive. They obviously thought everything was going to blow up in their faces."

We lapsed into a phase of seriousness and wondered if Stan and Vince were still alive. As far as I was concerned, Stan was likely to be dead. He'd been on the way out on the first night of the E&E, and I couldn't imagine him suddenly improving.

"Bastard!" I said. "I gave him my bobble-hat."

It genuinely annoyed me that he still had my hat and was dead and didn't need it any more.

"That bastard's always got all the kit," Dinger said. "I bet he's already nicked God's anorak."

We weren't sure about Vince and Chris. On the assumption that if anybody was alive they'd be with us now, they, like Bob, were either still on the run or dead.

The only question we didn't have an answer for was why they had put us together. What did it mean? That they believed our story? That they hoped we were going to start waffling and they would listen in? The only conclusion we came to was that we wouldn't waste time and energy thinking about it, we'd just take advantage of being together.

The crash of the bolt being undone on the door at the far end of the corridor concentrated our minds wonderfully. Footsteps echoed again on the tiled floor, and the glow of Tilly lamps invaded the cell. Boots thumped against the door to force it open. Oh shit, oh no, I thought, they're going to split us up now.

Two guards appeared. The first presented us with a pitcher of water. The second guard was carrying bowls that were steaming.

The blanket, the water, the soup—it was like staying at the Ritz. This was all rather pleasant, room service coming in and pampering us like this. I wondered if I could trouble them for a copy of the *FT*.

We looked up at them with our blanket around our shoulders, grinning like a couple of grateful refugees.

"American?" they asked.

"No, British."

"No Tel Aviv?"

"No. British. England. London."

"Ah, London. Football. Manchester United. Football. Good."

"Yeah, Liverpool."

"Ah, Liverpool. Bobby Moore! Good."

We didn't say a word to each other until the door

had slammed firmly shut. Then I turned to Dinger, and in unison we muttered "Wankers!" and had a giggle.

The bowls held a hot liquid that tasted vaguely of onions. In the pitcher there must have been four pints of water, and it tasted better than vintage champagne. In theory, you've really got to take your time and sip it slowly. In practice, because you can't trust the bastards not to come in and whisk it away again from under your nose, you are forced to rush it. The big danger then is that all you achieve is the feeling of wetness on your throat and a swollen belly.

We tried to settle down. The handcuffs dictated that we had to lie on our backs. We got the blanket over us, and I stared at the ceiling. Very soon my nose started twitching. Dinger stank, he absolutely stank.

"Your poor wife," I said. "Imagine sleeping with a stinking mess like you every night—it must be like kipping next to a grizzly bear."

Just a minute or two later, I was gripped by a fearsome urge. It must have been the onions.

"Dinger, mate—I wanna go a pooh-pooh."

Dinger grudgingly hauled himself into a half-lying position with his hand in the air so I could get as far away from him as possible.

I struggled to get my trousers down, trying hard not to tighten the ratchet on the cuffs.

"For fuck's sake get on with it," he moaned. "Let's get our heads down."

At last I was in position, and I emptied my arse. Wet, gooey shit sprayed all over the place.

"Oh, fucking cheers," said Dinger indignantly. "This is my house, this—would you do this in your own place?"

I couldn't help myself. It kept on coming.

"No consideration. I had to work hard for all this. You invite people over, you offer them dinner, and how do they repay you? They drop their arse all over your nice carpet.''

I was laughing so much I fell back into it, and there wasn't much I could do except pull my trousers back up and lie down. It wasn't the best of situations, but at least there were three compensations. I'd done it in his cell, not mine, it was warm on my legs, and it would be his turn next.

We put half of the blanket under us for insulation and got snuggled down, sharing body heat.

During the night we heard the guards coming and going and doors banging. Each time I'd dread they were coming for us, but they always passed by and kept on going.

At one point we heard a door in the distance being kicked open and the muffled screams and shouts and moans and groans of somebody getting filled in. You strain to hear, but you only get bits and pieces. To hear somebody else in pain like that is a horrible thing. You're not particularly worried about who it is. You don't know, so you don't care. But it's so demoralizing, because you're so defenseless and you know it could be you next.

We heard, ''Naughty boy. Stand! Bad boy. Bad boy.'' Then the sound of something like a plate being thrown across a room and banging on to the concrete.

Could it be ''Stan'' they were saying? We tried our hardest to hear more, but the noise subsided. At least we knew there was somebody else in the equation, even if we didn't know whether it was one of us. But whoever he was, he could pose a threat. Dinger and I were reasonably content that our stories squared up; another person on the scene, however, a person we couldn't get to speak to, could mean that the rug was about to be pulled from under us. I felt my happiness evaporate. The only thought I could console myself with was that Dinger and I were still together.

Suddenly, as if it was sent deliberately to calm me, I heard the welcome noise of bombers going through the sky about a mile away. I felt an instant surge of hope. If we took hits, then we had means of escape.

We spent the rest of the night together. Every time we heard doors banging we thought they were coming to separate us, and we said our goodbyes. Finally, some time in the morning, our cell door was kicked open. I was handcuffed and blindfolded and taken away.

I knew I was being taken for another interrogation; I knew the route so well. Out of the door, turn right, up the corridor, turn left, over the cobblestones, up the step, along the pathway, past the bushes, into a room. I assumed it was the same room.

They pushed me onto a chair and held me there.

"Good morning, Andy," The Voice said. "How are you this morning?"

"Fine, thank you very much," I said. "Thank you for the blanket. It's very cold at night."

"Yes, it is very cold. As you can see, Andy, we do take care of you. We take care of people who help us. And you will help us, Andy, will you not?"

"Yes, I've told you, I'll help as much as I can."

"There are just a few matters that we need to clear up this morning, Andy. You see, we are not totally convinced that you're not Jewish. We need proof. Tell us if you are, because this will stop a lot of pain and discomfort for you. What is your religion?"

"Church of England."

"What is Church of England?"

"It's Christian."

"Who do you worship?"

"I worship God."

"I see. And who is Jesus?"

I explained.

"Who is Mary?"

I explained.

"Andy, do you understand that we worship the same God, you and I? I'm a Muslim, and I worship the same God as you."

"Yes, I understand."

"Are you religious, Andy?"

"Yes, I am religious. I take my religion seriously."

"Tell me how you pray in the Christian world."

"We can pray on our knees, we can pray standing up, it all depends, it doesn't matter. It's a very personal thing."

When I was a junior soldier at Shorncliffe there was a battalion church parade every fourth Sunday. You had to wear your best uniform and boots, and march smartly all the way from the camp to the garrison church. It was a bind, because as a boy soldier you only get one full day off a week, which was Sunday—and that was only if you weren't behind the CO on the Friday morning cross-country run: otherwise it was another run on Sunday. Even then you couldn't go home because you weren't allowed out until nine in the morning and had to be back by eight at night. So all in all I wasn't best pleased with church parade and never paid much attention to what was going on. Now I was desperately trying to remember all the bits and pieces of the services and make myself sound like the devoutest Bible-thumper since Billy Graham.

"When do you fast? When do Christians fast?"

Did we fast? I just didn't know.

"We don't fast."

His tone changed. "You're lying to us, Andy. You're lying! We know that Christians fast."

He told me about Lent. You learn something every day. I hadn't known that Catholics fasted.

"I'm a Protestant," I said. "It's different."

He seemed to calm down.

"So tell me about the festivals. What foods do you eat? What foods don't you eat?"

I was racking my brain trying to remember what happened at times like Harvest Festival and Easter.

"Protestants eat all foods. We actually celebrate the fact that we can eat what we can, when we can. It's a very liberal religion."

"So you don't have to keep away from pork?"

"No."

"Look, Andy, just tell us if you're a Jew, that's all we need to know. If you're lying to us, you know you will be punished."

Another bloke to my half right joined in, also speaking in good English. He told me he'd been to Sandhurst.

"When is St. George's Day?"

I didn't have a clue.

"St. Swithin's?"

Same response.

"How do you have burials? How do you mourn? How long for?"

I ducked and weaved for the next two hours.

Finally The Voice said, "What would you say, Andy, if I was to tell you that we know you are Jews and can prove it?"

"You're mistaken. I'm not a Jew."

"Right. Tell me what you know about Judaism."

"You've got orthodox Jews with long matted hair, and they don't eat pork. That's all. We don't mix with the Jewish community."

"Well, tell me, have you ever had a Jewish girlfriend? Do you know any Jews in England? Tell me their names and where they live. How would you know if they were Jews?"

"I've never had anything to do with Jewish women."

"Why not, Andy, are you homosexual?"

"No, I'm not homosexual, but in England we have definite racial groups, and there's not too much intermixing. The Jewish community keep themselves to themselves, and you don't really have that much contact with them because they're very insular."

"How big is the Jewish community in England?"

"I have no idea. We don't really mix."

The questions went on and on, and the answers I could give became more and more limited. I was getting boxed into a corner. Then I suddenly had a thought. I couldn't believe that it hadn't come to me sooner.

"I can prove I'm not a Jew."

"How can you prove that?"

"Because I have a foreskin."

"What? What is a foreskin?"

There was lots of gobbing off in Arabic, and the sound of paper rustling. Perhaps they were checking a dictionary.

"I can show you," I said helpfully. "If you undo my hands, I'll show you what a foreskin is."

Still they couldn't comprehend what I was talking about.

"How do you spell foreskin?"

I could hear the bloke scribbling away. A soldier on each side clamped a hand on my shoulders, and somebody undid one of my handcuffs.

"What are you going to do, Andy? You must tell us what you are going to do first."

"Well, I'll unzip and get my penis out, and I'll show you that I have a foreskin."

I stood up and pulled out my cock. I got hold of the foreskin and stretched it as far out as I could.

"See, I have a foreskin! Jews are circumcised as part of their religion. They have the foreskin taken off."

The room rocked with laughter. They were rolling up. As I did myself up, I was pushed back on to the chair. The handcuffs went back on.

They were having a huge giggle about this foreskin business. They babbled on in Arabic, occasionally throwing in the word "foreskin."

"Would you like some food, Andy?"

"Yes, thank you very much, I'd love some food," I said. And as everybody was in such a good mood, I added, "And something to drink, if I could, please."

A hand came up and put a date in my mouth.

They all carried on laughing as if I wasn't there, and I was rather pleased with myself because things were going rather well. I didn't get anything to drink though. I sat there with the stone in my mouth, wondering what I was going to do with it. I didn't want to swallow it because it would stick in my throat and I didn't have anything to wash it down with. The Sandhurst officer must have realized my problem, because he gobbed off at the guard and the bloke put his hand under my chin and I spat the stone carefully into his hand.

The room was still buzzing with chat about foreskins.

I had a sudden thought. I didn't know what everybody else's condition in the patrol was, whether they had foreskins or not. It dawned on me that Bob looked dark and Mediterranean. If they had his body, they could have taken him for a Jew, and we were getting the good news as a result.

"Of course, Christians as well as Jews get circumcised, for medical reasons," I said. "Some parents want their children circumcised at birth. So it's not just Jews that are circumcised."

"Tell me more, Andy. You told me Jews are circumcised at birth. Now you're telling me that Christians are circumcised at birth as well. This is confusing. Are you lying to us?"

"No, it all depends on the parents. Some people think it's more hygienic."

They found this ever so funny, and I was chuffed that there was a bit of laughter going on. I wondered how I could keep them going.

"We shall talk some more very soon, Andy," The Voice said.

I was dragged to my feet and taken back to my old cell. Once again, I was on my own and handcuffed.

I heard Dinger being put back into his cell some time later. Then there was silence, and we were both left to our own devices for a number of hours.

Later that afternoon they came for me again.

"Tell us more about the helicopter, Andy," The Voice said as I was pushed onto the chair. "What sort of helicopter was it?"

"It was a Chinook."

"Why a Chinook?"

"I don't know why it was a Chinook; that's just the helicopter we used."

"Where did you land?"

"I have no idea where we landed. It was nighttime. We're soldier medics, not navigators; we just sit in the back."

"Do you know if the helicopter took off again?"

"I have no idea what happened to it."

"If it crashed on the ground and you know where it is, we could find it for you and maybe find the rest of your friends."

There was a brief pause, and then he said, "Look, Andy, we can find no aircraft anywhere. It must have taken off and left you, or you must be lying."

"No, I'm not lying."

I went through the story again. As I spoke, I was interrupted constantly by questions.

"Andy, I'll ask you again, one more time. Do you know where you landed?"

"No, I've no idea where I landed. I've told you, I can't tell you any more. I don't know anything else. Why keep on asking me? I really don't know. I want to help. All I want to do is go back to England."

His tone was shifting now. He was getting more grave. "How much fuel does the helicopter hold?"

"I haven't got a clue. I don't know anything about that. I just get in the helicopters, I don't know anything about them."

And that was more or less true. I had never known anything technical that I didn't need to know. With a weapon, all I want to know is how it works, what kind of ammunition it fires, and what to do when it goes wrong. I don't want to know the muzzle velocity and stuff like that, because it is immaterial. You aim, press the trigger, it goes bang, it fires a round. The same principle applied to helicopters and other bits of kit. I am downright wary, as most professional soldiers are, of anyone who can come out with all the statistical facts. Sometimes people use these to mask their inadequacies. They might know all the bumpf, but it's "hands on" that counts.

This line of questioning was irrelevant anyway; they could have got any of the information out of *Jane's*. It was taking up time though, which couldn't be bad—and I wasn't getting beaten. I sat there, acting confused and humble as usual. The only problem was that they were getting more serious about it and accusing me of not helping. But I must have sounded genuine because I was. I didn't have a clue.

"How does the ramp come down?"

"Somebody presses a button."

"Where's the button?"

"I don't know . . ."

They gave up, and I was taken back to the cell. It was dark. My blindfold was off, but the handcuffs were still on. I had long since lost all sense or feeling in my fingers and hands. The flesh on my wrists had now swollen so much it covered the bracelets. My hands were like balloons.

I heard them toing and froing with Dinger as well, and then they came back for me. It was the third interrogation within what felt like the space of twenty-four hours. This was the scariest, because they fetched me in pitch darkness.

The Voice started by going over some of the helicopter stuff again. Then I got questions on the big war plan.

"Schwarzkopf and his Allies—how do they plan to invade?"

"I don't know."

"Will they invade Iraq?"

"I don't know."

"How many aircraft are there?"

"I don't know."

"How many Syrian soldiers are preparing to invade Iraq from Syria?"

"I don't know."

"Do you think it is a feasible idea that they should invade Iraq from Syria?"

"I don't know."

"Will Israel invade Iraq?"

"I don't know."

"Well, how many soldiers have the British got here?"

"That I do know. I read it in the newspaper. Forty to fifty thousand, I think. It doesn't really interest me, I'm afraid."

"How many tanks are there ready to invade Kuwait and Iraq?"

"I don't know."

"Aircraft?"

"I don't know."

"Does Bush realize that he's killing our women and children?"

This was weird stuff, but wonderful: at least I wasn't getting filled in, and they weren't bringing up the fact that they had lost a lot of men during the contacts.

Again there were lots of pauses, and: "Andy, you're

not helping me. You must know how many aircraft there are."

I was profoundly tired. It had been more or less impossible to sleep, and I was very hungry and thirsty. I was gagging for a drink.

In daylight, with the usual scary noise, the guards kicked the door in and brought me a pitcher of water. It was horrible minging stuff that looked as if it had been dredged up from a drain, but I wasn't particularly bothered. It was wet. And even if it made me ill, at least I was rehydrating—unless I brought it up again.

They wanted to take the pitcher back with them, so I was to drink it all in one go. They took off my blindfold for the first time since the first interrogation, undid my handcuffs, and stood over me as I sat on the floor and grasped the pitcher in both hands.

I started drinking. My broken teeth exploded with pain as the cold water hit the stumps. As I looked past their legs and out into the corridor, I saw Stan. Stan was about 6'4", and he was being dragged by men who only came up to his armpits. The whole of his head, including his beard, was dark red and matted. On one side his scalp was split open in a big, glistening gash. His trousers were caked with blood and mud and shit. His eyes were closed, and he was moaning and groaning to himself. He was totally and utterly gone. He was hobbling and stooped, well past the "injured and confused" stage of bluffing. He made me feel like I'd just come out of a health farm. It was the first time I had seen him since we had tried to contact the jets with the TACBEs.

I remembered the night Dinger and I had heard what we thought was guards commanding somebody to get up. "Stand, bad boy! Stand!" So they *had* been mispronouncing his name after all.

The guards turned and saw what I was looking at.

They kicked the pitcher out of my hands and went berserk with their boots.

"No look!" they screamed. "No look!"

It was the first kicking I'd received since the very first interrogation, and I could have done without it. Whether they had screwed up by leaving the door open or it was all intentional, I had no idea.

I curled up on the damp concrete. My teeth were raging but I counted my blessings: the guards had forgotten to put my handcuffs back on.

I felt sick, but I was trying hard to keep it down. I didn't want to dehydrate. Finally I couldn't help myself, and retched. All the precious fluid I had gained I lost again.

I heard Dinger being moved; I didn't hear Stan being brought back. A short while later they came for me. It was routine by now. They blindfolded and handcuffed me, and dragged me off without saying a word.

There was a long, long silence as I sat on my chair. I could hear feet shuffling and pens scribbling. I could smell all the same smells.

Nothing happened for what seemed like an hour.

"Andy," I heard. "Today we want the truth out of you."

It was The Voice, but in a new guise. Firm now, impatient, no nonsense.

"We know that you've been lying. We've tried to help you. You're not helping us at all. Therefore we will get the truth out of you in other ways. Do you understand what I mean?"

"Yes, I understand what you mean, but I don't know what you want. I've told you everything I know. I am trying to help."

"Right. Why are you in Iraq?"

I went through the same old story. Before I had even finished, he was up and walking around.

"That's all I know," I said, blindly trying to locate where he was in the room.

"You're lying to us!" he screamed in my face. "We know! We know that you're lying!"

My face was pulled up, and The Voice started slapping me hard. Guards on either side held me up by the shoulders.

It stopped, and he shouted at me, from so close I could feel his breath on my cheek. "How do we know that you're lying? Because we have your signals operator in hospital, that's why. He's been captured, and he's told us everything."

It was possible. Maybe Legs was still alive, and in his physical condition he might have said anything. Or everything. But The Voice hadn't told me what Legs had said. Was it a bluff?

"You *are* lying, aren't you, Andy?"

"No, I'm not lying. I can't help you any more. I am trying to help but I just don't know anything."

I was doing the pleading bit now, because I was flapping good style. I was trying to think of a reason why they should have told me this.

More slaps and I went down. They picked me up and took off the handcuffs. Before I had time to wonder why, they started to strip me. I had sudden visions of them cutting my cock off.

They ripped my shirt off and pulled down my trousers. This is it, I thought: this is where they fuck me.

But they pushed me down on to the chair and held my head forward. I took a deep breath and waited.

It must have been a piece of four-by-two or the end foot or so of an oar. *Whoomph!* The shock of it hitting me—*whoomph! whoomph!*—I screamed out like an idiot. They worked their way all over my back and head with it. I must have been unconscious before I hit the floor.

I came to, groaning and mumbling, and they hoisted me up and put me back on the chair.

"You will tell us everything, Andy. We want it from you. We know what has happened. We have your signals operator. He's told us he's your signals operator."

That had to have come from Legs. He was the signals operator. Was he in hospital?

I denied, denied, denied.

They punched and slapped, smashed the paddle in a frenzy on my back. Then they stopped for five minutes, as if they were resting, getting their strength back.

"Why are you doing this to yourself, Andy? Just tell us what we need to know."

They started up again.

I got my first hit with what felt like a metallic ball on the end of a stick, like some sort of medieval mace. It thumped into my neck and arms and kidneys with terrible precision. I went down again, screaming my head off. This was way out of control. This was when I was going to die.

As I hit the floor, the lads behind me started to give me a kicking. I screamed again and again.

The Voice screamed back at me. "You're lying! You will tell us!"

It went on and on, I didn't know for how long. They'd kick, get me back up, slap me around the face, whack me with the metal ball and wooden paddle. I could hear them breathing hard with the exertion of it all.

The Voice would shout at me, and I would shout back.

"Fucking hell," I bawled, "I don't know, I don't know anything for fuck's sake!"

He gobbed off at the boys in Arabic, and they started up again with another kicking.

I went down time and again.

Pain upon pain.

It hurt, it really hurt.

They stopped kicking and lifted me up. I was dragged out of the room, my chest bare and my trousers still round my ankles. As soon as we got out into the courtyard, there was the reception committee. I was kicked and punched all the way down. I got one kick up the arse, and I really thought they'd split my rectum. I thought my insides were falling out. I went straight down, howling like a pig.

They threw me into the cell, blindfolded, handcuffed, and naked, and left me. My breathing was very shallow. When I had recovered sufficiently to sit up, I checked myself for broken bones. I clung to the memory of the lecture by the Marine aviator. The Viet Cong had broken every major bone in his body during the course of his six years in jail. In comparison, I was having a picnic.

"I was told the bigger and harder you were the quicker they would leave you alone. This I soon discovered was untrue. They can do whatever they want with you. The only thing they cannot break is your mental state. Only you can let that collapse. My head stayed clear, and every day it said to me: 'Fuck 'em.' That's what kept me alive."

My body was in far better condition than his had been, and my mind was definitely clear. So then—fuck 'em.

It was dark. I had been lying there for ages. I hadn't noticed the cold at first: the pain had blocked out such trifles. Now I was starting to shiver. I thought, if this carries on for many more days, I've had it—I'm going to get well and truly done in here.

I could hear screaming and shouting in the other rooms, but I wasn't taking much notice of it because I was too involved in my own little world, my own little universe of pain and bruises and broken teeth.

The others would be getting the same as me, but it

was a world away. It was in the distance, it did not concern me. All I did was wait for my turn again.

From then, and for what must have been quite a few days, it just carried on. Hour after hour, day after day, beating after beating, taking my turn with the other two, lying curled up, cold and in pain, waiting for the terrifying noise of the door being kicked open, the worst sound I had ever heard.

"Andy, this is your last chance; tell us what we need to know."

"I don't know anything."

I knew one thing. I knew the other two weren't giving up because otherwise my interrogations would have stopped. I kept saying to myself, It's not going to be me, I'm not going to let them down, I'm not going to be the one to put the others in the shit.

It was a haze. Two or three interrogations per twenty-four hours. Day after day. Always the same stuff. Always a little bit harder to bear.

Then they found new ways of hurting me. Twice they held me down on the seat, pushed my head down, while they flogged me with a whip with thick thongs. And when they had finished, the others joined in with the paddle and ball.

After one session I was sitting on the chair, still naked, my mind a blur of anguish. The Voice talked quietly and conspiratorially in my ear.

"Andy, we need to talk. You're in very bad condition. You're going to die very soon, but you're still not helping us. I cannot understand it. We'll get the information out of you, you know we will. One of you will tell us, there's no big problems. Why make it harder on yourself? Look, do you want me to show you how bad we can be?"

There was a rubbing sore on the inside of my thigh about two inches in diameter. It was a weeping, seeping thing, red and raw. I heard the chinking of metal and the hiss of a paraffin heater being turned up. Hands gripped my shoulders and pinned me to the chair.

The back of the spoon was red-hot as he ran it over and over the sore. The stench of burning flesh made me gag. I howled like a dog.

Spoon. Scream. Spoon. Scream.

He rubbed it in small circles and little crisscross grids.

I jumped up, so violently that the blokes couldn't hold me. I yelled and yelled in an effort to release the pain.

They got me back on to the chair.

"Do you see, Andy? It's pointless. Just tell us what we want to know."

Legs told them fuck all. They wouldn't be doing all this just to get his information confirmed. And they hadn't said what information Legs was supposed to have told them. It was a load of old bollocks. If he could hold out, so could I.

11

People came in and out of the cells all the time now. The sound track was just screaming and shouting and the horrific banging of the sheet metal doors.

The guards must have had a beasting roster. Teams came in every two hours or so, hollering and shouting and filling us in. We were still handcuffed and blindfolded.

"Stand up! Sit down!"

As you're trying to do it, they're punching and kicking. Sometimes I'd fall into a semiconscious state after just a few punches, sometimes I'd just be there, breathing heavily and taking it. Sometimes they'd come in with a length of hose, which hurt incredibly on my kidneys and back. My body was becoming even more of a mess, but the worst bit about it was hearing them in Stan's or Dinger's room. Not so much because I was concerned for them—there was nothing I could do to help, and they were big and ugly enough to take it—but because it meant that it was going to be my turn soon.

One time, by way of a change, the interrogation started off all rather pleasantly.

"You're in a terrible condition, aren't you, Andy?"

"Yeah, I'm in terrible condition."

My mouth was so matted with scabs and swellings I could hardly get the words out.

"How are your teeth—they were giving you some problems before?"

"I've got some smashed in at the back. They hurt." I continued to play the humble dickhead. And at this stage I was totally out of the game anyway. My teeth were agony—more painful than the worst toothache I'd ever had, and then some.

"I have arranged for somebody to come in and sort that out," The Voice said soothingly. "We have a dentist here. In fact, he worked in Guy's Hospital in London for nine years. He's one of the best."

My blindfold was removed. The dentist appeared and said, "Hello, Andy." He got me to open wide, and gently and reassuringly he peered into my mouth. He sounded sympathetic as he took some instruments from a bag.

"Open wide again, Andy, please," he said in perfect English. "Oh, dear, that is bad, but I'll soon sort it out for you."

I had my suspicions, but there was nothing I could do. I opened as wide as I could for him, and the cunt gripped the first stump of tooth with the pliers and twisted hard.

I screamed and blood gushed from my mouth.

"Do you really think we're going to help you?" The Voice laughed. "Do you really think we're going to help you, you despicable heap of shit? We could just leave you to die, you know—you're so irrelevant to us. Who do you think is going to help you, Andy? Your government? You can't believe that. John Major doesn't care about lumps of excrement like you. No, Andy, the only one who can help you is yourself. Why are you doing this to yourself? You're going through this for nothing. You're stupid, a stupid, misguided fool, and your teeth are going to come out one by one."

I couldn't answer. I was screaming. I knew that I was going to die. And I knew now that it wouldn't be clean and quick.

We had been stripped of all clothing for several days now and left exposed to the damp and bitter cold. We were getting beaten regularly in the cells and tortured to the point of unconsciousness during the interrogations. We were put in stress positions in the cells, blindfolded and handcuffed, and we had to stay that way. They'd come in and beat us when we toppled over. The combined effects were taking more and more of a toll.

There was bombing every night, and sometimes it would be close. On one occasion the place was rattling on its foundations, and the guards were yelling and running around.

I was lying on the floor listening to the noise, and I heard myself screaming at the top of my voice: "Do it! Fucking bomb me! I'm down here!"

I really thought they were going to carry on with it until I was dead. I wanted it over with now. I wanted the pain to stop.

Heavy ordnance makes a buzzing sort of sound as it falls. I fixed my attention on each buzz and willed it to land in my cell. The building rocked and trembled. I felt the pressure waves of high explosive. It was the first time I had ever wanted to die, and I just wanted and wanted them to do it. I had reached the lowest point of my life.

For fifteen minutes one night I found God. The Supreme Being was in the top right-hand corner of the cell, and I had a little discussion with him.

"Come and help me now," I pleaded. "If you help me now, I'll be your best mate for ever. If you're there, fucking do something about this. We need your help now—all of us. If you're there, do it, and I'll be putting pennies in your pot every day."

I said as much of the Lord's Prayer as I could remember from school, but nothing happened. God did not exist.

I was slowly dying. Your body tells you. The cell was awash with my shit and piss. I slept in it. It covered me.

Sometimes they'd bring me a drink.

One night a gang of guards came in.

"Tel Aviv, Tel Aviv," one of them said.

"No, British," I mumbled, "I'm British."

"Foreskin," he demanded. He'd obviously heard the story and wanted to see for himself.

I motioned that I couldn't do anything because of the handcuffs, and they undid them.

Still blindfolded, I fumbled with my swollen, numb fingers to find my cock. I stretched out the foreskin, and they roared with laughter.

Two of them grabbed my arms from behind. One in front of me was slapping something in the palm of his hand. I heard a slight swishing sound, then all my world was pain. My knees buckled. The guard in front of me had raised something like a riding crop in the air and tonked it down hard on the end of my cock. They hooted as I screamed and writhed on the ground.

They bent over me and prodded and flicked at my bollocks. Again I wondered if I was going to get fucked, but the difference this time was that I was way past caring. But that wasn't what they had in mind. With a final kick to my balls that left me retching with agony, they handcuffed me again and left, still chortling.

One day they came into my cell, screaming and shouting. One of them was carrying a newspaper. The front-page story that he shoved under my nose was of the

Allied bombings the day before. The Iraqis had lined up all the bodies of the children that had been killed. There was a photograph of their distraught mothers weeping over their little forms. The guards slapped and punched me furiously, as if I was personally responsible for what had happened. It developed into the normal filling in, followed by a 10-minute recovery period, and another filling in. When I finally flaked out, they left me.

When I came to, I saw that they'd left the newspaper behind. I crawled over and checked the front page for something that I remembered from previous trips to the Middle East. I found what I was looking for. The only thing in English on the whole page was at the top, near the title: the figure 4.

It was the 4th of February.

That meant they had been torturing us for five days.

I was dressed just in my socks and a big, baggy pair of army-issue skiddies I'd been given when I arrived in Saudi. They were black now, smeared with shit and permanently wet with piss.

I lay shivering on the concrete, handcuffed and blindfolded.

Guards came into the cell and poked me with their weapons until I made donkey noises. When I did, they kicked me.

"Bush, pig," they said. "Thatcher, pig."

I had to repeat it. They laughed and giggled and gobbed on me. Sometimes they sat me up against the wall, pulled back my head, and held my face while they ranted at me. By now it was like water off a duck's back.

There was one major shift in their tactics, however. They didn't hurt my face any more. It was slapped, but no longer damaged by punching or butting as before.

*　*　*

I was hauled out of the cell in my socks and skiddies for another interrogation. It was several days since I'd even been able to stand up unaided.

At first, nothing happened. There was a long, long silence.

There was lots of sighing and: "Oh dear, what are we going to do with you, Andy? You're simply not helping at all, are you?"

"I'm trying to help," I mumbled. "But I don't know anything."

I'd got to the stage where I'd said it so many times I believed it was the truth.

"Andy, you know that we have one of you in hospital. He's had two pints of Iraqi blood, and he should be very proud now to be one of us. We have demonstrated to him that we're not barbarians. We've helped him. But we can't help you, because you won't help us."

Possibly there might be somebody in hospital, and my mind flashed back to an incident when the guards had come in and pointed at my feet and gone "bang bang." At the time, I'd thought they were going to shoot me in the foot. After all, they played lots of games with me, like making me put my mouth over the muzzle of their weapon while they cocked it. But maybe what they had really been getting at was that one of us had been shot in the foot.

I didn't know whether to believe him or not. "Thank you very much," I said. "I'm glad that you've saved him."

"You need to tell us what was happening, Andy. Why were you in Iraq? Your friends have all told us what was going on, but we just want to hear it from you. Are you going to help us? We've got no more time for you, you know. We'll let you die. You're nothing to us. Have a think about it."

They took me back to my cell.

Was it true? Had they actually got people in hospital? It couldn't be Legs. He had exposure; he wouldn't have been needing blood. Had somebody else survived a contact? It seemed very unlikely.

During the day I heard Stan and Dinger being taken away. Towards last light they came for me. This time there was no talking. It was just straight in and a good beasting with the plank.

I went down, only semiconscious.

"You're the only one that's not helping us, Andy," The Voice said. "We need the truth from everybody and you're not helping. We have told you that we have your people in hospital and we're willing to let them die."

I didn't answer.

"We actually have two of your people in hospital, Andy, and if you don't tell us what we need to know, we'll simply let them die. There are no consequences for us. The only reason they're alive is because of us. So therefore we can kill them, and we can kill you, too. There are no problems with this whatsoever. Nobody knows you're here. You would not sign anything for the Red Cross when we offered you the chance; therefore we have not told the Red Cross that we have you. This is your fault, Andy. Everybody else has signed the papers."

I didn't believe him.

"If you don't tell me what I need to know, Andy, we will simply let your friends die. You know that your signals operator is in hospital. I've already told you this. And also you know that one of your men has had two pints of blood. Now we will let them both die, and that will be your fault, Andy. And everyone else will also die because of you. Five men dead, simply because you're stubborn.

"We know you're the commander," The Voice said impatiently. "We know you're a sergeant, you're in charge of these people. It's down to you now to tell us;

otherwise we're simply going to let your men die. Do you understand?''

"Yes, I understand, but I can't help you because I do not know anything.''

It wasn't an act of bravado. Far from it. I just needed time to think. They knew that I was the commander and were changing their tactics. Now it was down to me if people lived or died, because they were getting nothing from anybody else.

"Well then, we cannot do anything more for you. What is about to happen is your fault. Remember that. You are responsible for these deaths.''

They picked me up and dragged me back to the cell. When we got to the open door, they launched me against a wall. I crumpled to the floor.

"Stupid, stupid, you're stupid,'' the guards shouted.

They left me alone all night. I started to go through the options in my mind. As far as I was concerned, we would all be dead in another two days. Stan probably even before that, going by how he looked. So what it boiled down to was: I was the commander and it was up to me. It was decision time.

It was a fact that there were three of us in prison. I had to take it as also true that there were two others in hospital. Dinger had seen Legs being taken away on a stretcher, and there was the possibility that somebody else was also there. At the back of my mind, the correct thing to do was to let the interrogators have something that was going to keep them happy, and in turn keep all of us alive.

I came to the conclusion that we'd held out long enough. This was eight days since capture, plenty of time for the damage assessment to have been made back at the FOB. It was time now to think of ourselves. OPSEC was no longer our problem. We'd held out long enough. We'd done our bit.

It was a tough decision. Pride shouldn't have come into it, but it did.

So, what could I actually give them? I'd keep the Regiment out of it, because that would make the situation even worse. There was no doubt they knew that the boys were screaming around like lunatics. They'd know this from the acts on the ground as well as from the media. They watched CNN like everybody else.

No one had said a word to me about the Regiment since the time I was captured, and there had been no indication that they suspected Special Forces. I wanted to keep it that way. But what was I going to give them? As far as they were concerned, we were part of the eight-man team that they compromised on the MSR. I had to come up with something congruent with that story. What were we doing there?

I could hear the screams every hour or so as Dinger and Stan got filled, but I was left on my own. Twice guards came in and taunted me, but they didn't beat me.

On the second occasion, in the early hours of the morning, I told them that I wanted to see an officer. They didn't understand.

"Officer," I repeated. "I need to see an officer."

They seemed to think that I was saying that I was an officer and was disgusted with my treatment. They laughed and came into the cell and gave me a kicking. I heard them coming to attention and making a mock rifle salute, and I realized there was no way I was going to get through to these people. I'd just have to leave it and wait.

During the day, one of the guards came in and spoke to me in reasonable English. "Andy, you're very stupid. Why don't you help?"

"But I want to help. I want to speak to an officer."

"We shall see."

An hour later, another guard came and shouted through the window. "What do you want?"

"I need to speak to an officer. I might have something that he needs to know."

"Maybe."

Two or three hours later, I was taken into the same block as usual, but to a different room. It was very cold. I was pushed down onto a chair. I heard a different voice, one I'd never heard before.

"Andy, what do you want to tell me? Why have you waited so long? Why have you gone through all this stupid pain for yourself and other people? We cannot understand: why does it have to be like this?"

"I was told yesterday that there are people in hospital, and I am worried for their safety and ours. I just hope that you will look after these people."

"Of course we will. What do you think—that we're just going to kill them? Don't be naïve. If you help us, everything will be fine. We told you that in the beginning. So this is the reason you're doing it, because of the other people in your patrol?"

"Yes. I don't want people to die."

"Andy, don't worry about them. You must do it for yourself, for your family. Don't worry about the other people in the patrol. You help us and we'll look after you."

"Well, I'm concerned about the people in hospital. I don't want them to die."

"Think about yourself, Andy. Do this for yourself. Now tell us, why are you in our country?"

"I am a member of a COP platoon."

There was a buzz of chatter in Arabic.

"What's a COP platoon?"

"A close observation platoon. Every infantry battalion has one. They do the forward recces for the battalion. We were flown in, told to go to the MSR and count the number of military vehicles passing in each direction and to report them."

I couldn't tell if they were buying it or not. In theory, that was correct tasking for a COP platoon, except that it would never have been behind enemy lines. But it sounded feasible, and there had been Sandhurst-

and Staff College-trained officers present during the interrogations. Hopefully it would ring a bell with them.

There was more gobbing off, and the sound of people leaving the room and returning.

"Why would they want this information?"

"I don't know: we're only told what we need to know. As I'm sure you know, at the beginning of the orders brief, there is the reminder 'Need to know.' We're not told these things because we're just the troops on the ground."

There was the sound of general agreement.

"How long were you planning to stay in our country?"

I had to assume that they had got all our kit and had rummaged through it. If nothing had been pilfered, they could assess how long we planned to stay by the quantity of rations.

"It was going to be for up to fourteen days," I said.

"How many of you were there?"

Again this was easy enough to work out by the number of abandoned bergens.

"There were eight of us."

"Where did you land, Andy?"

"If you take off my blindfold and my handcuffs, and give me a map, I'll be able to help you."

There was a heated discussion between themselves.

"We'll take off your blindfold and your handcuffs, but you remember, Andy, we consider that you are all very dangerous men, and if you attempt to do anything, we will shoot you. Do you understand this, Andy?"

"Yes, I understand."

Even if I'd wanted to do anything, I didn't have the strength left. They took off my blindfold, and in front of me, sitting down, was an officer in olive drab uniform. Another officer, who was sitting in the top left-hand corner of this room, was dressed in a camou-

flaged bomber jacket over a flying suit. Instead of military boots, he wore the Chelsea boots they all seemed
to have on.

The bloke in olive drab was doing the talking. I'd
never heard his voice before, but he spoke excellent
English. He looked like an Arab version of Richard
Pryor, with normal, swept-back Arab hair and a very
clean, very smart, very well-pressed uniform. There
were three or four other people sitting down, smoking
cigarettes and drinking tea out of small glasses. They
were all wearing cheap and nasty, badly fitting suits.

I was facing a window. Beyond it I could see trees
and a wall. Sunlight was streaming into the room.

There was a guard on either side of me. One of them
held a pistol to my head in case I started running
around doing karate chops or whatever else they considered I would do.

On the table was one of our own escape maps.

"Is it all right if I get up off the chair and come to the
table?"

"Get up."

The two guards lifted me up and took me over to
the table. The gun never left my head.

I pointed out the general area where we had landed.

"Yes, Andy, that's correct. We know about that. We
know when you landed because you were heard. You
landed two nights before, didn't you? You're helping
us. This is very good."

Some of the lies I told them would have to be based
on the truth, as all good ones are. This wasn't just
training: it was a lesson I had learned in childhood.

"Show us where you went to hide."

I indicated the bend on the MSR.

"Yes, good, we know that. This is good, Andy,
you're helping us. How many people again?"

"Eight of us."

"Give me some of their names."

This was no problem. They knew there were eight of

us. If they had, in theory, five of us—dead or alive—
they'd know our names, because everybody was wearing dog tags. And it appeared that I was helping,
which was good—for now. Later on it might get totally out of control, and I'd spend the rest of my days
answering questions. But at this stage I had no choice.
Was I supposed to call their bluff and see if they would
carry out their threat? I had to take it as real.

I gave the names. They wrote them down.

"We know this."

I didn't know if that meant that they had everybody,
or if it was all bluff. I played on my concern for the
people in hospital and acted scared and humble, but
inside my head I was racing to think about what I had
said and what I was going to say.

"Please, look after the people in hospital."

"Tell us more about the COP platoon. What does it
do?"

"We just report."

"Does this mean that the British army plans to invade Iraq?"

"I don't know. We are never told. All we're told is to
go out and do the job. We're not told why. We're just
squaddies."

"How many COP platoons are there?"

"There's one for each battalion."

"How many battalions here?"

"I don't know; I've never really bothered to find out.
It's of no consequence to me. I'm just a soldier."

I was so glad that we hadn't had vehicles with us.
We were unlucky not to have them when we got compromised, obviously, but we were lucky now because
vehicles might have linked us to the Regiment.

Things were going well at this stage. They seemed
happy with what I was telling them. There was a potential problem in that they might come back to the
other two and say, "Right, we know what you're doing. You tell us now." However, the chances were

slim. The boys had said nothing so far, so why should they suddenly cave in?

If I didn't tell them something, they were going to let people die. If I did tell them and they found out it was another load of old bollocks, then I might be committing everybody to going through this system again, and they would die. But I couldn't see that there was anything else I could do.

"Thank you very much for helping us, Andy. Things may get better for you now. If we find out you're lying, they won't. But things might get better. And I'm glad that *you* have had the sense to help us."

His words made me feel a complete shit. Had I done the right thing after all, I asked myself? Was this going to go on? Was I going to be used now? Was I going to go on telly and be "the British lad who helped us?" I had visions of Vietnam, of people getting prosecuted and persecuted when they got home. They were marked down as collaborators by people who had no conception of the circumstances in which the so-called "betrayals" took place.

But here was Richard Pryor telling me we were now best mates, and it was hard to take.

"You've done well, Andy. This is good."

I knew I was right to have taken their threat as real. The way they'd been treating us, I wouldn't have put it past them to kill the ones in hospital. They'd had ten years' practice at this sort of thing.

"Do you want a cigarette?"

"No, I don't smoke. But my friend Dinger does."

"Maybe we might be able to give him a cigarette one day."

"Now that I've told you, is it possible that we can have some clothes and maybe some warmth? We are very cold."

"Yes, this will be no problem, because now we are friends. You can go back to your cell now, Andy, and maybe things will change. Meanwhile, we'll check on this."

They put the blindfold and handcuffs back on, and took me back to the cell.

Half an hour later, they came back and threw me my clothes and removed the blindfold and handcuffs. But they hadn't finished with their little games quite yet. As I tried to get dressed, they kept pushing me over.

I woke up still wondering whether I had done the right thing. I was lying in the same old corner. You seem to go to the same place all the time, maybe because it makes you feel more secure or more covered up.

The guards came in, accompanied by a sergeant major. He spoke very good English.

"Ah, Andy, Andy. Our friend Andy," he said, his mouth full of pistachio nuts. "My name is Mr. Jihad."

He spat shells on the floor.

"Good morning, Mr. Jihad." I knew that couldn't be his name, but I went along with it.

"It's good to see that you've got your clothes back now, and you are feeling better. You are feeling better?"

"Yes."

"Unfortunately we can't give you any medical attention because we don't have it ourselves. The children are dying in your bombing; we have to give it to them first. Do you understand?"

"Of course, I understand."

"It's Bush and Thatcher and Major. They're stopping all medical aid coming in. But we do have some food for you this morning. You would like some food?"

"Thank you very much, I would like some food."

They brought in water and a one-inch cube of margarine in a paper wrapper. I opened it up and started eating.

"About escape, Andy. You've been here a long time. You may be feeling that you want to escape. Escape would be very, very useless; it would be no good for you. You're in Baghdad. There's nowhere for you to go. And we're friends now, aren't we, Andy?"

I nodded and agreed, my mouth slippery with grease.

"Let me show you what happens when people try to escape." Mr. Jihad lifted up his trouser leg and showed me a huge scar. "When I was a young man, I was in prison in Iran for six months. My friend and I tried to escape. We got away but we were captured the next day. They took us back to the camp and decided to make an example of us. So they got us on the floor, face down, and two soldiers stood over us with their rifles and bayoneted our legs through the back of the knee. They forced our kneecaps right out. If you try to escape, Andy, I will have to do the same to you."

I wasn't going anywhere. I could just about stand up.

I smiled. "I just want to go home to my family."

"This cell is very dirty, you know, Andy. You people might live like this, but we Muslims are very clean. You will clean this up."

"How do I do that?"

"You clean it with your hands, Andy. Come on, clean this place up. We do not live in this mess."

He stood over me and watched as I got down on my hands and knees and scooped all my shit into a pile. Then he gave me two bits of cardboard to put it on, and they left the cell.

I looked at the walls and saw fresh bloodstains on the surfaces. They were mine. At least I'd added to the ambience of the cell.

I began to feel apprehensive. What would happen now? Would we go away? Would we stay there?

Richard Pryor had said to me: "England is a nice

place. I was there fifteen years ago. I was at college in London. I know London well. Maybe one day you'll get back.''

Yeah, maybe.

12

Some time in the afternoon of the 6th, they came in and handcuffed and blindfolded me again. They picked me up, and I thought I was off for another interrogation. I went outside and started to follow the old familiar route, but this time we took a strange turning, and I found myself being put into the back of a vehicle.

I leaned forward, head down to release pressure on my hands. It was lovely and warm in the car, and I could hear the birds singing. It was gorgeous weather. I was full of dread.

The car was big. An old American thing, I assumed, like they all seemed to be.

"If you try to escape," somebody said, "we will kill the other two. And if they escape, you will be killed. So you see, it is pointless."

Did that mean that Dinger and Stan were coming too? I waited for someone else to get into the car, but no one did. Both doors were closed. I was alone in the back. There were two fellows in the front, and they both spoke excellent English.

"Do you know where you're going now, Andy?" the driver asked as we set off.

"No, I have no idea."

"We're taking you to the British Embassy. You will now be going home to your family. No problems."

"Thank you very much."

They started laughing to themselves and I went along with it, playing the idiot.

"No, we are only joking, Andy. You'll be going home one day, but not yet. Not for a long time yet."

We drove for a few minutes in silence.

"Have you heard of Ali Baba?" one of them asked.

"Yes, it's an old film which they play every Christmas. They always have Ali Baba and the Forty Thieves on."

"Yes, well this is where you are. You're in the land of Ali Baba, in Baghdad. The thieves of Baghdad. A very beautiful city. But no longer, because everybody's dying. You people, you are coming in and bombing our places. Children are dead. Entire families are dying. It's no more the great land of Ali Baba; it's all demolished. But when we win, we will rebuild, no problem. Fantastic place. Ali Baba."

I nodded and agreed. They turned on the radio and scanned through the stations. Every one sounded the same aggressive rhetoric or wailing Arabic songs. They were enjoying themselves, driving along with the windows open, not a care in the world.

I listened to the sounds of the city. We stopped at lights, hooted, and people gobbed off. Music blared out of shops; there was all the usual hustle and bustle of a city. The characters suddenly started laughing and chattering.

"We're just looking at your two friends in front of us," one of them said. "They are leaning against one another, sleeping. They must be very good friends."

This was great. It confirmed that Dinger and Stan were with me. It was a fantastic feeling.

The boys started smoking and were very jovial. We drove on for another 30 minutes or so.

"Yes, we're going to somewhere else in Baghdad.

You'll enjoy this place. Very good place. We were only joking about the embassy."

People reached in through the windows when we arrived at what they announced was the military prison, slapping me on the head, pulling my mustache. Nothing too serious, all very neighborly stuff.

I heard barriers being lifted, gates being opened. We drove forward a bit more and stopped. They got me out of the car and put a blanket over my head. I was led up to a door and along a wide corridor with concrete floors. There were echoes of talking, of bolts being opened and closed, the jangling of chains and keys.

This place wasn't damp, but it was freezing cold. They led me into a cell. I was made to sit on the floor, and my handcuffs and blindfold were taken off. I saw soldiers dressed in olive drab and red berets, wearing the old '37 webbing-pattern belt and gaiters, all immaculately blancoed in white. They were military policemen. I spotted an officer and a couple of blokes in civvies. They closed the door and left me.

The door to the cell was something that the sheriff would put you behind in a western. The bars were covered with a blanket to stop me seeing out. There was one fluorescent light, right in the middle of the ceiling, which was about 15 feet high. Also right at the top was a small slit window. A shaft of light beamed through. The bottom half of the walls were painted red, the top magnolia. And at first glance, that was all there was to see. Then I saw the scratchings on the wall, in Arabic. There were more pictures of doves with chains around their legs, and a drawing of a woman.

I paced out the cell. It was about 12 feet by 9.

I strained my ears and heard other doors being opened and closed. I assumed that Dinger and Stan were getting banged up as well. At least we were all in the same place. And compared with the interrogation center this was Buckingham Palace.

Had they finished with us now, or what? I wasn't too sure and I didn't really care. I loved this place. It was wonderful.

Fifteen minutes later the doors opened again. I thought I'd better start switching on and showing some respect. To turn the situation to your advantage you have to make an effort, get some sort of friendship going.

As I got slowly to my feet, wincing with the injuries, a new character came into the cell. He was wearing civilian clothes, but with a DPM combat jacket over the top. He was about 5'3" tall and had white hair. On his face he had a pair of really thick glasses and a big happy smile.

"Would you like to be with your friends?" he beamed.

"Yes, I would, very much."

He took me by the arm and led me to another cell three doors down. It was empty.

Yeah, I thought—good fucking stitch! For a few moments there I'd been all happy that I was going to see Dinger and Stan. I sat down on the floor and tried not to show my feelings.

Two minutes later the door opened and there was Dinger. We had a big hug and a shake of hands. Then another couple of minutes later Stan came stumbling in, supported on either side by guards. In his hand he carried a tray of rice. As the guards locked us in and left us we looked at one another in disbelief, then started gobbing off.

"Chris and Vince?" I asked.

"Vince is dead," Stan said. "Exposure. I got split from Chris; I don't know what happened to him. What about the other three?"

I said that Mark was dead, and probably also Legs and Bob—despite what the Iraqis had told me.

We fell into silence and started eating. We heard the sound of footsteps and keys in the corridor and stood up again. The door opened and a major entered. He introduced himself as the prison governor.

"What happened where you were, I was not responsible for," he said in better English than mine. "I am only responsible for you now. We will feed you and we will look after you. If you are good, we will be good to you. If there is trouble, you will be punished."

Just 5'6" tall and small-framed, he was smartly dressed, well groomed, and fresh smelling. He seemed genuine. If we played the game, we should be Okay. As he spoke, however, I couldn't help noticing that the guards behind him didn't seem to have the same benign smile on their faces. They looked every bit as brutish as the people we were used to. They were very young, and they would have things to prove to us— and to each other. I didn't doubt that when the cat was away, the guards would play.

Once the major had gone, we came to certain decisions based on experience, training, and the advice of the Marine POW.

We would remain always the gray man, never allowing ourselves to show a reaction or become overconfident. We weren't out of the woods yet, not by a long way.

We would show respect to the guards. Being young bastards, they were almost certain to tear the arse out of the situation if we were abusive or truculent. By being respectful we might also be able to get information or take some advantage, which would take us halfway towards another aim, which was to get some form of relationship going. Sometimes it works, sometimes it doesn't, but you don't know until you try. We didn't know how long we were going to be there for— it could be days, weeks, or years. We would try to get some sort of fraternal thing going, based on us all being soldiers together, which might bring us medicine, food, and little goodies.

We'd use this time as best we could to sort ourselves out and prepare ourselves for escape, adjusting both physically and mentally. I still had my escape map and compass, and so did Dinger. Physically we'd sort ourselves out, hopefully helped by more reasonable supplies of food, and mentally we'd spend as much time as we could doing map studies. We knew we were in Baghdad, so if we learnt the surrounding area we'd have some form of chance if we managed to escape. The escape maps were not detailed enough to show the city in street form, but they indicated the main features on the ground like rivers, salt lakes, and high ground. All we had to do was get out of Baghdad.

The first thing to do, as ever, was just to tune in to the new environment, hoping that there was going to be some sort of routine. We didn't want to screw up the fact that we were all together. We would use the system, rather than fight against it.

During the course of the first day and night, guards were coming and going nonstop. Each time we'd stand up and face them. They were still in their teens, most of them, which made them more authoritative and overbearing. They never appeared in groups of less than three, and they always carried pistols. They were clearly very wary of us. On one of the visits our boots were taken away from us and replaced with white pumps without laces.

I asked for water. They came back with a pitcher and a cup. We drank some, and then put the pitcher back down on the floor as if it was going to stay there. They didn't question it.

"How do we go to the toilet?" Stan asked.

"You go when we say you go."

"We're suffering from diarrhea and stomachaches,

and we're being sick. We need a bucket or something so we can go."

A bucket turned up. They were small victories, but encouraging signs that we could manipulate our circumstances. That first night was a happy, giggly, taking the piss sort of time. We heard mumbling in the near distance and guessed that there were other prisoners. We eventually worked out that they were right next door to us. How many of them, we couldn't tell.

There was a door right at the end of the corridor, and once the guards had slammed that shut they seemed to be out of earshot. Nobody had told us that there was a no talking rule, but it was safer to assume that there was.

Tapping on the wall with our tin mug, we knocked out a simple identification code to see if the person in the next cell was an ally. Only a Westerner would recognize the friendly pattern of knocks you would do on the front door of a friend's house: tap, tapetty, tap tap —to which the reply, of course, is: tap tap. We got the answer we were hoping for. The contact was good for our morale, and probably theirs. It was a good feeling to have got something going on the very first night.

We started to speculate about our situation. Were the other members of the patrol here? Was this a staging post? Would we be here for the duration?

"We didn't know where the hell you guys had got to," Stan said. "Vince was babbling about aircraft and TACBE, and Chris and I remembered hearing jets. We worked out that Vince was telling us that you'd stopped and tried to make contact with them. We sat on high ground looking through the night sight, but there was no sign of you. We tried to raise you on TACBE, but no answer. In the end we decided to press on, hoping you'd keep on the bearing and we'd meet up."

* * *

They carried on for about four hours, and then it was coming to first light. Chris and Stan were worried about being caught in the open. Vince was out of the decision making; he stood swaying in the wind and rain as the others ran around looking for somewhere to hide.

Stan found a tank berm about 6 feet deep, with tank tracks leading away from it that were about knee deep. They led Vince into one of the tracks and lay down either side of him. Throughout the night Chris and Stan took it in turns to sleep. The man who was awake kept a watchful eye on Vince.

First light came and Stan had a quick look around. To his horror, he found that the tank berm was only about 600 meters from some sort of enemy position—either a hut or a box vehicle with aerials, it was hard to tell. They were stuck there now until last light.

It started to snow. Soon the snow turned to sleet, and the tank track filled with slush. They were soaking wet. The temperature dropped. They had very little food left, just a couple of packets of biscuits between them. Everything else had gone in the bergens.

As it started to come to last light, they crawled into the berm and stood up. They'd been lying in freezing water for twelve hours. Stan had lost all feeling in his hands and feet; Chris's joints were frozen. They moved around in circles, frog-marching Vince between them. When darkness had fallen and it was time to leave, they were so cold that the only way they could pick up their weapons was by cradling them in their arms.

Vince was soon lagging behind. He stopped in his tracks at one point and called the other two back. He complained about his hands, muttering that they had turned black. Chris looked at them and saw that he was wearing black leather gloves. "They'll soon get better if you put them in your pockets, mate," he said.

The next time they stopped, Vince was totally incoherent. Stan and Chris huddled around him, but it wasn't much use. They had to keep going or they'd freeze. They were on high ground, crossing bare rock and large patches of snow. Chris was in front with the compass, but the cold was getting to him. He was doing everything in slow motion.

The three men spread out as they climbed a gradient at their different speeds. Stan stopped to let Vince overtake him; he wanted to keep an eye on him. But Vince didn't appear. Stan turned around; Vince was nowhere to be seen. Stan called to Chris and they both went back. Visibility was down to a few feet in the blinding blizzard as they retraced their footsteps in the snow. They got to a large area of bare rock. They couldn't find the trail the other side.

They had to make a decision. They were both going down with hypothermia. It was agony standing still; they had to get moving again. In the end they just looked at each other, then turned and headed back up the hill.

Stan and Chris walked all that night, coming off the high ground at about 0530. They came into a shallow wadi about three feet deep and cuddled together. As first light came the weather cleared; the sun came out, and for the first time in several days they felt warmth on their faces.

The sound of goats came at about 1400, and sure enough they got compromised by an old herder. This one was wearing a tattered tweed overcoat. Stan couldn't help thinking how warm it looked and how good it would be to eat warm goat meat.

The old boy seemed quite friendly as he pointed east. Drawing pictures in the sand, he indicated food, a house, a vehicle. Chris looked at Stan. Did they kill him? It would protect their concealment, but was there anybody else about who was expecting him?

Stan was keen to investigate the vehicle. "I'll go down, bring it back, and we'll shoot off. We'll be at the border by tonight," he said.

They made their RVs, actions on, and warning arrangements, and Stan set off due east with the old boy and his goats. He left his belt kit with Chris to look less conspicuous, and wrapped his shamag around his head.

After a short while the goatherder wandered off at a tangent but again pointed east. Stan continued.

The hut was exactly where the old man had said, but there were two vehicles parked outside instead of one. Stan OP'd it for about twenty minutes. Nothing stirred. If the keys were in the vehicle, he'd just take it there and then and go. If they weren't, he'd make a room entry on the house. He'd get to the door, kick it in, and take on whatever was there.

As he started to approach the vehicles, an Iraqi soldier came out of the house. He looked as surprised as Stan was. He made for the first vehicle and tried to pull a weapon out. Stan downed him with his 203, and the body slumped over the driver's seat. The house was less than 60 feet away, and the door was open. Six or seven squaddies came flying out in confusion. Stan got three hits off, and then he had a stoppage. It was too late for stoppage drills. He ran to the nearest vehicle, the one with the body in. The soldier was still groaning. Stan pushed him aside. No key in the ignition. He was still fumbling for it in the man's pockets when he felt the muzzle of a rifle jab into his ribs.

Stan turned around and stared at them. There were five jundies left. They appeared very undisciplined, screaming and shouting at each other. They fired into the air and into the ground each side of him. He wasn't expecting to survive. They came forward cautiously and then one of them summoned the courage to smash him with a rifle butt. The others piled in.

They put him into the other vehicle and took him to a military installation near the Euphrates. Stan entered the tactical questioning phase. He was interrogated for most of the night, handcuffed and blindfolded. The interrogators spoke very good English. Some had trained in the UK. A major who had trained at Sandhurst said, "Everyone's very sad with you at the moment. They want to take your life."

Stan denied everything except the Big Four. They beat him badly and only stopped when he fell unconscious. When he came to, he started to go into the cover story. He told them he had done a medical degree in Australia and gone to

London. Because of his medical experience he had got roped
in through the TA to become part of a search and rescue
team.

"I want to cooperate in any way I can," he said. "All I
am is a doctor who dropped out."

He was questioned on medical techniques, and they
brought in a doctor to confirm his story. It went well, but
the rest of his story was starting to fall apart. They searched
the area in which Stan said the helicopter had crash-landed
but could find no sign of wreckage. "Possibly the aircraft
took off again," he said, but they looked dubious.

Two or three days later, Stan was moved to an interrogation center. The reception party beat him with batons. He
was made to kneel in front of the panel of interrogators. He
was thrashed with hosepipes, whipped, beaten with a pole.
At one stage they pulled back his head and held a red-hot
poker in front of his eyes. They didn't carry out the threat to
blind him, but they did use the poker elsewhere on his body.

We told Stan our stories and finally collapsed into
sleep. I woke up in the night with my stomach tugging
at me. We'd all had four or five liquid shits in the short
time we'd been there. We were dehydrating drasti-
cally, but at least we could replenish the loss now.

It was pitch-dark. Lying on the floor, feeling relatively safe, I started to think about home.

There was another bombing raid in the distance.
Flashes of light came through the high slit window. As
ever the bomb blasts were rather nice, giving a sense
of security, a feeling that we weren't the only ones
there. And best of all, they also gave us a possible
means of escape if we took direct hits.

The main gate of the block was opened after first light.
We heard chains rattling and keys going into locks,
and then the sound of a metal, corrugated-type door
the other side of our wall being opened and people
talking and walking about. We heard the base of a

metal bucket clanking on the floor, followed by the sound of the metal handle hitting the side.

Then we heard, "Russell! Russell!"

There was a mumbled reply.

Further down the corridor there was the same banging of buckets. Then "David! David!"

This one was definitely American. When he heard his name called, he replied with a resounding "Yo!"

The guards were shouting at this David character. They shut his door and came down the corridor to our cell. The door opened and we got to our feet. We didn't know what to expect. There were three of them: one little bloke who said we were to call him Jeral, one big fat thing with glasses, and a really young kid with curly blond hair. Jeral carried a bucket while the others covered him, pistols drawn. They seemed keen to throw their weight around with the new blokes on the block.

"Names?" the fat one demanded.

"Dinger. Stan. Andy," Dinger said.

He handed us three small plastic bowls, into which he tipped a small ration of rice and water mixture from the bucket. We were issued with two more mugs and given a brew of cold black tea from a battered old teapot. I thought it was Christmas.

When they left we had our first chance to look around the cell in daylight. There was a nail high up one wall, sticking out a couple of inches from the cement surface. Deciding it might come in handy, I as the lightest was given a leg up and jiggled it until I managed to prize it free. Dinger used it to mark where the light was shining on to the wall, as some sort of check on the passage of time.

We sat down and ate the rice, licking the bowls clean. We took sips of cold tea as we pondered what might happen next. The same three guards returned ten minutes later with the major.

"You're in my prison now," he repeated. "I want no

misdemeanors from you. If you cause me trouble, I will return the compliment. You're only together because the officer yesterday decided to put you together. He says to inform you that we know that you are dangerous men, and that if we have any trouble with you, we are to just shoot you."

It must have been a reference to the COP platoon story, which made us an unknown quantity compared with the airmen they were used to. Either that, or because we looked like wild men of the north with our matted beards, scabs, and bruises.

"Any attempt to escape or to aggravate us and we'll shoot, it's as easy as that," he said.

"Is there any possibility of emptying our bucket, sir?" I asked. "We have bad stomachs and it is filling up."

He gobbed off to one of the blokes and said, "Yes, take the bucket." Stan picked it up and followed a guard.

The major said, "You will be fed, and you're lucky

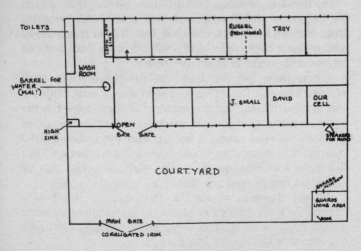

Prison

to be fed because you've come over here to kill our children. There is to be no noise—no talking, no shouting. Do you understand?"

While he was talking, Dinger spotted the outline of a cigarette packet under his shirt.

"Excuse me, sir, is it possible that I can have a cigarette?"

Dinger was smiling away. Nothing ventured, nothing gained. We were trying our hardest to come over as friendly, nice, polite, and courteous. The major unbuttoned his shirt and took the pack from a pocket in a T-shirt underneath. He handed Dinger a cigarette, but he didn't give him a light, so that was Dinger fucked. He spent the rest of the day looking at it wistfully and holding it under his nose.

Stan had tried to gather as much information as he could. All he could tell us was that there were a number of cells, with the doors sealed with blankets or rice-sack covers that were marked, ironically, FROM THE AMERICAN RICE BOARD TO THE PEOPLE OF IRAQ. At the bottom of the corridor there was a gate, and another corridor that led out into a courtyard, with yet another metal gate beyond that. That was as far as he had been able to see. Everything seemed to be self-contained within the one unit, with only one way in and out.

It appeared that we shared the ablution block with the guards. Their washing was hanging on lines. In one corner was a large oil barrel which was filled with water. There was a long concrete sink with about four or five taps coming off it, and normal Arab toilets which were blocked as usual. According to Stan the whole place stank.

A week passed. Sometimes they would come into our cell three times a day, sometimes twice, sometimes six or seven times. We could hear squaddies continually toing and froing, doing their washing, and just generally mooching about.

We were fed irregularly as well. Sometimes the bucket would come at breakfast time, sometimes in the late afternoon, sometimes at last light. Meals always consisted of rice soup or boiled rice, real dreggy stuff with grit and mud in it. They always told us we were lucky to have it. One time we were given bones that people had been chewing. We tucked in hungrily.

They must have watched one of those prison films where you get indoctrinated by radio, because every morning at first light they turned on a radio that then blasted away outside our window. It was like having a loudspeaker blaring into the cell, aggressive rhetoric punctuated by the occasional English word like "Bush" or "America." Then there would be prayers, then the rhetoric would start up again. It only stopped at last light, and it drove us all crazy.

We were bombed every night. There had always been sporadic firing around the city from antiaircraft guns, some of which were sited in our compound. We'd feel the shudder of the guns on our roof and hear the sounds of the gun crews arguing and shouting. What they never seemed to realize was that by the time you've heard an aircraft it's out of range anyway.

On the night of the 13th there was a massive amount of small-arms fire in the streets around the prison, which went on for twenty to thirty minutes.

"What the fuck's going on here?" Dinger said.

He and Stan lifted me up to the slit window, and I just managed to pull my head up high enough to see tracer going horizontal. It was bouncing everywhere.

"Must be some form of revolution or coup going on. That is one major firefight."

A few nights later we decided that we'd try and make contact with the characters in the other cells. We knew that the bloke next door was called David and was an American. We weren't sure about Russell. We decided to initiate some form of contact with them. We risked a beating or worse if we were caught, but we decided it was worth it. If they were released or escaped, they could report our names.

Last thing at night, when the guards finished their duty, they would close up the main gate from the corridor and then go out to the courtyard. It was a fair assumption that once we'd heard the final gate close, they would be out of earshot. I got right up to our door, covered by its rice bag, and called for help. If a guard responded, I would just say that one of us was really ill and needed attention.

We heard nothing.

I called out, "David! David!"

We heard rustlings, and then "What? What?"

"How long have you been here?"

"A few days."

He said that he and another transport driver, a woman, had strayed over the border and been shot. He had received a stomach wound, but had no idea what had happened to the woman.

"Who's further down?" Dinger asked.

"A Marine aviator called Russell."

"Russell! Russell!"

He responded and we all swapped names.

"What have you heard?" I asked him.

Russell Sanborn had been shot down by a SAM missile while at 10,000 feet over Kuwait. He'd only been in the prison for a couple of days. We concluded that we were the only prisoners and agreed we would try to talk again.

One morning, on about the 15th or 16th, the guards came in, and we stood up as usual and smiled at them. We'd got a bit of a routine going now. We'd say "Good morning," and they'd say "Good morning" back, and one of us would then go out and empty the bucket.

There were no smiles this morning. The guards were accompanied by a young officer, who pointed at me and said, "You—you come with me."

He had a white bandage blindfold that he put around my eyes. My hands were cuffed in front of me, and a blanket was put over my head. Escorted by guards, the officer started leading me away from the prison. He held my arm under the blanket and dragged me along. I looked down through my blindfold and watched the ground. We went through the gate, stopped awhile while he spoke to somebody, then carried on.

We were moving fairly fast when he walked me straight into a lamppost. The surprise of it knocked me over. My nose started to pour with blood. He thought it was brilliant. We went into a building, up some stairs, and into a room. I was pushed up against a sideboard and told to sit down and cross my legs, facing the wall. The doors closed. I didn't have a clue what was going to happen next, but assumed the worst. A minute later the blanket and blindfold were ripped off, and I was told to stand up and turn around.

I was in an office. The lighting was strong and harsh. There was a chair against one wall and a video camera set up facing it, with a microphone on a boom. Now I knew why they had stopped hitting my face.

I was facing the prison governor. When he saw the state of my nose, he went apeshit with the young rupert. I was in shit state to look at anyway, so I don't know what difference a nosebleed made. They took me next door to a sink and told me to wash off the blood. I used the blindfold as a flannel. I was then given a comb and a mirror and told to tidy up my hair. There was nothing I could do to it. It was just too matted with old blood.

It was the first time I'd seen my face since I left the FOB. I looked like Ben Gunn after somebody had taken a shovel to his face. I had a dirty, scruffy beard and the skin was flaky. My mouth was scabby. I couldn't believe they were going to use me in a video. I cleaned myself up a bit to make them happy, but not too much: I didn't want to look too healthy for my public.

I sat in front of the video, thinking hard about an appropriate way of showing that I was doing this against my will. I remembered that during the Vietnam War, people were going back to the States and getting persecuted purely because they'd signed something or said something to save their life or that of somebody else. People learned that they should do something that was out of the ordinary while they were exposed to the media, or do their signature with their left hand, so anyone knowing them would recognize that something was wrong.

I decided that I would try for as long as I could to keep my right index finger straight and constantly bring it up to stroke my left eye, under the pretext that my eye was hurting after walking into the lamppost.

I sat and waited. A jundie appeared with three glasses of tea and offered me one.

"We're going to ask you some questions, Andy," the major said. "I want you to answer them truthfully for the camera. Then, who knows, maybe you might go home soon."

"Oh, thank you very much."

He asked all the questions they'd asked before. Name, number, rank, date of birth, religion. Details of the helicopter and COP platoons, and what we were doing in Iraq. There was a bloke wearing dark glasses behind the camera, behind the lights, whose face I couldn't see properly. He would talk in Arabic into the speaker system on the video, then ask the question in English. I would answer, and he would translate. I kept rubbing my eye with my finger and never looked directly to camera. I tried all the time to make myself appear drowsy and incoherent. It was worth a go. Either I'd get away with it or they'd give me a bit of a slapping. In fact they didn't react to it at all.

"That's it," the major said after about twenty minutes. "You're going back now."

As I got up to leave, the fellow with dark glasses said, "You know your side will never win, don't you, Andy?"

"Why's that?"

"Because you're far too technical."

I was blindfolded and taken back to the prison and put into another cell on my own. I was depressed. I thought that now they'd done the film I was going to spend the rest of my time in solitary.

The guards went into the cell with the blindfold in their hands and said to Dinger, "You're next."

Dinger took one look at the blood on the bandage and roared: "Fucking hell!" He thought that either I had been slotted, or it was all going to happen again. Either way, if they were going to do it, they'd have to do it to him in the cell right there and then. There was what Stan later called a "bit of a scuffle" until other guards rushed in and put guns to their heads. They led him away, and Stan thought: And then it's me.

In front of the camera Dinger was given a cigarette. When it came to smoking, Dinger was very much a man of the thumb and forefinger school, but in front of the camera he smoked elegantly with the middle fingers of his left hand, like some character out of a Noel Coward play.

Stan decided that he would stroke his hair continuously with both hands and look down at the ground. While he was being interviewed, I got moved back in with Dinger. We tried to work out why we'd done these videos. We prayed that they were going to be shown to the media, so people back home would know we were alive.

* * *

We talked to the guards as often as we could about their families.

"How many children do you have? Do you miss them? Do you see them?"

I landed up scoring with Jeral. He was really skinny and young, in his early twenties. His English was very good; he spoke as if he was apologizing, with his shoulders shrugged up.

"I'm a drummer really," he said. "I play for a group called Queen at the Meridien Hotel in Baghdad."

His favorite groups were Boney M and Michael Jackson, and every time he saw me he'd start singing, "He's crazy like . . ."

"Oh Andy, I want to come to London," he said to me one day. "When I come, will you show me London? I want to play in a hotel there."

"Yeah, sure," I shrugged, "once the war is over we can be friends. You can come to London."

"Yes Andy, I love you." He stared longingly into my eyes. "I love you. Do you love me?"

"Yes, I love you too, Jeral."

I got a fearsome slagging from the other two the moment he left.

"I'll give you a month's pay if you let me watch," Dinger said.

"Give me a year's money, and I won't tell the squadron," said Stan.

Jeral was a nuisance, but we did get extra bread and little titbits of information from him. At some stage there was an initiative by the Kremlin, and Jeral said, "The war's going to be over soon. Gorbachev's going to organize everything."

There was indeed some sort of peace initiative, because we heard lots of chanting in the streets and small-arms fire. Some guards burst in, and Jeral said, "The war's over!"

"How do you know?" I asked.

"Saddam Hussein has signed a treaty. He has explained to the nation that he cannot let so many of the enemy die. He is a very compassionate man."

Our gauge of whether he was bullshitting or not was whether there was any bombing that night. In fact there was. Jeral wasn't correct that time, but he did tell us when the ground war started.

Stan got on quite well with a sergeant major who couldn't speak a word of English. There was some sort of affinity between the two of them, and Stan would speak to him through another of the guards. He would ask how many children he had. It turned out he had two wives and five children. Stan said: "Oh, very strong man," and the man loved it.

We did have some slight problems with the guards. We'd get filled in now and again while we were taking the bucket down. They'd make sure you were on your own, then come and pick on you. On one occasion they made Dinger do a Michael Jackson moondance. We just let them get on with it. It was just a kicking and a few punches. You'd go down, they'd have their little laugh, and that was that.

Another time, the toilets were blocked with their shit. They marched me down there and made me pull it out with my hands. Afterwards, they made me lick my fingers clean. They thought this one was a cracker.

Stan went to the ablution block one morning with the bucket, and when it was clean, they offered to let him fill it up with water from the oil barrel. Thanking them for their kindness, he dropped the bucket into the barrel and received a massive electric shock that threw him against the wall. We heard his screams and their hoots of hysterical laughter. The generator was running, and they'd wired up the barrel to the mains.

Baghdad was still getting attacked every night. If a bomb fell too close or somebody lost a friend or family member, the guards would come in and make sure we knew about it. They began dishing out many more serious kickings in the toilets. The three of us made a pact that if they went for it when we were together, we weren't going to stand for it.

One night during the bombing we took a hit near the compound. From the beginning we had maintained that if ever there was a crack in the structure big enough for us to get through, we would go for it. If bombs were falling that close and you didn't start moving, you'd probably end up being killed by your own ordnance anyway.

They took casualties that night. We could hear the screaming and shouting, the pressure waves, all the windows in the area shattering. The town of Ali Baba was really getting the good news. There was shouting by the gate to the outer courtyard, and then the sound of the gate being pushed open. We could guess what was going to happen. Sure enough the guards came in, and they gave it to Russell and David.

Then they came to our cell, two lads waving their Tilly lamps and hollering. They had their helmets and webbing on. Their weapons were slung, and they carried batons.

We stood up as they charged into the cell. They could kill us with those batons: it only takes a good twat around the head to do the business. In the films the hero gets beaten unconscious, then comes to a few minutes later and goes off to save the world; but in real life if you put your arm up to defend yourself, it will be broken. Something in our eyes must have told them that we were prepared to fight. They stopped in their tracks and stared at us. We stared them out, and they edged towards the door. They stood in the doorway, shouting and pretending to cock their weapons, but they backed off and slammed the door behind them. We couldn't believe it. We might have laughed if we hadn't had to listen to the moans and groans from the other lads further down.

We went through the same scenario one other time,

but this time it wasn't a bomb that sparked it off but an American. They seemed to have an irresistible urge to communicate with their fellow countrymen, even if to do so resulted in a good hiding. The Americans in our block knew now that there were others around, and that set them off.

David called out: "I'd kill for a Burger King."

A guard who happened to be in the washroom overheard him, and minutes later the blokes tore in. But it was Russell, not David, who carried the can. His cell was nearer to the washroom, and they must have come to the wrong conclusion. He got a severe going over and was dragged off to a punishment cell. They came back and gave David a few slaps as well, and then they came to us.

There were three of them, in helmets and wielding batons. We greeted them with a look that said: "Come on, then."

They backed off, shouting, "We're going to split you up." The threat was more horrifying than a beating would have been.

Miraculously, nothing happened. We could only surmise that the boys didn't report the incident in case their lack of bottle came to light.

We became a sideshow. The guards would bring in friends and local dignitaries, and stamp about and show their authority, cocking their weapons and pointing them. One big fat bastard came in one day with his Makharov pistol. He cocked it, brought it up, aimed it at Dinger, and pulled the trigger. The hammer came down on an empty chamber. The guards loved it. The fat bastard started laughing, all his mates started laughing, and we joined in. Then Dinger somehow managed to turn the whole thing to his advantage and ended up getting a cigarette out of it, which made his day.

We continued doing our ground studies of the map

every afternoon, trying to memorize every detail so that when we escaped and got out of the built-up area we'd have some form of identification of where we were. I think we got so good after a while that as soon as we saw a roadsign, we'd have known exactly where we were.

Map studies took up a lot of time, but in idle moments we just sat there and waffled. I went through my life story several times, until everybody knew Peckham and my three ex-wives almost as well as I did. Stan would talk about his time in Rhodesia with his family. They had donkeys and used to paint their hooves in bright colors. He told us one particularly good story about the day he'd watched as a herd of elephants came and ate all the windfall apples from an orchard. The fruit was so old that it had started to ferment, and it wasn't long before the elephants had flaked out on their haunches, completely pissed. While they were sleeping it off, a group of monkeys appeared and ate the remaining apples. They went up into the trees to rest after the feast, and it wasn't long before they also were pissed. One monkey was so gone that it fell off its branch, bringing down two other monkeys with it. They landed on the head of a pissed-up elephant, which then came to and started charging around the place.

Another story had a much darker side. Stan's family had a houseboy who lived with his family in a small bungalow on the estate. One night, a group of rebels got hold of him and shot him because he worked for the white man. They dragged the body back to the bungalow and left it on the doorstep as a warning to the rest of the family. The warning was heeded. Soon afterwards, Stan joined the army and became part of the rapid reaction force. When independence was declared, Stan left the country in despair.

We tried to educate Stan in the finer points of punk music. It took us three days to remember all the words of the Jam song "Down in the Tube Station at Midnight," and then we tried to teach it to him. He soon gave up. "I don't understand all this British shit," he complained. "Don't you guys know any Rolf Harris?"

Poor Stan. He had a thing about storing food: even if he was hungry, he would try and save it for a rainy day. He'd spend a lot of time and ingenuity hiding it from the guards, and then we'd wake up in the morning and insist that he share it. After all, what else are friends for?

We also passed the time doing exercise or assessing our injuries. I worried a lot about tooth decay. The guards nearly always spat in our food, and I imagined foul Iraqi bacteria attacking my broken stumps and rotting them, and then all my other teeth falling like dominoes.

We kept tabs on the date, and I felt especially low on the 24th. I couldn't help myself thinking about how I would have spent the day if I'd been in England. Would Katie have been with us for the day, or would I have just phoned her to wish her a happy birthday?

Towards the end of the month the major began turning up much more often, normally just before last light. He talked to us a lot about how wonderful it was to be an Iraqi since the revolution. There was a comprehensive health-care system, he explained, and everybody got a handsome pension at retirement age. Saddam also provided free education for all, up to and including university level—even if that entailed studying overseas.

"Our children read Shakespeare at school," he said one time, showing us a copy of *Hamlet*. "Last night I was going home, and a bomb dropped behind me. To be or not to be—it is Allah's will, no?"

None of us said anything, and after a while he muttered, "You know, you have been well treated here."

It was our best clue yet that the war was nearly

over. We didn't tell him what his guards were up to when his back was turned. That would only have made matters worse.

"Just remember that what happened before is nothing to do with me," he repeated. It must have been obvious to him that the war was going against them, and he was covering his arse.

One night we heard the gates opening and the sound of moaning and groaning. I hated hearing the gate open at night: it made me feel very insecure. It was clear from the sounds that a prisoner was being brought in and put into a cell. There was lots of mumbling, and suddenly a long, loud burst of screaming. We made contact with him the following night. His name was Joseph Small, call sign Alley Cat. He was a major, an aviator in the US Marine Corps. Poor bastard, he had been shot down on what he was able to tell us was the last day of the ground war. He had a bad parachute landing that left him hanging in a tree. He had sustained an open fracture of the leg, and all the Iraqis had done was give him an open-cast splint and let him get on with it.

It was wonderful to hear the news. The ground war had not only started but nearly finished, and Iraq was on its arse. But the problem Joseph Small brought with him was that the more Americans there were, the more chat there was. They wouldn't listen to make sure there weren't any guards around: they would just spark up, and the fallout was bad for all of us. I was still concerned that we could find ourselves separated.

Joseph was quite amusing because he was gagging for a cigarette and he was always asking for them, but he always asked aggressively and they just fucked him off. But Dinger, the model diplomat, every time the major turned up now he'd get a fag out of him.

In the end we decided not to initiate any more conversations with the Americans. We let them start their own, and waited to see if there was a reaction from the guards. If there wasn't, we'd join in, always trying to get as much information as we could. Had anybody been reported to the Red Cross? we asked. Did they think that we were dead? Did they know we were alive?

Joseph Small was able to say that nothing about us had been reported to the Red Cross; we'd all been posted as missing in action. Bush had just announced that if all prisoners were not released, the Allies were going all the way to Baghdad. That made us feel good in one respect: at least we were winning, and there was a good chance that we'd be released. But there was also a chance we wouldn't be freed. We knew the Iraqis had contact with the PLO. Were we going to land up best mates with Terry Waite, cuddling the same radiator?

There was a funny side to it as well, though.

"Who's that?" a voice boomed out.

"Major Joseph Small, Marine Corps."

"Russell Sanborn, Captain, Marine Corps."

"Aviator?"

"Yes, sir!"

It was real good gung ho stuff, straight out of *Top Gun*.

The day after Joseph Small turned up, a medic sergeant called Troy Dunlap was brought in on a stretcher with spinal injuries. He had been with a woman doctor who had broken both her arms and was also taken prisoner. The rest of the Black Hawk crew were dead after being shot down. Inevitably, the Americans made contact with him straightaway.

"Major Small? Major Joseph Small? Shit, sir, I'm your search and rescue mission!"

We made sure he knew our names as well, in case he got repatriated early because of his injuries.

Around this time the bombing stopped, which confirmed Small's story. We were using the bombing as a barometer. If it started again, we would know that things had gone to rat shit. In the afternoon two bangs sounded off in quick succession. After the first the birds flew away very loudly, and there was lots of shouting. Our hopes of an early release faded with the echo of the boom.

I tried to think positively. The Iraqis were getting their arse kicked by ground troops as well now. Small's information indicated it would be a matter of days rather than weeks until the end. And things must be going well for there to be daylight raids. But I hadn't heard any antiaircraft fire. Jeral confirmed that it had been aircraft going supersonic over the city—theirs or ours he didn't know.

Early in the morning of March 3, the outer gate of the courtyard opened up and then the gate into the main prison. There was lots of noise of keys clanking, voices raised, and shouting. David's cell was opened. We were all straining to hear what was going on.

We heard the words: "You're going home."

We looked at one another, and Stan said, "Fuck, mate, this is good shit."

Our door burst open, and a guard stood in the doorway with a clipboard in his hand. "Stan. Dinger. You are now going home. Wait here."

No Andy. It was one of the worst moments of my life. Our worst fears had been confirmed. They were going to keep back hostages.

I turned to Dinger and said, "If you're going home, make sure you speak to Jilly."

Dinger and Stan shook my hand before leaving. "Don't worry," they said.

Don't worry? I was flapping fit to take off.

Left alone in the cell, I spent the first couple of hours feeling severely sorry for myself. I felt happy for the blokes that were going, but that didn't stop me from

feeling abandoned. After so many weeks of comrade-
ship, the sudden loneliness was almost a physical
pain. I forced myself to work through the options. The
war must have ended; there was no doubt about that.
We knew that Small's sortie was just about the last to
be flown, and that was days ago. So why had only
three of us been released? *Were* they being released?

In the afternoon the major came in with all his entourage. "Yes, it is true," he said. "Your two friends
have gone home. They will be home with their families very soon. Maybe you will be going soon. Maybe
one day, maybe two days. I don't know. But remember, what happened at the other place is nothing to do
with me. What happened here is my responsibility.
You've been well looked after."

I was nodding and agreeing like a lunatic. He gave
me two oranges, which I ate as soon as he had gone,
peel and all. I began to feel better.

Later that afternoon I was dragged out and put into
the courtyard in the sunlight. I sat there soaking up the
rays for five minutes and was joined by two guards
who started talking about the pop charts. They were
about two decades behind in their news, but I wasn't
going to tell them that. Instead I discussed the merits
of various Boney M and Abba hits, nodding and
agreeing as much as I could without my head falling
off. Everybody was being all rather nice, so I knew
something was afoot.

I got the sun on my bones for an hour, and it felt
wonderful. They took me back in when the sun went
down, but I was feeling more and more hopeful.

Something strange happened to Joseph Small that
night. I was lying on the floor of my cell when I heard
his door open and people go in. There were
mumblings; then about a minute later the door closed,
and the noises receded. At last light the guards left us
alone. The three of us got talking, and I asked him
what had happened.

"An Iraqi soldier came into my cell," he said. "He was in combat dress and in bad shape. He had a rough beard, he had his webbing on, helmet, his boots were in shreds from rock cuts. He came in, looked at me, saluted, and left. Weird, Andy, fuckin' weird."

We could only surmise that he had withdrawn from Kuwait and for some odd reason wanted to see a prisoner.

We spent the next half hour trying to work out why two lots had gone but not us, but didn't get far. For the second night I didn't get any sleep. The first time it had been because I was so down in the dumps. Tonight it was the excitement of what the morning might bring.

In the early hours of March 5 the gates opened, and I jumped to my feet, eager with anticipation.

Russell's door opened.

"Russell Sanborn? You're going home."

Then Joseph's door.

"Joseph Small? You're going home."

The next one was the stretcher case.

And the last one was me.

"Andy McNab? McNab? Yes, you will be going home soon."

They handcuffed us and took us out of the cells one by one. We went through the gates that led onto the courtyard, and then through those gates, and were put onto a bus. For the very first time I saw the bodies that belonged to the voices from other cells. Joseph Small was much older than I had imagined, a man in his mid-forties who looked good considering his injuries. All I had ever seen of Russell Sanborn was an eye and finger that pulled down a small flap of blanket so he could look out and see people slop out as we walked past his punishment cell. There was no light in his cell apart from this hole. He had a deep, booming voice,

full of authority, and I had expected a man mountain.
In fact he had a very slight frame.

They moved down the bus and blindfolded everybody. We drove along the road for another 75 feet and
stopped. We seemed to be picking up another batch of
prisoners, who sounded like Saudis. I guessed we'd
been staying in a mirror image jail that had two identical wings.

We drove for about forty minutes. We stopped and I
heard aero engines. This is great, I thought: We're just
going to get on the plane and fuck off. But only the
Saudis disembarked. The guards then started to call
out our names.

I went forward when called, still blindfolded, and
was taken into a building. The echoes indicated it was
a low structure; I imagined it was a hangar. We were
arranged in a long line, handcuffed and blindfolded.
There was a loud hiss of Tilly lamps, and the noise of
soldiers moving around. I could hear the breathing of
people either side of me. We were held there for a long
time. My stomach was playing up again, and I was
feeling weak. I leaned forward, and my nose brushed
against a brick wall.

A sudden flurry of commands brought me bolt upright. I heard the ominous, metallic echo of weapons
being cocked.

Well, there you go, I said to myself. So much for
getting released: we're going to get topped. I took a
deep breath and waited for it.

Nothing happened. We stood there for five minutes
in total silence, everybody holding their breath.

I was feeling more and more ill as we stood against
the wall, and finally I buckled, collapsing on to my
knees.

"I've got to go to the toilet," I called out.

Somebody grabbed my arm and propelled me away,
but by the time we got there I'd sprayed myself with
runny stuff. I was taken back and put in the queue.

They took us one by one into tiny cells. The handcuffs were removed, and I could touch either side with my hands. But there were three blankets, a real luxury, and a little window. I needed to bang on the door every five minutes during the night. A guard appeared each time and dragged me down to the toilet, then stood over me while I dropped my arse. We spent the whole night toing and froing.

At first light we were given a good breakfast of egg, jam and bread, and hot, black tea. It was rather encouraging. I looked out of my cell and saw piles of old uniforms arranged on the floor, and yellow prison POW pajamas with pumps. I thought, this is the ticket.

An hour after breakfast, my cell door was opened, and I was led along a corridor to a room where there was a chair, table, mirror, water, and a razor.

The "barber" started to shave me, so clumsily that he ripped small chunks out of my face. Blood trickled down my chin.

"Can I do it myself?" I asked.

"No, you are a dangerous man."

They wouldn't let me rinse my face afterwards, either. I just had to wipe the soap and blood off with my shirt.

I was taken back to the cell by two soldiers who told me to strip. They presented me with one of the yellow uniforms and took my clothes away. I said a sad, silent farewell to my escape map and compass.

"Name?"

"McNab."

"You'll be going home today. Very soon."

The blindfold was put back on.

The cells were opened one at a time. A soldier checked our names, removed the blindfolds, and we came out and got in line. Somebody came up to the left of me and grabbed my hand enthusiastically.

"My name's John Nichol," he beamed.

I shook his hand. He noticed me looking at the green RAF polo neck under his yellow top.

"Fifteen Squadron," he said. "Tornadoes."

He was a really happy bloke, but not as delirious as the Americans. They were behaving as if they were already back in the States, and a few of the guards were getting twitchy about it. I was still keeping myself in check. The light was at the end of the tunnel, but who was to say it wasn't just another guard with a Tilly lamp coming towards us?

We were blindfolded yet again and marched off in a big crocodile. After a few meters they stopped us again, and a soldier walked up and down the line spraying us with women's perfume. I gritted my teeth. I could live with the smell, but the alcohol stung my badly shaved face.

We boarded a bus and after half an hour or so were told that we could take our blindfolds off. The bus had curtains, but I managed to look out through a gap and saw bombed bridges and buildings. Daily life was still very much going on, however. It was quite a happy time on the coach. The pilots were saying "Hi" to each other, and the guard at the front just sat there and let them get on with it.

It could be the world's biggest bluff, however, and I decided to keep myself to myself.

We pulled up at the door of the Nova Hotel. The place was teeming with soldiers and camera crews, and there was a fleet of Red Cross vehicles. I began to feel slightly more at ease.

The main foyer was crowded with what I at first thought were Iraqis, but who turned out to be Algerian medical staff. Part of the trade-off between Saddam and the Red Cross had been that they provide medical staff for Baghdad. The Algerians lived in the hotel and helped in the local hospitals.

We were taken into one of the reception rooms and segregated by nationality for documentation. The hotel had no heating, no hot water, no lifts. There was lighting, but the Red Cross had brought everything else with them, including their own food.

This was the first time that the Red Cross had had any news about any of us from the Iraqis. Even then, the lists being handed over were corrupt. It was a breach of the Geneva Convention, but a rather minor one compared with the rest of our experiences as POWs.

I was keen to find out about Dinger and Stan.

"Have there been prisoners released before us?" I asked one of the women.

The Red Cross personnel appeared to range from women in their mid-twenties to men in their late fifties. They were incredibly brave and professional people. I wouldn't have done their job.

"Yes. They got out via Jordan."

"Is there any chance you can give me the names of the Brits?"

She checked a list for me and found the surnames of Dinger and Stan. There were no other names that I recognized.

The girl confirmed that we were the last batch. So we had been the only three all along, I thought. All the stuff about wounded signals operators was a load of bollocks—a good bluff that had got me to gob off. Legs had probably been dead from the time Dinger left him.

Once the administration was done, we were given a little Red Cross ticket and a number, and the Europeans were taken upstairs to the third floor. I noticed that the fire escapes were boarded up, leaving only one way in and out through the central staircase.

Everything we needed was on the third floor. A Red Cross waiter brought us anything we asked for—if he had it. We got boiled eggs that weren't boiled properly. When we opened them they ran, but they were the best eggs I'd had in my life. The others followed theirs with croissants and chocolate, but by that time I

was in the toilet, bulking up. I started again with an
empty stomach and settled for a bottle of beer and
some bread. We sat around talking, and I listened to
everybody saying, "Well, that's it, we're away."

I couldn't believe what I was hearing. After all that
we'd been through, people were taking the Iraqis at
their word.

It seemed the intention that we were going to be held
in the hotel for a couple of hours and then taken away
to an airfield. One of the Red Cross blokes asked if
anybody was cold.

"Fucking right," came the reply.

Two hours later he came back with a jumper for
each of us that somebody had gone and bought downtown. The patterns were weird and wonderful, but
they were warm.

The main man of the Red Cross appeared and said,
"Is there an Andy McNab here?"

"Yes."

"Somebody downstairs wants to see you."

As he led me down the staircase I said, "We fly out
this afternoon?"

"We don't know yet because of the weather. We
could also be delayed because we can't get the aircraft
back from Saudi. It's very difficult to get communications—the Iraqis won't let me set up my own satellite
comms. It's all third-hand information, so I'm just sitting here and waiting. It's a terrible setup: they won't
give me any help at all. We brought all these Algerian
medical teams to help them with the civilian victims of
the bombing, but they've moved the civvies out of the
hospitals in Baghdad and told them to go home, to
leave hospital beds for soldiers who are coming home
from the front. There's so much unrest they have to
give priority to the soldiers.

"That's why you are on the third floor. We put the
Algerians at the bottom because they are in no danger.

We have the Red Cross personnel next, and then you right at the top, because they are after you. They want some of you for hostages and bargaining power. If you come down these stairs, you must only come down with me or another Red Cross member.

"We can't get the badly wounded up to the third floor because the lifts do not work and we can't maneuver them around the staircases. Unfortunately they've got to stay downstairs. It's quite possible that they'll raid the place and take people. The only defense we have is our Red Cross status."

We went into the main foyer, and I spotted two sinister-looking Arabs sitting by the reception desk.

"Secret police," he warned.

If they hadn't posed such a threat, they would have looked laughable in their big, baggy suits with turn-ups, white socks, and swept-back hair.

"Believe it or not," the official went on, "the soldiers out there are protecting you."

It was ironic. I saw the soldiers stop two other men in suits from coming in. You could tell by the body language that there was obviously some friction between them. Rumors were already circulating that fifty generals had been executed after a failed attempt to change the system of power.

We walked through the foyer.

"When you go into this room," the official pointed, "you must stay there. If you want to move outside, one of us must be with you."

A Red Cross girl was sitting in a chair, blocking the door. She was quietly reading a book, and on the floor by her side she had a small bottle of wine, a bit of bread, and some cheese. Brave, unbelievably brave.

Four or five people were on stretchers. I recognized Joseph Small and Troy Dunlap and waved. Then, looking along the line, I saw Mark.

"I gave them everybody's name to see if any of you were here," he grinned.

I wanted to hug him and say "Great to see you," but the words wouldn't come out. I shook his hand instead.

"What happened to you?" I said, hardly containing my amazement.

He was wearing a dish-dash. His body looked wasted, and he still bore the bruises and scars of severe beatings.

"When we had that last contact and we both went down, I went left and got caught up in fire. There were people all over the place. I ended up lying in a small drainage ditch. They were following up and were a foot away from me at one stage. Then I moved off a bit, trying to edge my way out of it. After about half an hour I saw some torches, and as they were fanning about, they caught me in the beam. There was a big cabby, and I got shot through the foot and across the elbow. Look."

He lifted the dish-dash. The round had skimmed all the way around his elbow. He was incredibly lucky. A 7.62 round could have taken his arm off.

"The foot wound fucked me up," he said. "I couldn't move. They gave me a good kicking, dragged me onto a truck, and took me to a location. It was fucking hideous. My foot was just bouncing up and down on the wagon floor because I had no control of it, and I was screaming my head off. They thought it was hilarious. They were laughing their bollocks off."

Mark lost a lot of blood and thought he was going to die. He received no medical attention for his foot; the gaping wound was just bandaged and left to heal by itself. He was handcuffed naked to a bed all the time he was in prison, and basically left to rot. He went through the same system of interrogation as the rest of us, the only difference in his case being that the interrogation took place in his room.

"They'd dig at my foot," he said, "and shake my leg so my foot rattled around. It was grim. But one funny thing was, they'd piled my clothes on the floor by my bed. Every day I looked down at the gold, wrapped up in the masking tape, and the fuckers never found it until halfway through my capture. I still had my escape map and compass and all."

He had two blokes that used to come in and take him out for a shit. He called them Health and Hygiene because they were such dirty, minging old things. When he was on his own, he used to get the pitcher of water and try to clean his wound. The actual hole was clogged up with human skin and gunge, trying to heal itself over. His foot was swollen to the size of a marrow.

"Sometimes I'd call out that I needed a shit, and they'd come in and put a bowl under my arse and leave me for hours. Piss was going everywhere because I can't organize myself, and there was shit up to the brim of this little bowl."

He got filled in by the guards quite a few times. The blokes would come in and play with his foot and generally give him a hard time. All along, he kept up the same old story as the rest of us. During one interrogation, somebody recognized his New Zealand accent. He was accused of being a mercenary, working for the Israelis.

I told him that Dinger and Stan were away and should be in the UK soon, and gave him our theories of what we thought had happened to the others. As we talked about events, he reckoned he could have been in the same prison as us: it certainly took direct hits at exactly the same time.

The Red Cross were knocking out sheds of coffee for us, and then a cooked dinner turned up.

Mark had lice, like we all did, and generally stank. But his stink was something special, and he was worried that it could mean gangrene. We talked about the possible scenarios that could happen now, but kept drifting back to swapping horror stories, each of us trying to cap the other.

I was just telling Mark about the situation outside with the secret police when one of the Red Cross guys came around and said that there was a delay. We couldn't go until the next day because of the aircraft: it had gone to Saudi to pick up prisoners for an exchange, but because of adverse weather it wouldn't be coming back until the following morning.

The Red Cross people were tense. They posted sentries in the corridors and at all the entry points, and armed them with candles and food. It was obvious that they were expecting this to be a rough night.

Mark and I had a beer and then turned in. I planned to kip on the floor next to his stretcher in case of trouble. That was the plan but it didn't happen. I went back upstairs to get some food and chocolate and fell asleep in a chair. Red Cross people, awake all night, sat among us in groups of two and three.

I woke up early. An official appeared and announced with a grin that it was time to go home. Mark and I had a problem now of security, because men from the Regiment are required to keep their faces out of the press at all costs. I went up and saw the pilots, and explained my concerns to the Red Cross.

"No problem," they said. "At the same time as the coach comes to the front of the hotel, ambulances will be going to the back because we can only get the stretchers out through the service area. You can go in one of the ambulances with your friend."

The aircrew agreed to put on a diversionary show for the media, pulling their jumpers over their heads to get the cameras clicking. Footage of these camera-shy "Special Forces" lads was broadcast all over the world.

We moved off in a convoy. We had two Red Cross guys in the front of our ambulance, and as we drove

along, one of them said, "We'll give you a tour of
Baghdad, if you like. If you look to your left," he said,
adopting the voice of the typical tour guide, "this is
the Ministry of Information. It was a whole system of
buildings, and just one building was dropped. Talk
about precision bombing. And on your right you have
the Ministry of . . ."

Posters of Saddam and the symbol of the Muslim
crescent were on every street. There was devastation
everywhere, but by the looks of things the precision
bombing had indeed been excellent. Without a doubt
they'd been hitting their military targets. Civilian
buildings right next door to the ruins were relatively
unscathed.

He started talking about the Iran–Iraq prisoner exchanges that he'd been involved in. He said they'd
been exchanging prisoners in their twenties who
looked over forty, they'd had such a terrible time of it.
Their life was gone. Some of the injuries were horrific,
open wounds that had been left to fester.

"This is actually the most successful exchange yet,"
the bloke said. "I think that's because of pressure from
the military, who probably want their manpower back.
There is a lot of concern about stability. A coup seems
imminent. The sooner we get you out the better."

"I'll second that one," Mark said.

I read the road signs towards Baghdad International, and as the kilometers ticked down, I felt my
apprehension building. There seemed to be a lot of
administrative cock-ups because we'd drive a little
way, then stop, then drive on, then stop. I couldn't see
any aircraft.

"We have this all the time," the driver said. "The
bureaucracy is mind-boggling."

We rounded a corner and saw a convoy of buses full
of Iraqi prisoners. They didn't look very happy with
themselves. The main terminal was deserted. We sat

through two hours of petty administration before the call finally came for us to be put onto an aircraft.

The walking prisoners went up the steps at the front of the two Swissair 727s. The stretcher cases were maneuvered up the stairwell at the rear. I stayed with Mark. The Swissair crew greeted us like VIPs, and straightaway the coffee came out—with cream. It was nectar.

As the aircraft lifted from the runway, we roared like a football crowd. I looked at Mark and grinned. This time we really were going home.

13

The head boy of the American contingent, a colonel, came over the loudspeakers. He wanted to orchestrate it so that all his men were dressed only in their POW kit, to look good for the cameras. They had to bin their pullovers. He also organized them so that they came out in strict order of rank. I couldn't believe it. Five minutes out of an Iraqi jail and he gets his military head on again.

Mark and I were unaffected by this crap because we knew we wouldn't leave the aircraft until the media had dispersed. We were getting in amongst the sticky buns and coffee when the captain announced that our pair of 727s would soon be getting an escort of F15s and Tornadoes.

No sooner had he said it than two American F15s came up alongside, one flying slightly higher than the other. They maneuvered until they were flying right over the wings of our aircraft. The Yanks were up and giving it lots of "Yo!" One pilot responded by taking his mask off and giving it the old "Way to go!" arm swing in the air. He fired off chaff and banked away. It really was a fantastic sight.

Then the pilots got their aerobatic hats on. One spun off and did a victory roll and landed up over the other wing; then both F15s landed over the starboard wing.

Now it was the turn of the RAF Tornadoes. They came up so close that I could see the pilots' eyes. One flier took off his mask and mouthed the word "Wankers!" with, of course, the accompanying wrist action. John Nichol, the RAF prisoner who had shaken my hand, went up forward and spoke to some of them on the radio. They fired off chaff and were spinning around the sky as well—and doing it all a bit better than the Yanks, I thought.

"These jet pilots think they're the only ones that can do that," said our captain. "So, fasten your seatbelts, please, and hang on tight."

With that he banked the aircraft steeply and put us into a perfect barrel roll. The other Swissair jet came up level with us, and both aircraft flew in concentric circles, meeting up again in the middle.

There was another big roar as we passed into Saudi airspace, and then all the jets came down, hoiked down the chaff, and were off, afterburners flaming in the brilliant blue sky.

We landed in Riyadh to a tumultuous welcome. Every pressman and his dog was there, and every bit of top brass—Stormin' Norman included. Mark and I peeked out from behind the blinds and saw that some of our people were there too. It was just a matter of waiting. The Saudis disembarked first, followed by the orderly exit of correctly dressed Americans. The rear door was opened and the stretcher cases were loaded into the ambulances. Our people came on board.

"We're going to throw you in the back of one of the ambulances," one of them said. "You'll then go straight around the corner into a C130. We'll fly out, land at another airfield, and pick up a VC10 which will take you straight to Cyprus, where you're going to hospital."

We got onto the C130, and the rest of the Brits joined us. We flew for about twenty minutes, landed, and

picked up our connection for Cyprus. The interior of
the aircraft had been thoughtfully rearranged so that
the seats faced one another. We were each given a day
sack, in which was a Walkman, spare batteries, shaving foam, a razor, underpants, soap, and a watch with
both digital and analogue time.

It was dark when we landed at RAF Akrotiri. Again,
our own people were there to meet us. Each of us was
allotted a sponsor we knew. Mine was an old mate,
Kenny. His first words were: "Am I ever pissed off
that you're still alive. I was down to take over your job
next September."

There were lots of handshakes, and a bottle of gin
was circulating rapidly. A fellow sergeant called Mugger was in overall charge of the SAS recovery mission.
He was running around Riyadh with a borrowed Warrant Officer crest on his wrist to give his requests
added authority, as nobody from the Regiment was
wearing anything that showed who or what they
were.

"I wish you'd been delayed even more," he honked,
"because I've been running around doing the RSM bit.
It's fucking great."

We were put on a bus and taken straight to a segregated secure ward at the military hospital.

The massive, hulking frame of Stan loomed out of the
darkness, closely followed by Dinger, fag in hand.
Stan had hepatitis and wasn't feeling too good, but
Dinger was firing on all cylinders.

"I've phoned Jilly," he said. "I've got it all squared
away; don't worry about the phone cards. Our blokes
have rigged up a link through to the UK."

Mugger went down to the town to organize a few
videos for our entertainment, and the B Squadron sergeant major turned up with a hospital trolley loaded
with booze for a piss-up. We were smuggled out of the

ward and down to the library, where we set about getting blitzed.

Gordon Turnbull, the RAF psychologist and counselor, had arrived in Cyprus to oversee the recuperative phase.

"What have you got there?" he asked Mugger as he spotted him heading for the library.

"Videos for the lads."

"Mind if I have a look?"

Turnbull nearly had a heart attack. Mugger had bought us *Terminator*, *Driller Killer*, and *Nightmare on Elm Street*. "You can't do this!" he shrieked. "Those blokes are all traumatized!"

"Traumatized?" said Mugger. "They're pissed out of their brains. Come and have a look."

Turnbull saw us and blew a gasket.

"Don't worry about it," Mugger said. "They were all fucking barking to start with."

I helped Mark into the bath, and a big lump of skin the size of a bath plug fell out of the hole in his foot. I then went in search of our special phone.

The armed guard sneaked me down to the cellar and took me to where a couple of scaleys were guarding the phone to keep away freeloaders.

The link worked perfectly, and I got through to Jilly straightaway.

I staggered to bed after lots of "I love you." As my head hit the pillow, I worked out that this was the first proper bed I had slept in for eight weeks, three days.

For the next couple of days we had X rays and tests, and the dentists had a provisional go at my teeth. We had posttraumatic shock sessions with Gordon Turnbull, which lasted only a few minutes each. Poor Gordon, he'd thought it was Christmas with all these traumatized blokes coming back from captivity. He was good at his job, but the mentality of the blokes made them far more interested in taking advantage of everything else that was on offer. Our blokes had organized for us to get down to the town, and the Red Cross had given us a float of money. We wanted to buy our duty frees before it all disappeared.

The Red Cross went round asking if we had any special requests, which they would then go into the town and buy on our behalf.

"Why don't you just give us the money, and we'll buy our own kit?" I said to a distinguished-looking lady in her late fifties.

"You can fuck off," she smiled. "Do you think I was born yesterday?"

However, she eventually relented. I bought jeans, T-shirts and videos, and a suitcase to put it all in. Everybody had a good old shopping frenzy. After an hour we started running out of money, and Kenny was flapping because we put a £600 dent in his plastic. He knew he'd have a long wait before we paid him back.

The Belgians had a medical team there as part of their contribution to the war. They had a big going-away barbecue, and Mugger got us all invited. The night passed in a blissful haze.

The following day it was confirmed that I had hepatitis. Being made to eat our own shit just might have had something to do with it. Other medical checks showed that my shoulder had been dislocated, I had ruptured muscles in my back, scar tissue on my kidneys, burns on my thighs, and loss of dexterity in both hands, but I was keen to get back to the UK.

We packed our kit on March 10 and jumped aboard a VC10. Unfortunately it wasn't going straight to Brize Norton; we'd caught the military equivalent of a number 22 bus.

We flew to Laarbruch first to drop off a lot of the RAF personnel. We stayed at the back with the blinds down while whoever was in charge of the air force in Germany greeted his boys off the plane. Without a doubt it was a big homecoming. After the ceremony the top brass got into his car. His next port of call, and also our next destination, was an hour or so's drive away, so we now had to wait on the pan at Laarbruch to give him time to get to Brüggen. When we landed, he was at the other end to greet the second batch of RAF prisoners. The whole ceremony was repeated. We sorted out some crates of Grolsch and slowly got pissed.

We flew into Brize Norton, and as the aircraft closed down its engines, we could hear the familiar sound of our own Agusta 109 helicopters coming in to land. They came down right alongside the aircraft. My squadron OC was on board, and Mark's sister, who lived and worked in London. After a brief reunion we boarded the helicopters and lifted off for Hereford.

The camp was deserted. Two of the squadrons were still in the Gulf, and other teams were scattered as ever on various jobs.

The adjutant came out to the heli pad.

"Welcome back," he said. "Come into the office."

He popped a bottle of champagne. As he poured it, he said to Mugger, "Right, you need to be back here for half six tomorrow, because we're taking you straight back out. You're needed in Saudi."

"Fucking hell!" said Mugger, completely crestfallen. He had been looking forward to a few nights at home with Mrs. Mugger.

To the rest of us the adjutant very generously said: "There's no big rush at the moment. Take a couple of days off."

The families officer offered me a lift home. As my house came into view, I asked him to stop.

"I'll walk from here," I said. "I need the exercise."

14

We had the luxury of two days off.

On Monday Jilly and I went for a walk around the town. I was dressed in familiar old clothes that were a lot looser-fitting than the last time I'd worn them. We wanted just to bum around, doing nothing in particular, but ended up bumping into loads of blokes with suntans and swapping horror stories.

On Tuesday Katie came to stay and we spent our time watching the *Robin Hood* video and practicing our high kicks.

On Wednesday it was back to work.

The Regiment wanted to find out what had happened and why, and whether there were any lessons to be learned for future operations. The five of us sat down with maps and aerial photography and pieced together every detail of our movements from the time we got the warning order to the moment of our release.

We visited widows and families. Stan and Chris spent time with Vince's wife and his brothers, giving them details of what had happened and trying to console them. I visited Legs's wife and found her very switched on and down to earth. Meeting her was a help to me. I could talk things through without having to do the "never mind" bit.

On March 16 we got away for a couple of days to Aberdovey, a place Jilly and I had gone to when we first met. The first time we went there she told me it was the most wonderful holiday ever. She expected the same again, but we both sensed that this time things were different. We couldn't put our finger on anything specific, but things were a bit strained. We cut short the trip and went to see Bob's mother and sister in Bognor. The loss of their son and brother had hit them hard. They hadn't even known he was in the Regiment—nor had his divorced father, who'd had to stop working in the restaurant he managed in London. He was physically sick with grief.

The debrief took about three weeks. We then had a visit from Gordon Turnbull again and a two-hour session in the officers' mess, chatting away. He and one of his colleagues got us to do a simple tick test to evaluate our levels of stress. The higher you scored above 10, the worse your emotional turmoil. We all scored 11. Gordon got 13.

We decided that the wives and girlfriends had been more traumatized by the events than we had. They'd had a lot to go through: the pain of uncertainty, which they hadn't been allowed to share with anybody, and then the sadness of being told that we were almost certainly dead—only to see some of our faces on TV a few days later. Gordon Turnbull held a session specially for them, explaining in particular the symptoms of posttraumatic stress disorder.

Once the debrief was consolidated, it was announced that we would address the whole Regiment. We did a lot of rehearsals because we wanted it to go well. It is an unheard-of event for all available personnel to turn up to a debrief, but when we stood up, it was in front of a sea of faces. Everybody was there, from the heli crew to the search and rescue coordinator. General Sir Peter de la Billière—DLB as we know him—was seated in the front row with an array of army high command.

We spoke for two hours. I gave the initial brief of the planning phases and then went on to the compromise, up to the split. Then each person told his story, and what lessons he had learnt. Chris was last on. He had a remarkable story to tell.

When Stan went off with the old goatherder in search of a vehicle, the plan had been that if he didn't return by 1830, Chris would move out, leaving behind Stan's belt kit and some ammunition. This he duly did, heading due north on a bearing, aiming for the Euphrates. It was 36 hours since their water had run out.

Chris had only been going for a quarter of an hour when he saw vehicle lights behind him in the area of the LUP. He started to run back, thinking that Stan had managed to get a vehicle and was coming to RV with him. Then he saw a second set of lights. His heart sank.

Chris walked for the rest of that night. It was a clear sky —good ambient light for the night sight—but still very cold. At about 0430, looking through the sight, he saw the river below him. There were bits and pieces of habitation dotted amongst the irrigated land, and the sound of dogs barking. He was desperate for water, however, and started to move down towards the river. Without warning, he found himself up to his waist in mud. He floundered around, and it was a long time before he managed to drag himself clear. Exhausted and cautious, he crawled the rest of the way to the water's edge. He filled his bottles, drank, and then filled them again. The water was thick with mud.

By now it was nearly first light. He found a small wadi to hide in but realized only when it was too late that he was also just 1,600 feet away from a small village, and the top of the wadi was in full view. He was stuck. He tried to sleep but was so cold and wet that every time he dozed off he woke up again minutes later, shivering uncontrollably. Inspecting his feet, he found that he'd lost all his toenails, and that the blisters along the sides of his feet had connected up into long cuts that were weeping pus. So much for the £100 go-faster mountain boots.

He moved out again just after last light and was soon having to box around military and civilian locations. There seemed to be hundreds of them, and the result was that between 1830 that evening and 0500 the next morning he covered only 6 miles.

For his next LUP Chris climbed down a short way from the top of a 600 feet cliff face. He lay in a fissure in the rock, watching village life on the opposite bank—kids running around, women in black kit, people washing and fishing.

He moved off again soon after last light and found himself sandwiched between the river on his right and a road on his left. Cross-graining the wadis exhausted him, and he ended up practically walking on the road. At one point he heard the sound of a vehicle and jumped into the ditch. He peered through the sight at the Scud convoy that was thundering by overhead. He made a note of the time and place and moved on.

Soon afterwards, another vehicle went past on main beam and illuminated a road sign up ahead. Chris was gutted by what it said. He was 30 miles further from the border than he'd estimated. That equated to another two nights of travel, which depressed him severely.

When it came to first light, Chris couldn't find a decent LUP and started flapping. After a lot of running around, he eventually got into a big culvert under the main road. That seemed to be fine, until he heard the ominously familiar sound of goat bells.

A herd of goats was coming up the culvert—heading, he supposed, for the fields on the other side. Chris legged it from his hiding place and managed to scramble about 6 feet up the embankment before an old goatherder emerged, followed by a donkey and the world's supply of goats—and a pair of dogs. They were bound to scent him. He had a split second in which to decide whether to shoot the old man to be on the safe side, or just do a runner. The dogs made the decision for him, running straight past without looking up. The rest of the procession followed without a flicker. Chris couldn't believe it. He had been within spitting distance of them all. He could only think that the dogs had been put off by the scent of the goats—or that of the old boy's dirty dishdash.

They would almost certainly be going back that way before last light, however, so Chris knew that he'd have to move. He started crawling along a wadi, having to get down every time a vehicle went along—which was often. The ground had changed by now, from lush, irrigated vegetation to wadi systems and small mounds covered with thorn bushes. It was hard going. After about 5 miles he found a large depression in the ground and settled down for the rest of the day.

Chris had used up his supply of muddy river water and was dehydrating badly. He knew, however, that he had to keep away from the Euphrates, since every hut seemed to have a dog in it. He'd just have to keep going and hope that he'd find water elsewhere soon.

At last light he got up and headed due west, walking for several hours. At one point an air-raid siren went off ahead of him, and through the night sight he could make out an emplacement that appeared to consist of several S60s, together with radio masts and sentries who were patrolling. He boxed around the position and came to a small stream flowing over white rock. Not wasting a second, he undid his water bottles and quickly filled them. Then he moved on straightaway.

He kept encountering more and more enemy activity and eventually found himself at a road junction, wedged between a VCP and an antiaircraft site. It was nearly first light so he crawled into a culvert under the road. It had been used as a dump site for garbage, and the stench was overpowering.

His feet were in a very bad way by now, but there wasn't

anything he could do to treat them. He consoled himself by lying back on the rubbish and taking a big swig from one of the bottles.

His lips burned and blistered the moment the fluid touched them. He nearly shouted with pain. The emplacement must have been guarding something like a chemical plant, and the stream must have been some kind of outlet from it. Chris was in a bad way. He had nothing to rinse his burning mouth with, and his bottles were now unusable. For a short while he thought he was going to die.

As he lay in the culvert, Chris took stock. He hadn't had water for two days, and he now needed medical treatment for his mouth. Some cuts on his hands had turned septic, and his feet were so bad he could only just about put pressure on them. He knew he didn't have much time left.

He set off as soon as it was last light. It was very cloudy and dark, which meant he might be able to get past the VCP unnoticed. In fact he found some dead ground and staggered past, his feet causing him excruciating pain. He hobbled as best he could for about an hour when suddenly there was a flash in the sky. Thinking he'd triggered off a trip flare, Chris hit the ground. Then he heard explosions. Looking over his shoulder, he realized there was an air raid on the area of the chemical plant.

He knew he must be close to the border by now and was looking for the twin towers on high ground. He saw a town in the distance, brightly lit, and very soon afterwards encountered coils of barbed wire. Was the town in Syria, though, or was it on the Iraqi side and the wire was a false frontier?

A patrol in vehicles went past. Their existence seemed to confirm that this was the border, and he decided to go for it. He found a point where there were stakes holding the wire and started to climb. He shredded his arms and legs, but managed to get over. He sat down on the other side and made another appreciation. The town seemed to be in the wrong place. But whatever, it made sense to press on west.

Chris had just about had it by now. He was swaying

around as he shuffled along, well on the way down with dehydration. There was no saliva in his mouth, and his tongue was stuck to the inside of his cheek. As he walked, his head filled with a loud crackling noise like static electricity. He saw a white flash and must have passed out. He came to on the ground. He got back up on his feet and tried to move. The same thing happened. This time, he came to with his face in a pool of blood. He'd landed face down on a rock and broken his nose. He staggered into a nearby wadi and fell asleep.

He woke at first light when he heard Stan shouting to him to come on out, everybody was just around the corner. He got to his feet and started hobbling towards the sound of Stan's voice. He felt so happy that the patrol was going to be reunited. Coming out of the wadi, he realized at once that he was hallucinating. He knew that if he didn't get some water down him soon, he'd be dead.

There was a small house, probably a goatherder's dwelling, in the middle distance. Chris decided that even if he was still in Iraq, he'd have to go there and get some water—if necessary, by force.

A woman was preparing food by a fire. Children were playing around her, and he could see a man in the distance with a herd of goats. As Chris shuffled up to the fire, a lad in his late teens came out of the house and greeted him. The boy was friendly, shaking Chris by the hand and smiling.

"Where is this?" Chris said.

The boy didn't understand. He looked quizzically at Chris, then started pointing behind him. "Iraq! Iraq!" he beamed.

Chris got the picture. He shook the boy's hand again and said, "Thank fuck for that!"

He was invited inside and offered a big bowl of water. Gulping it down in one, he immediately asked for another. An old granny with tattoos on her face was feeding a child in the corner of the room. She gave him a toothless grin. Also stacked up in the same room were the whole family's bedding rolls and straw for the animals. Chris went over and sat by the paraffin heater and soaked up the warmth. The children who had been playing outside came in and showed him pictures they had drawn on scraps of paper. The drawings were of skies full of aircraft and tanks in flames.

The woman came in with a hot loaf of nan bread she'd just baked and presented it to Chris. He was touched. The bread had obviously been intended as the family's meal. He swallowed one mouthful and felt instantly full. His stomach must have shrunk dramatically. The lad brought him some hot sweet tea; as far as Chris was concerned, it was the best brew he'd ever had.

Chris tried to explain that he needed to find a policeman. The boy seemed to understand and said he'd take him to one. Chris took off his smock and webbing and stripped down his 203 to look less aggressive to anyone they met. He wrapped the parts inside his smock and put it in a plastic fertilizer bag that the boy gave him. They set off with waves and smiles, the boy carrying the bag, Chris limping along on his damaged feet. The children stayed with them until the hut was almost out of sight.

After they'd been walking for about an hour, a Land Cruiser pulled up alongside, and the driver offered them a lift into town. They sat in the back, and the driver and the boy exchanged a few pleasantries, but for most of the journey they drove along in silence. From time to time, Chris caught the driver staring at him in the rearview mirror.

Just as they were coming into the town, the vehicle stopped outside a house, and the driver shouted to somebody inside. An Arab in his late thirties came out, dressed from head to toe in black. The two of them had a long discussion, at the end of which the driver told Chris's friend to get out. He reluctantly did as he was told, and Chris noticed as he said goodbye that he looked very worried.

They drove on, and the driver, who appeared to speak more English than he had let on, started gobbing off about the war. He got quite agitated about it.

"You should not be here," he said. "This is not our war." Basically the drift was: "Fuck off back to Iraq, white eye."

Chris showed him his indemnity slip, which stated in Arabic that anybody guiding the bearer to a British Embassy or to the Allied forces would receive a reward of £5,000. The Arab glanced at the piece of paper as he drove, then stuffed it into his shirt pocket. Chris explained that the paper was no good on its own; there had to be a live body to go with it. Just to let him know that he meant it, he gave the Arab a bit of an evil look.

They pulled up outside a garage. Another Arab who appeared to know the driver came out of the workshop, went around to the passenger side of the Land Cruiser, looked at Chris, then turned on his heels and ran back inside. It seemed to Chris that he was going to get slotted here, and he started to pull the weapon out of the bag. The driver grabbed his arm, and Chris responded with a bit of good news with his elbow. He jumped out of the vehicle as the Arab lolled across the seats with his head sticking out Chris's side. Kicking the door so that it slammed on the man's neck, Chris did a runner—or rather, a fast hobble.

He rounded a corner and spotted a man in uniform, armed with an AK47, who was on guard outside a bungalow.

"Police?" Chris shouted.

"Yes."

"British airman!"

The man hustled him inside the building, which turned out to be the police station. Officers were lounging around the room in leather jackets and sunglasses, doing the sinister bit.

Minutes later, the driver of the Land Cruiser came in, holding his neck and cursing the British. Chris grabbed the indemnity slip from the man's pocket and showed it to the police. They laughed at what it said. Chris began to get the feeling that he had a problem on his hands. Just as he was contemplating fighting his way out of the station, one of the policemen went over to the driver and smacked him hard across the head. Others jumped up and dragged him from the building.

"Stupid twat," Chris grinned at them, "he's just done himself out of five grand."

They searched Chris's kit before taking him to the chief's office. The senior officer didn't speak a word of English—none of them did—but he got Chris to write down his name and details on a sheet of paper. Chris supplied his correct name but stated that he was a medic with an air rescue team.

The chief picked up his phone. He spelled out to somebody everything that Chris had written, letter by letter. Then he made another call, which Chris guessed to be internal by the number of digits dialed. One of the policemen appeared with a dish-dash and face veil and told Chris to put them on. He was hustled out to a vehicle, a policeman either side of him. Chris was left in no doubt that he was their prisoner, and he didn't have a clue where they were taking him. For all he knew they could have been heading back to the border.

They drove for about an hour along a desert highway and eventually pulled up behind a couple of Mercs that were parked at the roadside. Six heavies lounged against the black limos, all wearing sunglasses. One of them had a Makharov in his hand.

Chris was blindfolded and made to kneel on the tarmac. His head was pushed forward and he thought: Here we go, it's topping time. He was severely pissed off with himself for falling into the trap.

For several seconds, nothing happened. Then they hauled him to his feet and pushed him into the back of one of the cars. They must just have been having a bit of fun. They drove for another two hours, and Chris saw a big sign with an arrow and the word **Baghdad**.

One of the men in sunglasses said, "Yes, we are going to Baghdad. You are prisoner of war. We are Iraqi."

It was coming to last light, and the sun was setting in front of them. Chris was so confused by this stage that he couldn't remember whether the sun set in the west or the east. He thought back to his childhood in Tyneside and the times he'd watched the sun coming up over the coast in the morning. If it came up in the east, he reasoned, then they must be heading west.

He knew he was right when he started to see signs saying Damascus. It was dark when they hit the outskirts of the city. The heavies put out their cigarettes and started straightening their ties. They pulled up behind another car. A man got out and came and sat in the passenger seat of Chris's vehicle. Middle-aged and smartly dressed, he spoke excellent English.

"Are you all right?" he asked.

"Yes thanks, I'm fine."

"Good. Don't worry, it won't be long now."

It was clear to Chris that the other two blokes in the car were practically shitting themselves with fear of this fellow. When they reached a compound and stopped, both men jumped out and opened the man's door for him. Chris tried to get out and fell onto his knees. His feet had given up the struggle. The man snapped his fingers, and Chris was carried into the building.

He was shown into a large office and greeted by a man in a navy blazer, striped shirt, and tie. The man shook his hand and said something.

"Welcome," an interpreter translated.

The office had all the mod cons: teak furniture from Harrods, gold-plated AK47 on the wall, the lot. He worked out that they were in the headquarters of the secret police.

Through the interpreter, the top man asked if Chris would like a bath. Chris nodded and was ushered through a door into a bedroom, with bathroom and gym en suite. The man put a new blade in his razor and unwrapped soap and shampoo and put them on the bath as he left.

Chris was just starting to strip off when a young lad came in with a tape measure. He put it around Chris's chest, then took his other measurements. Chris hoped it was a suit he was being measured for, and not a coffin.

The bath water was black almost as soon as he got into it, so he ran another one. Yet another boy appeared. He presented Chris with a cup of coffee. It was good stuff. He started to feel more secure. If they were going to top him, they wouldn't waste good coffee on him.

The interpreter came back and asked him questions. Chris responded with the cover story. The Arab looked dubious, but made no comment. Chris got out of the bath and looked at himself in the mirror. He couldn't believe how much weight he'd lost. His biceps were the size of his wrists. Somebody else came in with clean clothes for him. It felt fantastic putting on fresh skiddies, then a white shirt and tie, socks, shoes, and—the pièce de resistance—a brand-new pin-stripe suit that must have been run up in the last half hour, when he was in the bath—in the middle of the night. The trousers were a little too big around the waist, and the chief gave the lad with the tape measure a fearsome bollocking. The boy gestured for Chris to take them off again and disappeared with them over his arm.

A doctor was brought in. He dressed Chris's feet and bandaged them up. As he was finishing, the boy came back with the trousers. This time they were a perfect fit.

The chief asked Chris if he'd care for a little food and led him to his dining room. The table was groaning under the weight of steaks, kebabs, vegetables, fruit, freshly baked bread. Chris knocked back a liter of water and then got stuck into a steak. He could manage only a few mouthfuls.

The chief was really getting into it now and offered him a night on the town.

"I'm sorry," Chris said, "but I think I should go to the British Embassy as soon as possible."

The chief looked really disappointed as he telephoned the embassy and arranged for somebody to come and collect Chris. He'd probably been looking forward to a night out on expenses.

When the driver from the British Embassy arrived, he, too, bowed to the chief. Then he picked up Chris's dirty kit and carried it to the car while Chris shook hands with his new bosom buddy.

The embassy sent messages at once to Joint Headquarters

*at High Wycombe and to Riyadh, and made arrangements
for Chris to fly out the next evening. It was the first news
anybody had had of Bravo Two Zero since the night of the
infil.*

Chris had walked more than 180 miles in the eight
nights of his E&E. In all that time he'd had nothing to
eat except the two small packets of biscuits that he had
shared with Vince and Stan, and he'd had virtually
nothing to drink. He had lost an enormous amount of
body weight, and his survival was attributed to his
system feeding on its own meat.

It was two weeks before Chris could walk again
properly, and six weeks before he got any sensation
back in his toes and fingers. The location where he
reported finding the water that burnt his mouth
turned out to be a uranium-processing plant. He had a
severe blood disorder and problems with his liver
from drinking dirty river water, but he was back on
operations very soon afterwards. It was one of the
most remarkable E&Es ever recorded by the Regiment,
as far as I am concerned, ranking above even the
legendary trek through the desert of North Africa by
Jack Sillitoe, one of David Stirling's originals, in 1942.

There had been many more troops than we'd expected
in the area. In fact, we now learnt that what we had
gone into was one large military holding area: two
Iraqi armored divisions were positioned between the
border and our first LUP. As if that wasn't bad
enough, every man, woman, and child in the area had
been told to be on the lookout for us. Children were
given the day off school to join in the hunt. All the
same, we gave a good account of ourselves: it was
established by intelligence sources that we had left 250
Iraqi dead and wounded in our wake.

The FOB received our Sit Rep of January 23, but in a
very corrupt mode, which must have confused the hell

out of them. On the 24th, at 1600 local time—the time of the compromise—another unintelligible signal was received. Later they picked up a faint TACBE signal and realized then that we were in trouble. And that was all they heard until Chris turned up in Syria on January 31.

Two rescue missions were mounted as a result of our lost comms procedure and the corrupt signals. The first, on January 26, had to turn back soon after crossing the border as the Chinook pilot was violently ill. It was just as well after all that we hadn't hung around for it. A second attempt was made on the 27th, and this time it was a joint US and British effort. Misled by the location of the weak TACBE signal, they flew up the southern corridor, but of course with no result. American intelligence reports were also coming in of an Israeli attack on the Syrian border, but because it was assumed that we were heading south a connection with Bravo Two Zero was not made.

What had gone wrong with the patrol radio? Nothing. In any area of the world only certain frequencies will work, and even then they have to be changed during the day to take account of changes in the ionosphere. The frequencies we were given were wrong, which was most unfortunate. It was a human error that you have to hope will never happen again.

And what of AWACS and the much-vaunted 15-second response time? For whatever reason, we were almost 200 miles out of range. There was a little hiccup in communication somewhere along the line, and it was just another thing that it was hoped would not happen again. The American pilot that we made contact with on TACBE reported the incident, but the report did not reach our people at the FOB until three days later.

One thing we got right was my decision to head for Syria rather than go back to the heli RV. The word "compromise" came through intact. However, without any other information what did it mean? Were they to read it as a possible compromise or a definite compromise? And whichever, should they take it to mean a compromise in contact or out of contact? There was simply not enough information for the colonel to act on, but he had to sit and decide whether or not to send a helicopter out to the RV, and he decided not to, even though the boys in the squadron were queuing up to go and giving him a hard time. But he was right. Why risk eleven men—the aircrew and the boys in the back—plus an aircraft, going into they knew not what? I was glad I hadn't had to make the decision. As we discovered from our interrogators, the infil Chinook had been compromised when it landed, so it was just as well another wasn't sent for the RV. The only thing we could have done with at the time of the compromise was a fast jet flyover. We could have spoken to them on TACBE and guided them onto the S60s, and then arranged an orderly exfil.

For the next few weeks we did debriefs to all and sundry. We gave a one-hour, edited-highlights version to Lord Bramall, colonel in chief of the Regiment, who entertained us to lunch afterwards. He struck me as a very switched-on man—deaf as a doorpost, but very switched on.

Schwarzkopf came down with his gang, and we spent two hours with him.

"I'm sorry for what happened," he said. "If I'd known what was up there at the time, you wouldn't have gone; it's as simple as that."

We had a great dinner with him, and he very kindly signed the silk escape maps we had half-inched from the briefing room in Riyadh.

The very last debrief was for B Squadron. Within days of their return to the UK most of the blokes had started to prepare for other jobs or had already left, but in August we managed to get together for the first time that year and hold our own internal postmortem. The SAS's achievements behind enemy lines were substantial. By January 26, only nine days into the war, no more Scuds were launched from the sector of western Iraq the Regiment had been assigned to—an area of land covering hundreds of square miles.

Mugger had taken part in one such mission. His half squadron group had been operating behind enemy lines since January 20. On February 6 he was tasked to attack a communications facility which was of vital importance to the operation of Scud.

The plan was to move at last light on the 7th to within 1 mile of the target, carry out a close target recce, giving confirmatory orders, and attack. The target, it was discovered, was protected by an 8-ft. concrete wall with a 6-ft. inner fence, and manned enemy bunkers to the left and right. Four men were detailed to destroy the two bunkers with antitank missiles and additional fire support from the vehicles. Eight men moved to the target across 600 feet of flat, open ground to carry out their demolition task. They couldn't locate the switching gear because of damage done by Allied bombing. Mugger was therefore tasked to blow up the steel mast. He and his gang managed to place charges with timers set on two minutes, but as they withdrew they came under fire.

The demolition party took cover on target, aware that they had very little time before the charges detonated. According to Mugger, as the seconds ticked away one of the blokes screamed out, "The timers! We need cover! We need cover!"

"Cover?" Mugger shouted back, mindful of the tons of steel that was about to fall around their ears. "You'll be getting all the fucking cover you need in a minute!"

As he spoke, the fire-support team aboard the Pinkies found their targets, and with the enemy temporarily suppressed, Mugger's gang was up and running. They regrouped back at the vehicles with the rest of the half squadron and successfully fought their way clear of enemy positions. There was a blinding flash followed by a pressure wave as the charges detonated. The tower was down.

Vehicles and equipment had taken many hits, but there were no casualties. The following day, however, it was discovered that it wasn't only Mugger and his gang who'd had a scary time: two blokes found bullet holes in the fabric of their smocks.

On another occasion, one of the patrol commanders had aborted his mission when he saw the flat, featureless terrain. Believing that it was impossible to achieve his aim where he was, he had got his men back on the helicopter and returned to base. He questioned his own integrity because of it. Personally, I feel that it was one of the bravest acts of the war. I wish I was made of the same sort of stuff.

The Iraqis found the body of Vince Phillips and delivered it to the Red Cross, who in turn had him brought back to the UK. The bodies of Bob Consiglio and Steve "Legs" Lane were on the same flight home.

Legs was awarded a posthumous MM (Military Medal) for what the official obituary described as "unswerving leadership." For me he showed this during the contacts and even more in the E&E. It was Legs who wanted us to find a better ambush point for the hijack, and it was just as well he did—otherwise it would have been two truckloads of troops we were stopping, not an old American taxi. And it was Legs who got Dinger into the water when swimming over a quarter of a mile of freezing Euphrates was the last thing he wanted to do. That's leadership.

Bob, too, got the MM that night. Either he made his choice or it was made for him, but he went forward like a man possessed and tried to fight his way out of the contact. In doing so he drew a fearsome amount of enemy fire, and this diversion, without a doubt, helped the rest of us get away. He was hit in the head by a round that came out through his stomach and ignited a white phosphorous grenade in his webbing. He died instantly.

As is the custom, we held a dead man's auction. All the men's kit was sold off to the highest bidder, and the proceeds given to the next of kin or squadron funds. The practice is not macabre; it's just the culture within the Regiment. If you worried about people getting hurt and killed you'd spend your life on antidepressants. The pressure release is to take the piss out of everything and everybody. A bloke fell off a mountain once when we were away, and it took us about three hours to get the body back down to our base camp. A helicopter came in to fetch it, and one of the blokes was straight into the kit to get his rum and all the other goodies.

"Well, he ain't fucking going to need them now, is he?" he said, and quite rightly so. Before anybody said a word, he'd got the man's jumper on and was away with all the rest. When we returned to Hereford, all the borrowed kit was returned and auctioned. It's accepted, but it doesn't mean to say you're not upset. The bloke who's dead is not going to worry about it, and anyway, he'll have been to other people's auctions and done exactly the same.

Bob had a big Mexican sombrero in his locker at work, a typical tourist souvenir that I knew for a fact had only cost him ten dollars because I'd been there when he bought it. I took the piss out of him on many occasions for wasting his money on such a bit of tat. At the auction, however, some idiot parted with more than a hundred quid for it. I kept it at home for a while, then took it to his grave with some MM ribbon for him and Legs.

We had some problems at the joint funeral in Hereford.

Legs was cremated, and Vince and Bob were buried in the regimental plot. Afterwards there was a wake in the club—curry and drinks. A group of Vince's male relations started to give me a bit of a hard time. As far as they were concerned, there was no way such a tough man could die of hypothermia. I tried to explain that it doesn't matter how good you are or how strong you are: if hypothermia hits you, there's not a lot you can do about it. I appreciate that grief takes different people in different ways, but I hope that in time Vince's relations will come to accept the truth.

The following week, taking advantage of British Airways' "two for the price of one" offer to Gulf servicemen, Jilly and I went camping in California. It was a fantastic holiday, and it really helped put everything behind me.

A fortnight later I went back to work. Mark was in a rehabilitation unit, where he remained on and off for the next six months before returning to squadron duties. Chris went to training wing as one of the instructors in charge of Selection. Dinger had already left on a one-year job abroad. Stan, too, was away within two months, and once the medics had finished with my hands and teeth, so was I.

Epilogue

Our heating bills have been horrendous since I got back. It's nice to be warm. When it rains now and I'm indoors, I get a big brew of tea and sit by the window, and I think about all the poor blokes stuck on tops of hills.

As my stress-test score showed, I'm not emotionally affected by what happened. I certainly don't have nightmares. We are big boys and we know the rules that we play by. We've all been close to death before. You accept it. You don't want it to happen, of course, but sometimes, there you go—occupational hazard.

In a strange way I'm almost glad I had my Iraqi experience. I wouldn't like to repeat it, but I'm glad that it happened.

Some things, however, will live with me for ever.

The jangle of keys.

The crash of a bolt.

The rattle of metal sheeting.

A hatred of zoos.

The smell of pork.

I joined the army to get out of the shit I was in with the law, but there was never any intention to stay in for the full twenty-two years. I've been very fortunate. I've been all around the world, doing things that were outrageous but great fun. Now it's time to get on and do something else. I'm 33 going on 17, because I've always been too busy playing the soldier. I want to do the things I've always wanted to do.

Our big joke in prison used to be, "Well, at least it can't make us pregnant," and I have learnt that nothing is ever as bad as it seems. Things that might have bothered me in the past are less likely to now—the car not working, red wine being spilt on our light-colored carpet, the washing machine flooding, something valuable getting lost. I know my limitations better now, yet I feel more positive and self-assured. I no longer take anything for granted. I appreciate simple, everyday things much more; instead of going downtown in the car, I'll make an effort to walk through the park.

The Regiment used to have priority; the job always came first. Now, if it's Katie's school sports day, I'll make the effort to be there and cheer her on.

During my time in Baghdad, and when I got back, I kept going over the decisions I had made, trying to work out if they had been right or wrong. The conclusion I came to was that I made some good ones, some bad ones, and some indifferent ones. But at the end of the day they had to be made. You're presented with a problem, you make your appreciation, and you make your decision. But make no decision at all and you're dead. Should I have gone for the border instead of hiding up? The answer undoubtedly is yes. Should I have appeared to give in to the Iraqis when I did? Again, yes—I know I did the right thing. Tactically, and morally.

As to the rights and wrongs of the war—well, that's never been a worry to me. I was a soldier; that's what I was paid for. It was very exciting; I got high doing it.

And as for the people who interrogated me, if I met any of them in the street tomorrow and thought I could get away with it, I'd slot them.

Maps

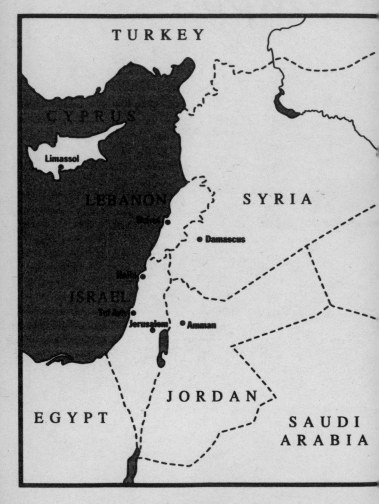

Iraq and neighbouring countries

IRAN

Mosul

Kirkuk

AREA OF DETAIL MAP

Baghdad

IRAQ

Basra

KUWAIT

Kuwait

KILOMETRES

0   100   200   300   400   500

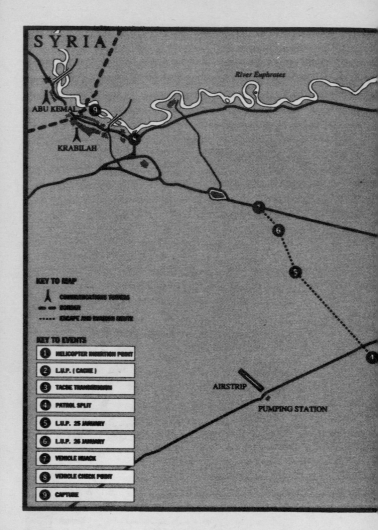

Route of Bravo Two Zero

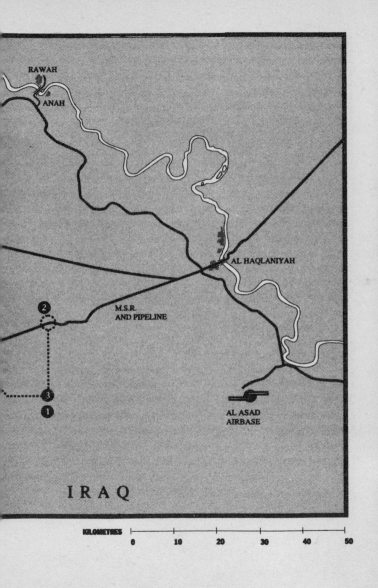

Glossary

203	*M16 rifle with 40mm grenade launcher attached*
2 i/c	*second in command*
66	*lightweight, throwaway antitank rocket*
AAA or Triple A	*antiaircraft artillery*
APC	*Armored Personnel Carrier*
AWACS	*Airborne Warning And Control System*
beasting	*army slang for a beating*
bergen	*pack carried by British forces on active service*
berm	*entrenchment for tank*
Big Four	*the only four pieces of information which, under the Geneva Convention, an enemy is allowed to ask for: number, rank, name, date of birth*
bone (adj.)	*stupid*

brew	*mug of tea*
buckshee	*free, without charge, surplus*
bulk up	*vomit*
cabby, as in "have a cabby at"	*fire your weapon at*
chinstrap, be on your	*really knackered, as in "I can't go on, I'm on, my chinstrap here."*
claymore	*antipersonnel mine used for area protection*
COP	*Close Observation Platoon*
CT	*Counter Terrorist*
CTR	*close target recce*
cuds	*countryside*
cyalume stick	*light-stick activated by squeezing*
DF	*direction finder/find the direction of*
Dinkie	*short-wheelbase Land-Rover (term first used during the Gulf War)*
DOP	*drop-off point*
DPM	*disrupted-pattern material (i.e. camouflage)*
E&E	*escape and evasion*
ERV	*emergency rendezvous*
FOB	*Forward Operations Base*
FRV	*final rendezvous*
fuddle or kefuddle	*getting together and having a brew or conference*
gob off	*speak*
GPMG	*general purpose machine gun*

green slime	*member of Intelligence Corps*
hard routine	*regime in the field that demands, among other things: belt kit on, weapons at hand, no flame or smoke, and all equipment packed away unless in use*
HE	*high explosive*
Head Shed	*nickname for anyone in authority. From Malaya days, this is what any form of leadership in the Regiment has been called—after the term for the start of a river course*
hexamine (hexy)	*small block of solid fuel*
ID	*identify/identity*
Jane's	*military encyclopedia*
jundie	*Iraqi soldier*
laager	*an armored vehicle LUP*
launched	*punched*
LSV	*light strike vehicle (dune buggy)*
LUP	*lying-up point*
MSR	*Main Supply Route*
NBC	*nuclear, biological, chemical (warfare)*
net	*radio network*
NVA	*night-viewing aid*
NVG	*night-viewing goggles*
OC	*officer commanding*
OP	*observation post*

OPSEC	*operational security*
PE	*plastic explosive*
pear-shaped	*got the hump*
pinkie (110)	*long-wheelbase Land-Rover*
Regiment	*Special Air Service*
remf	*rear echelon motherfucker*
rupert	*nickname for officer—not always derogatory*
RV	*rendezvous point*
scaley	*signaler*
scaley kit	*signals equipment*
Sit Rep	*situation report*
SOP	*standard operating procedure*
spook	*member of Intelligence Corps*
squaddy	*soldier*
stag	*sentry (also sentry duty)*
stand/stood to	*ready to fight in your position*
Syrette	*automatic one-time injector*
S60	*57mm antiaircraft gun*
tab	*forced march over a long distance, usually carrying a heavy load*
TACBE	*tactical beacon*
TEL	*transporter erector launcher*
VCP	*vehicle checkpoint*